God Will Make a Way

An Autobiography

Jon Los

GOD WILL MAKE A WAY. Copyright © 2018 by Jon Los.

All rights reserved. Printed in the United States of America. No part of this book may be used or reproduced in any manner whatsoever without written permission except in the case of brief quotations embodied in critical articles or reviews.

Unless otherwise indicated, all scripture quotations are taken from the Holy Bible, King James (American Version).

Book Cover Design by HCP Book Publishing

ISBN : 978-0-9997404-5-3

First Edition : March 2018

CONTENTS

Endorsements 4

Acknowledgements 5

Preface 6

Introduction 11

Chapter One: Starting Out 14

Chapter Two: Junior High School 30

Chapter Three: My Own Truck, Earl, and Feeding the World 57

   A Real Miracle 62

   Earl Fires up the Rocket 62

   Life Lesson Learned 63

   Angel Investor 64

Chapter Four: A New Chapter 84

   Angels Entertainment 91

   The Hand of God 92

   Hammer Down 97

   Death on the Highway 101

   My Amazing, Beautiful Baby Girl 104

   The Highway to Hell 108

Chapter Five: One Marriage Down **110**
   Ramen Noodles for Breakfast, Lunch, and Dinner 112
   The Guilty Flee When No One Pursues 114
   Faith For Your Needs, Not Your Greeds 114
   Richard's Big Faith Adventure 115
   Teresa 117
   One Knight in Rusty Armor Coming Up 119
   Dennis H 126
   It Worked 127
   In the Beginning, God 128
   Fundamentalist, Bigoted, Rightwing Christian 129
   The 63 Thing 132
   The System 134
   God Has a Plan 135
   Back To The Grind 152

Chapter Six: Despise Not Small Beginnings **156**
   One Third of a Bean Soup 169
   Pain In The Knee 171
   Heidi 176
   The Summer Kitchen 178
   Larry Black 193
   Soulish Prayers 195
   An Old Friend Gets Saved 205
   My Crazy Life Went On 207
   Getting Into The Word 208
   Unfinished Business 209
   The Prayer of Jabez 212

The Nipple Is On Fire 215
Going Home 222
Richard and Tammy 224
Richard M 225
James B 226
Nine Months Later, To the Day 230
Ricky 231
Rick's Salvation 233
God Moves Mountains, and Bureaucrats 235
Clean Up Time 239
I Need A Bath 242
Almost Started A War With The USA 245
Ask and You Will Receive 251
Bye-Bye Treehouse 253
The Sons of Belial 261
Fun with the Law 266
Driving Stories 276
Family of God 278

Chapter Seven: The Dream 282

Epilogue 285

Endorsements

I don't read often, but as soon as I got this, I couldn't put it down. I never had tears flowing so much that my collar had wet spots. I would have tears and giggles right after. I felt like I was sitting in the passenger seat. Very inspirational. You can't miss this opportunity to hear about God's gifts.

Kelly Kurtz

I met Jon as a talented storyteller with a fantastic story. Listening to him or reading his book is exciting, fascinating and takes me right away into his world with all its feelings. It was sometimes heart-breaking and touching, but full of joy and so inspiring to my own story.

Nicole Schulthess
Designer and Artist

Acknowledgements

First, and foremost, I dedicate this book to God. If it hadn't been for the Lord on my side, I wouldn't be here today!

I would also like to thank all the people who hurt me along the way. What they meant for evil, God intended for good.

Thanks to everyone who has encouraged me to write my testimony. It is while in the depths of depression that they reminded me of how far I have come, and of the many ways that the Lord has taught me to love unconditionally.

To Peter Talbot, a brother who believed in me. Thank you for being an incredible help.

To David and Heidi Lillos who took me in and cared for me, showing me what true hospitality is.

To Naomi Joy Ollor, who is in my corner praying for my success and who has never stopped believing in me.

To the Ditto family, who have blessed me by just being there when I needed someone to lean on.

To Isaac Peters, my brother from another mother who was a literal answer to prayer when I needed a friend.

To Don and Sandra Kwitkoski for their love and the spare room where I could rest my weary bones.

There are so many others I want to thank, but I simply ask that God blesses you all and that you prosper as your souls prosper.

Preface

In a dream, I was briskly "walking" across the prairies at a speed I was used to going when I was trucking. I came to a small town. It looked pristine and perfect. The trees were manicured. The lawns were all trimmed. There were white picket fences and beautiful houses. It was postcard perfect. But I didn't see a single person, bird, dog or any living thing.

As I got closer to the center of the town, the businesses all looked perfect too. There was a raised wooden covered sidewalk on either side, and I walked up the stairs. There were business shingles hanging in front of each door, all painted and hand-lettered. There was nothing out of place or dirty anywhere. Even the paint on the floor of the sidewalk looked brand new. Then I saw the General Store sign and went in.

When I got inside the shelves were fully stocked in perfect order, nothing was missing. The shelves were high, and there was a rolling ladder to access the items that were higher up. I went up to the front counter, but there was no one there. I rang the bell, but there was no reply. No one came. I heard a fan at the back of the store, so I went back there. It was a big oscillating fan on a stand, turning back and forth beside the door to what I assumed was the owner's residence. I peeked inside the door and saw a kitchen table all set and ready, so I called out. There was no answer. I was starting to feel creeped out, so I went back to the counter, still no one there. I went back outside and didn't see any living thing, anywhere. It was as if everyone had just cleaned the place and then left in a hurry, just before I got there.

7   Jon Los

I walked back to the road and headed out of the town. I was then back out on the prairies "walking" at 60 miles per hour.

I saw another town in the distance. There was smoke billowing up from it in a few places, as if there were fires burning there. As I got closer, I started to notice a foul odour. It became stronger and more intense as I got closer. It was making my eyes water and I was gagging by the time I got to the edge of the town. It was the exact opposite of the last town. There was garbage everywhere, burnt out cars on the roadsides and the buildings all looked like shacks with broken windows and peeled paint. I noticed that there was a trench that was in the middle of the road and there was open sewage in it, which appears to be the source of most of the smell, but the stench only got stronger as I got closer to the town center.

As I walked deeper into the town I saw long lines of people standing along the sides of the road. They were all impeccably dressed; men in suits and women in evening gowns. They were all holding containers. Some had pails and others had cups. Some had the cut off bottoms from plastic soda bottles. The scene was surreal. I noticed that they all had a snobby attitude towards each other. They would stand in little groups, not letting the others in. They sneered at me as I walked by. I could hear an evil sounding laughter coming from around a corner and the people were all laughing along whenever the laughter was heard.

I followed the line around the corner and saw a sight that disgusted and fascinated me at the same time. There, sitting in front of a huge pot over an open fire, was a sweaty fat man with no shirt on. He was the epitome of what I imagined a troll to look like, complete with warts. He was reaching into a giant pot with a ladle and scooping out the most foul-smelling slop and dishing it into the waiting containers. As soon as someone's container was filled, they would run to join their little groups and would loudly hiss and sneer at anyone who looked at them. It was a very odd sight indeed.

Although I had grown somewhat accustomed to the stench, it was still rather unpleasant, and I couldn't wait to get out of there. I saw the same scene played out repeatedly as I walked through the town. People started hurling insults at me once they noticed that I wasn't lining up for the slop. I was starting to fear for my safety as I started to run. I was running as fast as I could go. They started throwing rocks and other things at me while they cursed me. I found myself back on the prairies "walking" at 60mph, quite relieved to be away from that horrible smell and those evil people.

As I was walking across the prairies, I was trying to figure out what I had just seen in the two towns and how out of place it all seemed to be and what it could all mean.

I then saw what looked like an army barracks or Boy Scout camp, with all the long, low buildings exactly the same. They all had a door in the middle of each barracks with four steps each that led to a side walk. The road ended, and it became a crushed limestone path, about four feet wide. As I was observing the absolute uniformity of the place, I saw a huge dog turd in the middle of the path. I couldn't help but think how out of place it was. I stepped over it and continued. Then I saw another one, and another, and yet another one a few feet further. I looked up and realized that the amount of poo on the path only increased as I went forward. It got to the point where I was looking for places to step so I wouldn't step in it. Then it happened. I got some on the cuff of my pants. It was disgusting. I naturally went to wipe it off and now I had it on my hand. I was balancing on one foot, vainly looking for somewhere to place my other foot but there was nowhere to step without stepping in shit. I stepped in the places where I would get the least amount on my shoes, but it was hopeless. I now had shit on my shoes, pants and my hand from trying to wipe it off.

9   Jon Los

As I was standing there I suddenly became aware of a tall guy standing beside me. He was about nine feet tall. He looked like a hippie, with long hair and a beard. I looked down and realized he was standing in mid-air, about three feet off the ground. I asked him, *"How do you do that?"* He said, *"I never take my eyes off God. You can do it too you know."* I looked up at him and the next thing I knew, I was standing in mid-air and looking at him eye to eye. Somehow, I knew that if I looked down, I'd be right back in the poo, so I kept my eyes fixed on him. Then he started to walk, and I followed, watching the back of his head, but occasionally, he turned, looked at me and smiled. The reality of walking in midair was surreal. I just kept following the long-haired dude and watching him. It was too much for me and I glanced down, and immediately I was standing ankle deep in the crap. I felt like such a fool. I looked up at the guy and he was laughing at me. I couldn't believe it, and I was a little angry. He said, *"I told you, never take your eyes off God."* I was back up in the air again, following him.

I found myself standing on some cinder blocks stacked two feet high. There was a 16 feet long length of board laying on its side, spanning a boiling river of crap, and every other disgusting thing you could imagine. It was the only 'bridge' around so I knew I had to cross it. The tall guy says, *"I've been with you the whole way and you've made it this far. But you must walk across this bridge alone, and I'll be waiting for you on the other side. Just never take your eyes off me."* He was instantly on the other side, waiting. I looked down at the river of crap that was flowing by and felt like it was pulling me in. I remembered what He had just said, so I fixed my gaze on him and started across the 'bridge.'

Poop is slippery, and my shoes were getting covered in it. I was staring straight ahead into His eyes, feeling my way across the piece of board with my feet and taking very small deliberate steps. As I got to the middle, the board was sagging, and I could feel the contents of the river hitting the side of it. I wanted to look down so badly, but I saw that if my eyes were staring straight into his, I was making it across. Because the board was sagging, I had to walk up a bit but as the board started to level off as I got closer to the other side, I felt an incredible sense of accomplishment. He held his steady gaze and silently encouraged me to keep moving forward, and to not look down.

I made it! I was instantly clean. Even the poo that was on my shoes and pants from before was gone. He had a great big smile on his face and He said, *"Never take your eyes off me, Jon. There is nothing below you that you need to worry about. I am the Way, the Truth, and the Life. Now let's go!"*

Introduction

The purpose of this book is to encourage those who are struggling with this thing called life, especially if you are a Christian and you are wondering where God went. I have been there.

If your question is, *"Why does God allow bad things to happen to good people?"* Then you are looking at it from the wrong perspective. The question should be, *"Why do people do bad things towards a loving God?"* One word answers that question, *sin*. It's not a popular word these days but just because it is not polite to say at parties, doesn't negate its reality. We are all born into a fallen, messed up world where we find ourselves struggling to understand why good is evil and evil is good. Everyone's story is different, yet the same. Through no choice of our own we are, as Jim Morrison said in his song, **Riders on the Storm**, *"into this world we're thrown, like a dog without a bone, like an actor out on loan."* I used to really like **The Doors**. I still do, but the utter hopelessness they sang about never had an answer, and that left me, well, hopeless.

We all know intuitively that there is something bigger, and hopefully better, out there somewhere. As the Christian cliché goes, *"God has put a void in everyone's heart that only He can fill."* All those annoying Bible thumpers were right, God sent His Son Jesus Christ, a man like we are, yet sinless, to be our key to the lock on Heavens door. Some are fighting it tooth and nail, some are giving up in quiet desperation, some go insane, and some find the peace that surpasses understanding despite the trials, obstacles, and heartaches. God is not a big mean cosmic ogre. His heart aches and breaks over every lost soul as He tries repeatedly to get our attention, and we, being stubborn and proud, constantly turn our backs on Him.

I see God as a loving grandfather, sitting on His front porch in His rocking chair, waiting for His children to come and visit. But they rarely do. They drive up the driveway, sit in their cars and wave to Him, but they never get out of the car and sit with Him on the porch. He has great wealth in the house and He will gladly give it to His children, if they would just come and ask. But alas, they are too busy with the cares of this life. They might give Him a passing thought and think they really should go visit the old guy, but for some reason or another, they rarely do. If you were that old man on the porch, how would you feel?

This world is just a shadow of the reality of Heaven. Moth and rust don't stand a chance there; pain and tears are never felt or seen; death does not exist in that perfect place that our Heavenly Father has prepared for us. I guess you could look at it like a big test, but that outlook falls short of the bounty available to us in this life, if we would only stop by the old guy's place and sit with Him for a while. He loves us more than we could ever know, even when it feels like He's nowhere to be found. He's not tormenting us, He wants us to come to Him of our own free will, not under compulsion due to guilt, fear or shame.

The life that we have is a one-shot deal. There is no coming back to try again. It is appointed once for a man to die, and then the judgement. Many will argue this point and use that as their excuse for turning their backs on God, only to rob themselves of the incredible treasures that the old guy on the porch has for us. I was one of those lost doubters for many years, blissfully unaware of the riches.

As you read this, please understand that my journey has been very personal, filled with experiences and trials that were unique to me. Everyone has a story though, including you and yours is no better or worse than mine. The old guy on the porch is waiting for you to pay Him a visit. He's gone before you to prepare a way and all He wants is for us to come to Him in love, eager to receive the many blessings inside His cabin.

Chapter One

Starting Out

My parent's relationship was the proverbial "Oh No" to both sides of the family. My mother was the youngest daughter, born Sept. 7th, 1941, to a wealthy family from West Vancouver BC. She had two older siblings, Donna, the oldest, and Doug, the only son in the middle. My Grandfather, Charles Howard Rodgers, was an optometrist by profession but was also the general manager of Birk's Jewelers in Downtown Vancouver. He was the Worshipful Master of the Masonic Lodge in Vancouver for a time. He also owned the water taxi service that was based in Horseshoe Bay, where the BC Ferries main terminal is now. They were Presbyterians who attended Church regularly.

My grandmother was the head of the YMCA in Vancouver for many years. They lived in a big white house on the beach, on Park Lane, in West Vancouver. One of my earliest memories was of me sitting on a little stool waiting for the big steam locomotives pulling for the British Columbia Railway on the tracks that were just above my grandparents' home.

My father, born May 11, 1931, was the youngest of seven children. His family, all Catholic, immigrated from what had become Poland in the early 1930s. They landed at Ellis Island in New York. Upon arrival, he was asked what his name was. He couldn't speak English, so he didn't understand the question.

15   Jon Los

The person yelled the question until my father replied, *"Lauze."* His name was written down in typical impatient fashion as *'Loss.'* The family moved westward, then up to Canada, eventually settling in Manitoba on a homestead on the west side of Lake Winnipeg. My grandfather tried farming, but it was right at the beginning of the depression and he must have felt overwhelmed by his failure to provide for his family. He walked away from his farm and family when my father was five years old. The oldest son, Joseph, was twenty-five years older than my dad and assumed the role of provider. Hearing of the good life available in Vancouver, he moved his mother and six siblings there in 1937.

My dad was attracted to the marine industry, specifically diesel engine repair. He started as an oiler *(the young guy who makes sure all the moving parts are well lubricated)* and eventually apprenticed as a diesel engine technician. Upon receiving his Journeyman's certificate, he went to work for Kingcom Navigation, a small tug boat operation in Vancouver. My mom was a bookkeeper for Kingcom. She tells the story of how she would be waiting at her bedroom window in the family home on the beachfront, waiting for my dad to shine the spotlight at her house and blow the horn just for her. Well, hormones being what they are, they made me at Lumberman's Arch in Stanley Park in the back of my dad's new 60 Ford Fairlane. This was the early 60's. Pregnancy out of wedlock was still taboo. Dad did the right thing and married mom. Eight months later, trouble landed, me. I was the first-born male on my mother's side but in the eyes of the two families that wasn't a good thing.

Now these were two families who were not very happy about the situation. I was a bastard child, as far as they were all concerned. Protestants and Catholics went together like oil and water, so family get togethers were uncomfortable. My mom told me that my grandfather loved me very much, but he died of cancer when I was two. I have no memories of him, but I do remember the strange feeling of being unwelcomed and unwanted and the cause of much tension. I still struggle with those feelings today.

My mom didn't have the first clue about raising a child, let alone an adventurous baby boy. She had some help from the other women in her life, mainly her mom and sister, Donna Lee, but there wasn't a lot of love floating around. Someone gave her a copy of Dr. Spock's book, **"The Common-Sense Book of Baby and Child Care."** Dr. Spock's book is probably responsible for more messed up children than any other book on child rearing ever written. So, here I am, intuitively feeling rejection from before I was even born, alone in a crib in a dark room, howling at the top of my little lungs for someone, preferably mom, to come and hold me, feed me, or get the stinking diaper off my hinder parts. Mom, wanting to be a good mother, read that a child crying is only selfishly seeking attention. Leave it alone and it will settle down and be fine. Try explaining that to a child who feels completely abandoned as he gets so weary of crying that he bangs his head against the bars of his crib before he rocks himself to sleep. I still remember those feelings to this day. It took me years to stop rocking myself to sleep.

I remember staying at my Uncle Doug's for a weekend. In the middle of the night, Uncle Doug came in the room and shook me awake. It appears that I was slamming myself face first into the pillow while fast asleep. That wasn't normal. Sleepovers, anywhere, terrified me because I never knew what I was going to do in my sleep. Rocking myself out of the bed was common, as was humming very loudly. These traits didn't develop because I was just weird, they were the result of little to no intimate interaction with my mother. Don't get me wrong, I love and honor my mom. She did the best she could with what she had and considering that both sides of the family basically treated her as a pariah for having me, she was totally on her own. My dad was working at sea and gone for months at a time, so she did the best she could. Thanks to God, I have fully and completely forgiven her, and everyone else involved, but the memories and some of the after effects are still there. Even now when I feel stressed, I will rock in my sleep. My spouses have all had the experience of being kicked by me while I am sound asleep, and I wake up completely unaware that it happened. Thanks Dr. Spock.

One of my earliest memories is of Christmas. I was five years old. I was so excited that it was Christmas that I got up before anyone else. I waited. It seemed to take forever, and I couldn't stand it. There was a big present with my name on it. I opened it. It was a train set. I was thrilled and got right to setting it up. I had it up and running and was totally engrossed in it when my mom and dad got up. They were not pleased. I had no idea what the problem was since I didn't open anything else. I was hauled to my room and given a spanking and then I was banished while everyone else opened the rest of their presents. I wasn't allowed out of my room until dinner time. I was wrong to open my gift too soon, but was that fair punishment? I learned early that life was going to be a challenge.

I had an almost normal childhood. My dad made a good living and in those days my mom could afford to stay at home raising my sister, Susan, and I. My youngest sister, Patricia, came along six years after I was born. My dad was away from home for months at a time, so I was surrounded by women. Auntie Donna was perpetually single and liked to party. She was one of the founders of what is now 'Whistler/Blackcomb' which is the world's famous ski resort. She used to play with all those forbidden 'arts,' for example, palm reading, tarot, and all the other nice demonic crap. She bought my sister and I a Ouija Board once. Suzy and I went downstairs to give it a try. We were instructed to start with something simple, like spelling your name. I went first. We both put our hands on the little pointer and spelt my name. Nothing happened. Then we did Suzy's name. We moved the pointer to S, then U, then S, when all of a sudden it zipped all by itself to the A and then back to the N. We were totally freaked out. We ran upstairs, petrified by the new toy. Auntie Donna thought it was fantastic. We never touched the thing again.

My dad's mom was a typical Catholic worrier. She was nice, but I remember her crying a lot. My dad's family was spread out all over North America. He was the youngest, and the only one born in Canada. His older brother, Walter, lived in Calgary Alberta and was married to Aunt Cathy. They had three children, Greg, Grant, and Christine. I thought they were super cool cousins. They were well off and had all kinds of cool stuff, mainly musical instruments, for example, electric guitars, drums and keyboards. I always liked them. My Aunt Cathy was a hoot.

At the age of ten, I went on my first plane trip to their home in Calgary. Aunt Cathy picked me up at the airport and gave me a tour. I remember sitting at a red light when she said, *"I don't believe in starting out slowly when the light turns green."* When it turned green, she floored it and we shot away from it like we were in a dragster at the drag strip. From that moment on, as far as I was concerned, she was the coolest Aunt ever.

Dad's oldest brother, Charlie, lived in Seattle. He was married to Carol and they had two children, Gary and Marlene. They were the closest, so we saw them a lot. Gary was trouble. My mom and dad didn't want me to hang around him lest he rubbed off on me. I thought he was fun. He taught me how to make exploding balloons from ginger ale and Alka-Seltzer, among many other tricks. Rubbing off on me took on a whole new meaning one night when he climbed into my bed and molested me. I was around eleven, and had no idea what had just happened, but I knew I didn't like it. He died from a heroin overdose after being dishonorably discharged from the US Navy.

There was my Aunt Clarice and family in Los Angeles. Now they were cool. My three cousins, Karen, Arlene and Sandy were California cool. We only saw then occasionally but I always thought it was cool to have cousins from LA. The rest of his family were in Chicago, Toronto and Montreal. I never met some of them.

My first experience with school was a one room school house for kindergarten. I distinctly remember reciting the Lord's Prayer every morning. I liked school, until one morning when I had to pee really bad. I put my hand up to ask to go to the bathroom, but my teacher was busy at her desk and didn't look up. I had already been in trouble for talking in class, so I didn't dare say anything. I had my hand up for what seemed like hours, but she didn't look up. Finally, I couldn't hold it in any longer and let it go right at my desk. All the other children thought it was hilarious, but the teacher wasn't amused. In fact, I was punished by having my knuckles whacked with a ruler. It wasn't even my fault. That was the first real injustice that happened outside of my family. It was not the last.

They built a new school in our neighborhood, Buckingham Elementary School, just a block away from my house. In 1967 I started attending Grade one there. Prayer and Bible reading were basically outlawed in Canada around that time and I remember the teacher crying as she told us she was going to lead us in the Lord's Prayer and read from the Bible for the last time. I didn't understand the long-term implications of this then, but I sure do now.

My first memory of "church" is when I was five years old. My parents went to the Deer Lake United Church, not due to any religious inclinations, but back then everyone went to church on Sunday. It was more of a social thing that people do. I was carted into the basement to Sunday School. I can still remember the 'Bubble Letter' words on the wall of the Sunday School class, *'Love'* and *'Jesus.'* I had no idea who or what Jesus was but I had an idea of what Love was supposed to be, or at least, what it wasn't.

I have no idea what it was in that Sunday School class that scared the living daylights out of me, but something made me bolt. I remember stiff arming the door and running up the stairs outside and hauling the giant wooden door to the sanctuary open and screaming that I wanted to go home. My parents were mortified, since this was their offspring that had just disrupted the service. My dad came and got me and dragged me back to where they were sitting. My mom pulled my pants down and paddled my bare butt right there in the church. I was terrified, humiliated, and mad. That was the last time we ever went to church because I associated it with that horrible experience, and my parents were totally embarrassed.

I was a good student and got good grades in Primary School. Being born in late November, I was always the youngest and the smallest in my grade. I didn't notice at first, but it soon became obvious when I started getting picked on and beat up by the bigger kids. I tried to enjoy school, but it became increasingly difficult. I remember being chosen to pose for a picture that ended up in the local newspaper. It was 1967, Canada's Centennial year, and the school was planting a Dogwood tree in honor of it. I was chosen because I was the youngest child, not to mention the smallest. The oldest was a girl from the 7th grade. My mom still has the clipping.

Another observation from my early childhood was that truth seemed to be unwelcomed. It was around the time when the Americans landed on the moon. I was seven and I was always at my best friend, Ronny Boyce's house. They lived on Canada Way, which had just been widened to four lanes and had a lot of traffic on it. He lived on the other side from me, so I had to go to a controlled crosswalk. It had been drilled into me to only cross roads at a light or stop sign. There were two traffic lights and one was out of the way. The other was closer but went past a house that had a few big dogs that weren't chained or behind a gate. Either way, it was a long walk. The dogs were big and loved to scare the pants off anyone who dared to walk past their yard. But that was the shortest way to the closest crosswalk.

One day, after hanging out at Ronny's house, it was time to get home for dinner. I had a choice, go the long way and be late, but avoid the dogs, or go past the dogs and take my chances. I was seven years old and Canada Way was very busy during rush hour. I decided to take my chances. When I got to the dogs' house, I ran as fast as I could down the sidewalk, hoping that they wouldn't notice me. I made it. When I got to the intersection with the crosswalk, the traffic that was turning right didn't have to stop as there was a separate right turn lane. It was wall to wall and no one would slow down or stop for me. I stood there for what seemed like a very long time until I finally gave up and decided to go to the other crosswalk a good mile away, past the dogs. As I got close to the dogs' yard, they were standing there in the driveway. They knew I was coming. I didn't know which was worse, the dogs or getting in trouble for being late. I went with the latter. I walked towards the dogs. They came barking and growling towards me. I panicked and jumped off the sidewalk, right into the path of a moving car. It was a red Mustang convertible with the top down, a male driver with dark hair and sunglasses on, with a look of sheer horror on his face as he slammed on the brakes. I knew this was when I would die, but I didn't die. I found myself standing on the sidewalk and those dogs were whining and racing down the driveway as fast as they could go. This was a genuine miracle. I couldn't wait to get home and tell my mom. I thought she would be so happy.

When I got home, late of course, she wouldn't believe a word of it. She obviously thought my vivid imagination was at work. I was sent to my room without supper after a good swat on the rear end and told that worse punishment awaited when dad got home. I was flabbergasted, and indignant. I had just experienced a miracle and I was being punished. I have told many lies, for example, 'No homework today mom' and I was never punished. But when I told the truth, I was punished. I knew that was wrong, but I didn't like being punished for telling the truth, so I became an expert at making things up.

I had my first cigarettes and beer when I was eight. My parents liked to party and whenever they did, there was lots of alcohol and cigarettes around. The other partier's children, and me, would be at the doorway, watching for an opportunity to grab a beer and a cigarette when one of the adults would set one down and forget about it. One of us, usually me, would walk in, completely unnoticed by the adults, and pick up a smoke from an ashtray and a beer from the coffee table. We would go downstairs and have our own little party. I'm sure all the parents wondered why we were so easily put to bed later.

I was slowly being swallowed up by my sin nature, which no one bothered to explain to me. I found myself living in a very surreal world of my own. I was smart, got good grades and liked school, but I could spin a tale so good that even my parents believed it. Then came the summer of 1971. I had a best friend, Geoffrey, and we were inseparable. His father was from England and had taken to calling me *"Polack."* I had no idea what that was, but he thought it was incredibly funny and soon my friend Geoff started calling me Polack. I told my mom. She said the English were called Limey's, so I called Geoff and his dad Limey. Suddenly, I wasn't welcome at his house anymore. Go figure!

It became normal for the television networks to roll out all their new programs in the fall, just as school started. There was one year that All In The Family, with Archie Bunker, débuted. Calling his son-in-law the meathead and Polack were perfectly timed to start the most miserable time of my young life. I became Polack to everyone.

One of my so-called friends punched in me in the stomach and when I told the teacher, she said I must have asked for it. My friend Geoff was now my biggest enemy. I even had the Gym and Grade five teacher call me Polack. I was devastated and had nowhere to turn. Being small for my age made fighting back nearly impossible. I tried to tell my mom, but she didn't think it was a big enough problem to warrant going to the teachers or principal. I had to suffer with the shame of being a Polack by myself. It was a brutal time in my life. I was nine years-old. I gave up and quit everything. I deliberately got into trouble at school, but they only sent me back. The worst I got was detentions to clean lots of chalkboards. I slowly devolved into my own little world where no one could hurt me anymore than I had been hurt already. I never had a teacher who made a difference in my life. I had teachers who seemed to go out of their way to make my miserable little life even worse. I was pushed through school even though I only got D's and E's. They kept advancing me, even though I had basically quit. Soon I was so far behind that even when I wanted to catch up, it was impossible. When I did try, it didn't matter.

23   Jon Los

Once, in Grade 7, we were studying Scotland. We were asked to draw something Scottish, the only rule being that we couldn't trace it or use the overhead projector. I was up for the challenge and decided to draw a map of Scotland. It has one jagged coastline. So, with one hand on the pencil and a steady gaze at the map I started to draw. I simply moved the pencil where my eyes followed the coastline. I was amazed at how close it came out. I had to make a few adjustments but was rather proud of my accomplishment. I outlined it with red and blue, added some place names and historical facts and handed it in. I got an F. My teacher wrote across it that he rejected it because I had obviously copied it. I protested and swore, as I still do to this day, that it was completely freehand. He said he was adding lying and being obstinate to my report card and sent me to the principal's office. I was being punished for doing too good of a job. I lost it. I often heard my dad use words that I was forbidden to use, but I was so mad that I let loose a string of profanity that they kicked me out of school. I felt a righteous indignation like never before and I was not a happy camper. That was it for me. I didn't ever want to go back to that hell hole. My mom begged and pleaded with them to take me back, and I was forced to apologize to the teacher, principal and my whole class. I apologized for cussing, but no way was I groveling for forgiveness for something I didn't do. I was labeled as a *'problem child'* but they let me back in. As you can guess, I did my best to live up to my new title.

There was a kid one year younger but twice as big as me, who just happened to be our family doctor's youngest son. He was a total bully. I hated him and so did everyone else. He would push around and beat up the children who were smaller than him, myself included. I avoided him as much as possible but sometimes I couldn't avoid him. One day at lunch I was alone in my classroom eating my lunch, looking out the window at the sports field and the grassy hill that lead down to it. I saw him pushing kids around. I was filled with such a righteous rage that I flew out of the classroom, down the grassy hill and punched him in the face with everything I had in me. He didn't fall but he was shocked, and then mad. He started to lay a beating on me while the smaller children were hitting him. Like a giant, he swatted them away and proceeded to let me have it for daring to confront him. Some teachers soon arrived, and we were hauled into the principal's office. He lied saying he was protecting the smaller children from me. I was the 'problem child' so no one believed my side of the story. I told them to go ask the smaller children he was picking on. They refused saying that they were tired of my lies. I was given a note to take home and my mom was enraged. I was grounded. It was a good thing my dad was away at sea or I would have been beaten by him as well. So, once again, I was punished for doing the right thing and called a liar when I tried to defend myself.

I remember a new family moving in to the big stone house on Hazzard Street, about a block from our house. They had two sons and we became friends right away. They didn't know me yet. Their parents invited me to dinner one evening and I was glad to be there. As we sat down to eat, I noticed that no one was eating anything. I wondered what was going on. The mom asked me if I would like to say grace. I had no idea what she was talking about, but I said, sure. I said, *'Yeah, Grace. Hard to believe she has boobs as big as she does because she's only ten!'* There was a stunned silence. They never asked me to come over for dinner again and they didn't want me playing with their boys anymore. I had no idea what was wrong, but I felt rejection once again. They moved away soon after.

I had few friends. Most of the other children's parents didn't want me to be a bad influence on their children. The few kids I did have as friends were from pretty messed up homes themselves, so we all kind of fit together. One friend, David, was nice to me when we were by ourselves but as soon as anyone else was around he would get mean, even going so far as to beat me up. He stole stuff from my room and I was forbidden from going to his house because he told everyone that I was a thief. Then there was George, my closest neighbor. They had subdivided the farm that was opposite our house and theirs was the first one with another boy my age living in it. We hung out together a lot. His dad was an electrician and since I had always been fascinated by electricity, I had a million questions for him.

They built their house themselves and had more switches and wires in there than anyone anywhere. George and I were both kind of different. He was fat and kind of gross, I was small and the neighborhood weirdo. We were best friends. Then the new kid moved in next door to him. His name was Dean. He was a spoiled brat. He and his older brother were both jerks and it wasn't long before they decided they didn't like me. He stole George from being my friend and even incited him to fight me. I didn't want to fight. He knocked me to the ground and they all took turns kicking me until they were satisfied, then walked away laughing at me. I wanted to die.

My very best friend ever, Wayne Emery, moved in to old man Barnett's old shack that was across the street from our place. Wayne was the son of a family who took in foster children, and he himself had been adopted by them. He was a total screw up and we were best friends. There was no judgment from him and he even stood up for me a few times. I loved this guy. We had a bond forged in adversity. We always managed to find fun ways to get into trouble.

Once, we built a dam on the small creek that was a block away. We loaded it with firecrackers as we built it, with the express goal of blowing the thing up. We took extra care to keep them dry and we had some whoppers in there. We had it up to about the four-foot-deep mark when we decided to 'let her blow!' We lit the fuses, ran for cover, the firecrackers popped, but the dam remained intact. We were disappointed and mad. We took some poles and proceeded to demolish the dam. We never thought about what would happen to anything downstream and it turns out that a wall of rushing water and debris can do a fair bit of damage. The nice lady who had a big fence that the creek went under wasn't very happy that the stream wiped out her garden, bridge and fence. I guess there were some other neighbors who were hit by the deluge as well, but we just thought it was the funniest thing ever.

Our next project was to build a treehouse. We found the perfect spot where four perfectly spaced alder trees had grown out of the stump of the original tree that was cut down years before. It was right next to the lady whose garden, fence and bridge we had wiped out. We started with one floor, then two, then three, finally we had seven floors on that thing. It was impressive. We could look right over her tall cedar hedge into the old lady's yard. What we saw shocked us. The old girl liked to walk around naked. It was too much. We invited all to come and see for themselves, and we didn't even charge them. The next day, we found a very official looking sign nailed to our treehouse that read, NOTICE, THIS STRUCTURE IS CONDEMNED, AND MUST BE REMOVED IMMEDIATELY! By Order of the City of Burnaby. We were devastated. We fought to keep it and when my mom called the city hall they said they had no idea what we were talking about. We were a bit perplexed. My mom took pictures of it. Wayne said we would never win this one so we should just tear it down and use the materials to build another one somewhere else. I didn't like that idea at all. We had worked all summer to build that thing and I didn't want another one of my projects to end up in the trash. My mom figured that since the old lady was a painter, she must have made the sign. By the way, it is illegal to peer into naked old lady's yards.

It wasn't long after Wayne informed me that they were moving away. The owner of the house they were in had sold the property to developers and they had to move right away. I was destroyed. My only friend in the world was leaving me. Abandoned, again. I was so upset that I wouldn't even come to the door to say goodbye. The last I heard, Wayne was killed in a car accident a few years later.

My father, who I had idolized even though I barely knew him, came home to stay, no longer working at sea. I finally had a dad like all my friends. Then weird things started to happen. He would come home from work angry. I had no idea why, but I figured it must have been my fault because he seemed to take it out on me. He called me mean names, said he hated me and wished I had never been born. He would hit me and throw me around and I had no idea what I had done.

One day, my sisters and I were sitting in beanbag chairs in the basement watching TV. He came downstairs and picked me up and just threw me against the brick fireplace. I was terrified and got up and bolted out of the house as fast as I could go. He got in the car to chase me, but I hid in the bushes down the street as he drove back and forth looking for me. I was terrified. My heart is beating faster as I write this. I don't remember what happened after that but, it didn't do much for my already suffering self-esteem. What I thought was going to be great, turned into a nightmare. My dad drank and got mean, a lot.

I remember sitting at the dinner table with my mom and sisters, waiting for him to get home. We could literally feel the evil get closer when he was a block away. We just looked at each other. Mom would say, *'He's almost here, try not to do anything to make him mad.'* He would just sit there at the table, angry. Of course, having a strange sense of justice bubbling up to the surface, I had to do something to light the fuse. I felt the need to get it over with. I would say something and ran. It almost became a game.

One night, as I was down in my room, I heard my mom yelling *"No Eddy, NO!!!!"* I ran upstairs to find my mom on the floor and dad sitting on her back hitting her on the head repeatedly. My sister Susan was standing in the hall screaming and I lost it. All ninety-five pounds of me was filled with righteous indignation as I launched myself on his back and started punching him as hard as I could. He stood up with me still on his back, grabbed me and threw me across the kitchen. My sister was hysterical; my mom was crying, still laying on the floor and I was enraged by this bully who claimed to be my father. I charged at him again, but he just swiped me away. I ran as fast and as far away from home as I could go, not stopping until I was sure he couldn't find me. I had never felt such hatred towards anyone.

As is the norm with abusers, the next day it was all sunshine and lollypops. He acted like nothing had happened, but I hated him and was terrified of him. So off to school I went to be teased mercilessly and to learn how not to care. I hated liars even though I was branded as one. I hated bullies, even though I started to pick on smaller children. I hated life, I just... hated.

It's funny how resilient children can be. Despite my wonderful life, I still managed to go to school and even enjoyed art. I guess it was a good escape from my reality. It was the one thing that I was good at and was told that by my teacher. My mom registered me for some afterhours art lessons and it was nice to do something that others appreciated.

This was the early 70's, and rock and roll was a pretty big soundtrack in my weird and twisted life. I gravitated to it like a moth to a flame. It screamed out against oppression. It called out the hypocrites. It was loud and in your face. It was the perfect expression of rebellion and I was hooked. I had my very own theme music. I never liked the Beatles or the Stones, mainly because that's what everyone else liked. I had to be different, so I went for Procul Harem, Emerson Lake and Palmer, Grand Funk Railroad, Alice Cooper and pretty much anything that wasn't mainstream. I refused to get my hair cut anymore. I destroyed a barbershop when I was twelve and my mom never made me get another haircut. I started wearing the strangest clothing I could find. I didn't know it but God was allowing me to break free from the mold that everyone else was being conformed to. I had learned from the start what it is to be rejected by men and to be shunned as a leper. I was right where He wanted me to be.

I wanted to take guitar lessons. My mom agreed, and if I didn't get into trouble and did my chores, she would pay for them. So, at the age of twelve I started on my journey to rock stardom. We found this guy who owned a small music store and he gave lessons in the afternoon and evening. I would go there, straight after school on Tuesdays and Thursdays, catching the bus. It was kind of painful though. I have short stubby fingers and I just couldn't get the hang of the thing. I practiced, but my teacher said I would never be a rock star. I was heartbroken, but I kept on trying. One rainy afternoon I got on the bus and headed up the hill to my lesson. I got off the bus at the bus loop, which was right across from the music store. I had noticed a lot of police cars with their lights flashing as I went by on the bus, but I couldn't see what was happening because the bus windows were all fogged up. As I crossed the street and stood on the sidewalk, I saw my guitar teacher, soaking wet and face down on the sidewalk with his hair all matted, hands cuffed behind his back, with a cop's knee on him. He looked up at me and said, expressionless, *"Sorry kid, no lesson today."* Well, that wasn't expected. I ran with my guitar case over my head to protect me from the rain and got back on the same bus I had just got off. When I got home early, my mom wanted to know why I was home so early. I told her what I had just seen. She said that was it, no more guitar for you. It was obviously a drug bust and there was no way she was going to let me get in with that crowd.

Chapter Two

Junior High School

At last, a place where nobody knows me. I could try again and hopefully not get tormented anymore. It was great, for a while anyway. I soon learned that there were a lot of other kids who were from as bad or worse situations than mine. We found each other. Some would call us the losers club but I prefer to think of it as the survivor's club. There was always a crowd across from the school during recess and lunch and I soon found myself hanging out there all the time. We were distained by the jocks, nerds and teachers, but we didn't care. Some of these guys were tough and if they liked you they would beat the crap out of people for you.

My dad, despite his faults, made good money. My little sisters were all crazy about horses. Since there was an old riding stable a block away from our house, they spent all their time there. I had a friend from school who got a job there shoveling manure and looking after the rental horses. He took me there and introduced me to Ainsley Lubbock, a real old-fashioned cowboy who owned the place. He said he would give me a try. It was weekends only, but I had my first real job. He paid $2.00 an hour and 5 cents for every rat tail I could get. I was such a greenhorn that they all laughed when I asked about 'Rat tails.' Then my friend and new co-worker Rene pulled out his pellet gun and I clued in quick. I had never seen or held one, let alone shot one. It was only a pellet rifle but to me it was awesome. I couldn't wait to try it. We went around back and set up some targets. It was a spring, or break-barrel gun. One pump, load the pellet, close it up, aim and shoot. I was a natural. I was hitting targets like crazy and couldn't wait to kill some rats. Old Ainsley had an old air rifle that he let me borrow until I could afford my own and I became quite the sharp rat sniper. I discovered that their hides are tough, if you just hit them in the side or back the pellet would just bounce off them and they would disappear into their labyrinth for hours. To take one out you had to hit them in the eye or the back of the neck. I got so good at hunting the seemingly endless supply of rats that I was making more in rat tails than two hours of work. I was only working two hours a day, but there was a six-hour gap between the morning and evening hours.

Watching my sisters riding around on horses made me jealous so whenever there was a slow spell with no renters I would get on and practice riding. Rental horses are tough, devious and smart. They know when it's feeding time and if you are not in complete control, they will dump you in the blackberry bushes or mud (or both) and race each other back to the barn. I learned how not to take any crap from a horse. I would grab their ear and bite it, or hit them as hard as I could between the ears so they know who is boss. That usually works.

There was a tough guy from school, Tony, and he had a reputation of being one of the toughest guys at school and slightly crazy. I remember him luring a crow to himself with some bread, then once it got close enough, he grabbed it and bit its head off. We all respected and feared Tony. Tony and his girlfriend showed up one Saturday, and they wanted to rent some horses. I tried to explain that there were only two horses there and they were the toughest ones in the stable. If they didn't know how to ride, the horse would throw them off in the blackberries and race back for feeding time. Tony wasn't impressed, and he asked if I could ride them. I said yes. He said.

"*Let's see.*" So, I saddled up Gomer, a big old black gelding who knew every trick in the book. There were only a handful of renters who could ride him. I got on him and had him prancing like a Lipizzaner Stallion, not by my own doing, but because he wasn't happy that I was on him and he was rearing up to try and throw me off. I managed to stay on and take the old fart for a good run. When I got back, Tony was impressed, and he insisted that he and his girlfriend could handle them.

I saddled up Golden Boy, a beautiful older Palomino who was just as nasty as Gomer, and away they went, twenty minutes before feeding time. Like clockwork, we could hear the horses running back to the barn. As they came into view, without riders, we knew what was next. I was terrified that Tony was going to be mad at me but when they showed up, bloody and covered in mud, he was laughing and said, *"Man, you sure can ride. I like you."* The toughest guy in the school liked me. It was going to be different at school from now on.

My sisters moved their horses to the new horse barns at the end of the riding trails that led from Lubbock Stables. Since I was going back and forth on the trails anyway, and there were a lot of pretty girls at the other barns, I found myself hanging out there. There was one girl who I thought was the prettiest girl I had ever seen, April. She, and her sister, Angie, both had horses at the Burnaby Horseman's Association. One afternoon, while I was hanging around there, we heard that a girl had been thrown from a horse, so we took off running to see if we could help. We found the girl who had been thrown and she was fine. Her horse had taken off though and we all went to find it. It was standing in the tall grass and wasn't a problem. The girl got back on the horse and rode away, and April and I were standing there alone together. I was still very shy and not very mature for my age and she took my hand and we walked and talked all the way back to the barns. She became my first girlfriend. She liked me and I was terrified, but she was so easy to talk to and so relaxed around me that I felt relaxed around her too. We hung out together all the time and it was about a month before I had the courage to try to kiss her. She took over from there. I guess I didn't move fast enough for her. I was still a virgin and even though all my buddies were bragging about how they 'got some' I knew most of them were full of crap. I wanted to be sure because deep down inside I knew what a huge thing having sex was. This was the Seventies when disco was king, and everyone was having sex with everyone, but I felt it was just wrong outside of marriage. I don't know where I got that idea from, but I felt very strongly about it. April didn't feel the same way and one day she told me that she met another guy and that it was over with us. I was devastated. I thought there must be reward for doing the right thing. There was, but I just didn't see that far into the future.

Her friend, Brianna, figured I was still a good catch and it wasn't long before we were dating. I told her how I felt about sex before marriage and how hurt I was by April. She sympathized with me and said that she would never pressure me into doing anything I didn't want to. She lied. One night at her house, when her parents were away for the weekend, she had a big party. It was your typical teenagers party. Lots of beer, lots of pot and lots of kids throwing up. I could hold my liquor pretty good and while everyone else was puking and passing out Brianna and I were still going. She came up to me and gave me a big hug and whispered in my ear that it was *'time.'* I was as dumb as a post when it came to these things, so I asked her, *'Time for what?'* She laughed and started pulling me towards her bedroom. We started to kiss and make out when I got shot in the stomach. I felt so sick that I could hardly make it to the bathroom in time. I was no sexy hunk, but I was blowing chunks. She was disgusted with me and went to her room mad. I slept on her couch and I knew it was over the next morning. God had spared me from something I knew I wasn't ready for emotionally, physically or spiritually.

One of the characters that hung out across from the school was Mikey. He was smaller than me. The first time he laid eyes on me, he charged at me and wanted to fight. I stepped back, left my leg out, tripped him and sent him flying. He was angry, but I was laughing so hard that he just gave up and started laughing too. We became friends, the way most boys do. We would hang out at McDonalds, and generally just pal around together. We were never Best Friends, but we did hang out a lot. You might know him as Michael J Fox, the actor. There was an English and Drama teacher in our school who was obviously gay. He creeped me out and it was obvious that he didn't like me either. I opted out of his Drama class because having him for English was bad enough. Mike wasn't bothered by him though and the next thing you know, he's starring in a CBC sitcom called Leo & Me. The last time I saw him, he was driving his brand-new VW Beetle. He waved and honked. The next time I saw him, he was starring in the movie *'Back to The Future.'*

Since I gave up trying in elementary school, it was catching up to me and I was falling even further behind. I found myself day dreaming and watching the trucks go by outside the classroom windows. I still liked art. French was interesting. But as for the rest, I was lost. My math teacher was interesting. Mr. Kost was a former Russian circus performer who had defected when his circus came to Canada. He was old, but he could jump straight up on to his desk from a standing start. He got my attention, but it was too late to salvage my academic career. I was going to be a truck driver.

In art class we were learning how to do silk screening. The Steve Miller Band was coming to Vancouver and had an awesome ad in the paper. I copied it, transferred it to a clear sheet, put it on the overhead and traced it out. Did all the steps to silk screen print it. It was not a small project, with lots of little intricate cuts. It took me almost two weeks to finish before I was able to print anything. I was sick for a few days and couldn't wait to get back and print some of those posters. When I got to art class, I saw that this fat chick, who I didn't like and who didn't like me, had taken my silk screen and printed them out. She then claimed it as her work. I went to tell the teacher and the teacher took her side. I couldn't believe it. I went to the office to complain and was told not to make it any worse on myself and to apologize to fatso. I was now in trouble for someone else stealing my work.

I loved watching the trucks going past the school. I guess they represented freedom to me. The thought of getting in one and just keep going, leaving my pathetic life behind, was very appealing. I would get on my bike and ride around the truck dealers and repair shops just to be close to them. I took to building models of them and really enjoyed the *'mix and match'* capabilities of them. Unlike cars, they were infinitely changeable. I spent lots of time and money, alone in my room in the basement, breathing in the glue vapors and building my skill at model building, as well as turning out better and better results. When I was fifteen, my dad decided to take us to Disneyland in California. He rented a camper and my sisters, and I rode up top, at eye level, with the truckers. We stopped at a truck stop in California and I saw my first ever copy of Overdrive Magazine, **Voice of the Independent Trucker.** It blew me away. The super nice trucks were great, but the editorial content was a revelation. The editor and publisher, Mike Parkhurst, wrote about the injustices faced by the small, independent trucker. How they were up against the corporate machine that was destroying everything that their American forefathers had envisioned. How the independents had to suffer under excess taxation and incredible regulation burdens. How the United States Constitution was being completely ignored, even despised, by bungling bureaucrats. I was hooked. My life's problems were nothing compared to what these folks had to deal with, but I somehow felt a comradery with these people, even if I was just a punk from Canada.

As soon as we got home, I started my subscription. The tag line on the cover said, **"The Price of Truth, $2.50."** It was a magazine with kahunas, nice trucks and pretty girls. It was awesome. I entered one of my truck models in their Model of the Month feature and won a place in the magazine, 21st Anniversary issue. I was a part of something bigger than my own problems and it felt good to belong, even if at a distance.

My home life didn't really improve much. My dad still drank and got mean, but I had learned to simply avoid him. That wasn't always possible. One night he was on the war path and came storming downstairs. I flew into my room and slammed the door closed behind me. It opened to the outside, so he had to pull on it to open it, but I was holding it shut for dear life. I was hanging on to the door knob when it got quiet. Then suddenly, my barbell pole came through the closed door, just missing me. He was trying to kill me. I flung the door open and screamed at him, *"What the hell are you doing?"* He realized what he had just done and without apologies turned and went upstairs. I knew I had to leave that house, soon.

I was ashamed of my home life and didn't want anyone to know what a strange family I had. I loved trucks and idolized truck drivers, so I made up a fantasy family where my dad was a long-haul trucker. I look back with shame at how I felt. I had to hide my real family. I don't know why I made up a fake one, I guess it was because I was so ashamed of my circumstances. Whenever someone asked what my dad did, I told them that he owned his own rig and was away almost all the time. It became quite a chore to keep track of the whole thing and I eventually regretted ever starting the story. I felt trapped by my own lies and knew that wasn't going to be a very promising way to go through life but unfortunately, I had told the story to so many people that I felt that it was impossible to go back and tell the truth.

School was still a drag. I wasn't doing well in school at all. I wasn't stupid, just bored and left in the dust. I rode my bike to the local trucker's hotel, we didn't have a truck stop in Vancouver, and there was a driver outside of his truck working on it. I started talking to him and told him that I had never been in a truck before. He said he needed to go get some parts and asked me if I wanted to go for a short ride. I was all over it. We strapped my bike to the frame rails and away we went. I was on top of the world sitting there in the passenger seat. There was a girl I had a crush on from school walking on the sidewalk and when she looked up and smiled at me I was done for. I didn't ever want the ride to end, but it did. I was such a basket case that I broke down crying at the thought of it being over. I don't know what the poor trucker must have thought, but he went his way and I went mine.

I felt trapped by all the webs I had woven, as well as all the other troubles I was dealing with, so at the ripe old age of fourteen I tried to run away to the United States. I took a taxi from Burnaby to White Rock, near the American border, and got out and walked down the train tracks toward the border. When I got close, I went down a trail to the beach and simply walked across the border. I had my dog, Speedy, a husky/shepherd cross, with me and we came back up on the US side and went to Denny's. Not the smartest move, but I was hungry. I didn't have any American money, just Canadian, not to mention the big Maple Leaf on my backpack, so I was sticking out like a sore thumb. I sat in Denny's until day break then I walked over to the truck crossing and stuck out my thumb. A day-cab with a flatbed trailer stopped almost right away, but he said I had too much stuff and he didn't have room in his tiny cab. He assured me that another truck would stop and pick me up. He was wrong. I stood there for a good few hours and no one else stopped, except for a US Border Patrol agent. I discovered that they have jail cells at the border crossings. It was my first time in jail and my dog was tied up outside, barking loudly. Eventually I was picked up by the RCMP and taken to the Surrey BC detention center. I waited there for my mom to come and get me and Speedy. She wasn't happy about my actions, but she understood why I had run away. We were all afraid of dad.

It was around that time that I had my first introduction to drugs. Our school, Edmonds Jr Secondary, had a program where we could go and get skiing lessons on Saturdays. The thought of flying down a hill with a couple of boards strapped to my feet was rather appealing so I signed up. It was a blast. I loved every minute of it and had found a sport that I was good at, that I liked and where I didn't get the crap beat out of me because I was the smallest guy on the team. It wasn't long before I was doing acrobatic moves, jumping, and flipping all over the place. I had a great time. One afternoon, while riding the chair lift, the guy I was sitting with asked me if I wanted to smoke a joint. I had never tried it but wanted to, so I said yes. We smoked it as we went up and I was thoroughly stoned by the time we got to the top. It was surreal, and I was sure that everyone was watching me as I made my way to the slopes. Once I pushed off, all I can say is WOW, what a rush. I loved it. Being high and flying down a snow-covered mountain on a sunny afternoon was the best feeling I ever had in my life. I was so far away from my horrible existence and I never wanted it to end.

I found the guy who smoked me up and he gave me a small amount of pot. I saved some of it for school on Monday and at recess when I pulled out a joint, I was one popular kid. I suddenly had lots of friends and that was it. I was hooked, not physically but emotionally. I became quite the little pot head. I went from buying a little here and there, to selling some to keep myself supplied, to doing LSD and getting drunk regularly. My crowd of friends were some of the biggest losers around, but I didn't care, because at least I had friends, or so I thought.

I started to hang out with the wrong crowd at school. I had some pretty messed up friends. Looking back, we were all in similar situations, longing for acceptance and only finding it with each other. I started drinking more than just the occasional stolen mom's beer from the porch but was getting drunk regularly. I was with a bad crowd, but we accepted one another. We needed each other as we struggled with our demons. We laughed and partied. We broke into houses and stole cars. We were idiots, but we didn't care.

One night, one of the crew said he knew where there was a '69 Barracuda, easy to steal. We were all excited at the thought of the joyride and we headed to the car lot where it was. I was the smallest, so I was chosen to fit through the small broken window to get the keys. I found all the keys needed to move the cars in the way as well as to the Barracuda and we were in. There were six of us, and we all piled into the car and took off into the night. As we were driving the driver, Brock said we needed gas. No one had any money, so I knew what that meant. I wasn't into the idea of robbing any gas stations and we were right by my house, so I made an excuse that I had a test in the morning and needed to get out. If it wasn't for me, they wouldn't have the car in the first place and they all agreed that it was cool. He stopped the car and I got out and walked home.

The next morning, as I was getting ready for school, I heard on the news that a stolen car was involved in a gas station robbery and a high-speed chase. I knew it was them. They made it as far as Chilliwack, about 60 miles from Burnaby, when they came up to a road block. I'm guessing that Brock thought that he was invincible and that he could ram the roadblock like in the movies, so he did. Out of the five guys in the car, two died. Brock was one of them and the other was a kid I didn't know that well. The others were in the hospital with various injuries. I sat there stunned, realizing that I could easily have been in that car. No one ever ratted me out though and hopefully the statute of limitations is still in effect. Once again, my life had been spared.

Another so called friend was Billy. He was a funny little guy with frizzy hair and an attitude. He was from a really sketchy part of town and his family was even more messed up than mine. His dad was a total pot head and his older brother was in prison. His mom drank more than mine too. We all got along well, since we had so many problems in common. The one thing we had the most in common was that we had both gone out with April. It seemed ready weird to me that she would have ever gone out with someone like him.

There were a few other characters in our little crew of misfits. There was Bird who, strangely enough, kind of looked like a bird. Then there was Goots, which is stoog spelled backwards. He was a great guy, but one night the Hinchbergers put LSD in his beer, and he was never right after that. There were lots of others, but those were the ones I was closest to.

One night, Billy told us about this incredible building he had broken into. He said we would have to see it to believe it, so naturally we followed him. He pulled out his giant screw driver and with a good pry on the door, we were in. It was unreal. There were hard core pornography magazines from floor to ceiling in this warehouse. He said to follow him up a flight of metal stairs, so we did. When we got to the top, there it was, dope head heaven. There was every kind of drug paraphernalia you could think of; shelves and shelves of it. So, we started loading it into boxes and we spent the night cleaning the place out. All the stuff in that warehouse was completely illegal anyway so we had no fear of the cops finding out. We did have some trepidation about who might own it though. We didn't stick around to find out.

We must have had about fifteen big boxes full of Glass Head products, bongs, power hitters, a thousand roach clips and other stuff. Of course, we had no idea what to do with it, so we headed to downtown Vancouver to try and sell it. Talk about stupid. Billy got arrested with a bunch of the stuff, but he never ratted us out. Since the owners never reported it stolen, he was never charged with anything, but that brought it close to home. We knew that trying to sell it on the street was a bad idea.

I met this guy who seemed to be old. The reality is that he was probably no more than twenty. He said he knew someone who would buy all the stuff for a good price, so we loaded it all into his pickup truck and drove to a place in Vancouver. This nasty looking guy came down stairs and looked at it, then said he would take it off our hands for $500. That was a lot of money to us, so we said sure. We hauled it into his apartment and saw the sawed-off shotguns he had all over the place. We knew this guy was serious bad news. He told us to wait at the truck and he would be down with our money in a few minutes. He never came down. We sat there realizing that we had just been robbed and were feeling slightly outraged, knowing full well that going back up and asking for our money was suicide. We probably deserved that. I mentioned it to the others and they thought I was nuts and wanted revenge, but I was out of there. I told them what goes around just came around and we might as well just walk away. They refused to walk away, but I did. I heard that one of my friends got shot by the guy for something unrelated, but he didn't die. I was starting to get rather leery of these "friends." God was looking after this fool and I distanced myself from them, not wanting to die or go to jail.

One night, as we were sitting around getting high, I was overwhelmed by thoughts of things that were way bigger than me. I had no idea where it had come from so I asked them, *"Hey, have you guys ever thought of "the big picture?"* They looked at me like I was nuts, and we just dropped the subject. But, through my foggy mind, I knew there was much more to this life than getting stoned and stealing cars.

That wasn't the last time I ran away from home. When I was sixteen, I was caught with a small amount of pot and some Nunchaku Sticks. I was charged with possession of marijuana, a roach, and possession of a prohibited weapon. The latter sounds much worse than it was. My buddy Winston, a cool little Chinese kid from Hong Kong, showed me what Nunchaku Sticks were, so I made a pair out of an old dog collar and one of my mom's broom handles. I hurt myself far more than anyone else. Then I found out the hard way that they are illegal in Canada. There wasn't any 'Young Offenders Act' to protect me from the possibility of jail time back then. I was going to be tried as an adult and I was genuinely scared. Jail for small young guys is not usually a pleasant experience. So, with fear as a motivator, and my dog Speedy as my companion, I caught a taxi out to the Eastbound weigh scales at the Port Mann Bridge. I asked the scale guys if I could ask truckers for a ride from there and they said they didn't care one way or another.

There was an older American trucker in the scale who must have felt sorry for me, because he gave me an American $5 bill. I stood beside the scale platform and asked all the truckers if they were heading to Calgary. There was a steady stream of no's, until one driver said he was going to Edmonton and could drop me off in Kamloops. I got in and away we went. I thought I was in Heaven, in my own little world, and enjoyed going through the Fraser Canyon in a big rig. But, five hours later, we were in Kamloops and he had to let me off. I was sad and hopeful at the same time. I figured that if it was that easy to get a ride, I would be in Calgary soon enough. Except that it started to rain, and no one wanted a soaking wet long-haired kid and a wet dog in their car or truck. We stood on the road side for at least six hours until a car load of teenagers stopped and gave me a ride to the outskirts of Kamloops. They gave me a beer and smoked a joint with me, then dropped me off. It was a nice respite but very short and Speedy and me were standing on the roadside again twenty minutes later. We were there all night and I was getting tired so I dropped a hit of acid to stay awake. That was interesting because an old farmer picked us up shortly after that and took me as far as Sicamous, about eighty miles east of there. I started to trip while riding with the farmer and he must have known something wasn't right, but he drove me until he had to turn off. He let us out by the Monashee River bridge, in the pouring rain.

We ran across the narrow bridge to avoid getting smeared by a semi and I stuck out my thumb on the other side of the bridge. Speedy was interested in the river so I let him run down there for a bit. When we were done, and thoroughly soaking wet from the rain, we walked back up to the road. A bus went by, then stopped up ahead. I figured he was just dropping someone off, but I didn't see anyone get off and he honked his horn a few times. We ran up to the bus and the long-haired driver said, *"I'm going to Calgary, you need a ride?"* I was stunned and grateful. Once on the bus, I realized that it wasn't any ordinary bus because it was outfitted like a motorhome. The driver asked me if I had ever heard of Valdy. Surprisingly enough I had. He was a local country/blues artist who had a minor hit called **'Play me a Rock and Roll Song.'** He wasn't on the tour bus, so the driver was just taking it back to Calgary where it was stored in a warehouse when not being used for touring. There were a couple of other hitch-hikers already on the bus, and we were cruising in style. The driver fired up a joint and we all had quite a buzz as we climbed up and over Rogers Pass in the falling snow. When we were around Banff Alberta, the driver spotted another bus going the other way and stopped. He said that the guy driving that bus was the one who customized the one we were on. The other driver ran across the highway to our bus and then fired up a powerful joint. I let Speedy out to do his business and he was having a blast running around in the snow-covered field. There was a farmer on a tractor who stopped and leveled a rifle at my dog. I yelled and waved my arms until he saw me and put down his gun. Speedy had no idea how close he had just come to being mistaken for a wolf.

An hour later we were coming into Calgary and soon enough I was dropped off in front of the Highlander Hotel. I was completely stoned from all the pot and acid, and as I walked across the highway my sleeping bag came untied from my backpack and unraveled and dragged on the ground behind me like a royal robe. I gathered it up and went into the hotel lobby to use a pay phone. Calls were only a dime then and I had about $10.00 left. My dad's business partner's ex-wife and son lived in Calgary and he was the only person that I knew there that wouldn't call my parents. I searched the phone book under the last name 'Scott.' His first name was Kim, so I figured it wouldn't take long to narrow it down. I did get a female Kim Scott and I'm sure she was a bit shocked when I said, *'Sorry, wrong sex!'* There were a lot of Scott's in there. It took a while and I was getting down to my last dollar in dimes, but I finally found him. I told him where I was, and he got his friend to come and pick me up. I was so glad to have made it to my intended destination. Of course, his mother found out about me being there the next day and made a few phone calls. I guess mom and dad were a bit surprised to find out I was in Calgary. They weren't too happy with me, especially since I had court two days later. So, God bless them, they paid for a flight back to Vancouver for Speedy and me and I was in court on time. I lied and told the judge that I had just come back from Calgary where I had found a job. It wasn't a total lie since I was offered a job there, I just didn't really go there for that. I was sentenced for the pot charge. I was given a conditional discharge, six months' probation, two hundred hours of community service and a $150.00 fine.

I went to court in Vancouver a few days later for the possession of a prohibited weapon charge. I received the exact same sentence for that one and they later merged the two, so I only had to pay $300.00 and do some work at the local YMCA. I worked hard and it was obvious that I wasn't going to be a problem, so they ended my community service time and my probation a couple months early with a stern warning that if I got in any trouble at all, I was looking at serious problems. That was all the motivation I needed to keep my nose clean.

I was back at home and things seemed to settle down. My dad seemed to be genuinely sorry for being a jerk and we even tried hanging out a bit. He hired me on weekends to help him in his business repairing engines on ships and boats. It was okay, but I was always leery of him. He offered me a beer one day after work and I accepted. It wasn't my first beer. I had been stealing them from my mom's stash on the back porch for quite a while. I used to pride myself on not getting caught but after mom had had a few, she lost count anyway. As long as the empties were in the case, she was none the wiser. There I was having a beer with the guy who tried to kill me, but who really was a funny guy. I discovered that lots of people knew the old man and pretty much liked him. As I was working with him, he started to see that I might not be as big of a loser as he thought.

I was eligible to transfer to Burnaby Central High School for Grade Ten. I needed to start somewhere fresh, so I jumped at it. I managed to pass Grade 10 and went to work full time for my dad that summer. Now I had money and could buy lots of dope and alcohol to party with my friends. I had met a friend in High School, Kris Adams, and we hung out together a lot. He was a bit of an antagonist though and he didn't always act friendly towards me. I knew I was messed up, but I didn't need to be constantly reminded about it. He and I were always together though. We did lots of stupid stuff, but mainly we got stoned, a lot. We sort of drifted apart after a while. He was too much of a jerk and I had finally figured out that I didn't need to put up with that just to have a friend. He does reappear in the story, but in a way I never expected.

I started selling drugs. I didn't have to, since I could always work for the old man, but it just seemed like a cool thing to do, plus it was easy money, and I didn't have to get dirty. We met a guy who made LSD. John was his name and he seemed like a cool guy. He had a wife, a baby son, and a pet owl. He said he would let me make as much as I wanted on his acid if he got $2.00 per hit. A hit was selling for $5.00 at the time so I figured this would be super easy money. I was such an idiot. I had him front me a 'hundred lot' and I recruited my buddy Mike and we caught a bus to downtown Vancouver. Once we got there we were in business.

We were selling a little acid and found ourselves down in Stanley Park where we took a break. I had 100 hits when we started and had sold a few hits when Mike, like a complete fool, approached some really sketchy looking guys. I had no intention of talking to them, but it was too late. He told them I had some for sale and walking away would be a bad move. They said they were interested and we did the deal. They said they had some 'jungle juice' and asked us if we were into partying. I wasn't, but Mike was. So, I stayed and had a drink. Bad move. I honestly don't know what happened after that. I was told by some other guys a few days later that I had swan dived off the bus shelter onto the hood of a cop car, then was thrown into the back of the cop car by a female cop like a sack of screaming potatoes. I woke up in a jail cell that was too small to stretch out in. I checked for my acid, but it was gone. I was going to go to prison for trafficking. I screamed bloody murder. I lost it in that cell. Then I found it, one hit of acid in my pocket. I figured hey, why not, so I did it. Another bad move. Tripping on acid in a closet with a steel door was not good. I don't know exactly how long I was in there, but a guard came and unlocked the cell. He said I was lucky. I had no idea what he was talking about, but I was glad to not be in that cell anymore. He took me to a room where they gave me all my stuff back.

I was in shock. I couldn't believe it. Then a tall old grey-haired cop came in and got me. He walked me to an elevator. He looked too nice to beat the crap out of me in the elevator. As we started to descend, he hit the stop button. I thought for sure that I was about to be beaten to a pulp. But he put his hand on my shoulder and with the look of a loving grandfather said, *"Son, I don't know why you're being given another chance, but you are. Don't do anything that will get you in here again."* He then hit the button and let me out in the back alley behind the police station. I was free.

It was a long walk back to Burnaby on a Sunday morning before the busses started running. I had a lot to think about and to be thankful for. I wasn't going to prison. Good thing. I owed John $200.00 for the acid. Bad thing. I was told that John was a nice guy, until you owed him money. They said that he had beaten and even killed kids for less. I didn't know if it was true, but I didn't want to find out. He didn't know where I lived, but it was a small world and I knew that I couldn't stay in Burnaby and Vancouver. I called Mike and said, *"It's because of you that this happened, and you told me your sister lives in Calgary. Get packed buddy because we're going, today."*

I had I bought a couple of bus tickets and was off to Calgary to start my life away from home. We rode the bus to Calgary and called his sister and brother-in-law when we arrived. They lived in what can best be described as an off-campus Animal House. There was a party there seven days a week. We rented a room upstairs and I promptly set out to find a job.

I found a job at a transmission shop, pulling transmissions, and putting them back in. It was not very exciting. I lasted about two months before being told that I wasn't working out. Mike only lasted one day because he slept most of the time.

I found another job with a small trucking company that hauled explosives. It was okay, but one day in the lunch room I commented that I thought it was funny that I was working for 'suicide jockeys.' The place went silent. I was informed that they didn't see it like that. Then the Canadian government had passed a bill in which they basically were going to help themselves to all that nice Alberta oil revenue. I was laid off two weeks later.

The Animal House was a party central. All day and night, every day, there was something involving sex, drugs and rock and roll going on there. It was hard to sleep in that environment, let alone go to work every day, but I managed. After losing my second job and finding it nearly impossible to find another one I found myself partying, a lot. I had turned 18 on November 25th and since that was the legal drinking age in Alberta, I dove in head first. I had some savings from work and had applied for Unemployment Insurance, so it was full bore party time.

The UI took way longer to process than I had bargained for and I had spent my rent money. I found myself homeless in Calgary. That might not be bad when the weather is good but when it drops down to -30c overnight you can die. I made a call and found out that John, the acid guy, was in jail and I would be safe to come back. There was a small problem though, we only had two dollars. It was the middle of winter and the thought of hitch hiking was not that appealing. Then I had an idea, why not take the $2 and buy some basil and baggies from the supermarket, divide it up into four individual bags and head to the local arcade and sell it as pot. Sure, it was deceptive, but it wasn't illegal. No one is in jail for trafficking basil. We sold the four bags for $25 each and got the heck out of Calgary before anyone could figure out what we had done. We had enough left over to buy a case of beer and we sat at the very back of the bus and had a great ride back to Vancouver.

When I got back, I discovered that I was much wiser and more grown up than any of my peers. I went to the local arcade and saw it for what it really was, a hangout for children, and losers who still thought they were children. I went back to my parents' house, but dad had laid down the rules. If I was going to live there and not go to school, I had to get a job and pay rent and buy my own food. At 18 I should have been finishing High School, so I went back to try out Grade 11. I quickly discovered that I was the misfit of the century there since I had missed so much, plus, with the worldly experience I had, I thought they were all a bunch of loser little children anyway. So, like an arrogant idiot, I quit again.

I did meet an interesting character at the local arcade one night, Mikey. He was the same age as me and he had some worldly experience himself, so we had that in common. It turned out that he was swamping for furniture movers out of a local hotel that they stayed at.

I found out that you could get work as a swamper for the day, or longer if they liked you. The Lougheed Hotel was the main 'bedbuggers' stop in Vancouver. I ended up working regularly with a few guys whenever they were in Vancouver. One guy, Dale, drove for Banstra Transport out of Smithers and was in town once every three weeks. I would swamp for him as well as party and get him his pot. He was a great guy, and we became pretty good friends after a while. Three weeks after he headed back home, I expected him to be at The Lougheed. I saw his truck in the lot, so naturally I figured he was driving it. I went in to the restaurant and he wasn't there. There was a different driver who I had met briefly before. I asked him where Dale was. He looked at me and said, *"You haven't heard? He was in a fight and was messed up pretty bad."* I went to work for the guy, but he didn't know any more than what he had already told me.

I guess it was about a month later when I went into the restaurant and saw Dale sitting there. I was glad to see him, but I didn't see his truck out in the lot. I asked him what he was doing there, and he just pointed to his crutches and said with his head hung, *"I won't be driving anymore."* I asked him what happened, and he told me about it.

He was in Kispiox, a small isolated native village. He was in the hotel bar having a few beers when he ran out of cigarettes. He had a carton in his truck, so he went out to get a pack. When he got out to his truck he could hear a woman screaming. It was coming from behind his trailer. So, he grabbed his tire billy and slowly made his way back there. He found three young 'native Canadians' raping a young native Canadian girl so he did what needed to be done and beat the living tar out of them with his tire billy. He then helped her into the lobby of the hotel where he called the cops. The police came and took his statement and he went back into the bar to a hero's welcome. He was bought some more drinks and at closing time he headed back out to his truck. As he was climbing into the cab, he was stabbed in the back by one of the natives, who then disappeared into the night. They had severed his spinal column. He dropped to the ground and had to drag himself back across the frozen parking lot to get help. So, there he was, a month later at the Lougheed Hotel, bitter and angry at his situation and all Indians in general. I couldn't blame him one bit. Not only was he partially paralyzed by the attack, but the Workers Compensation Board ruled that since he wasn't in fact 'working' when it happened, they denied his claim. So, he was basically screwed. I offered to drive him around and help him in any way I could. I took him to doctors' appointments and helped him find a place to live. He only had welfare, so he couldn't afford much and since he needed to be near the hospital and clinics, he ended up in a pretty run down old flop house filled with the usual scary characters. He was miserable. And I was unsure if I was helping at all. I came by one day to see how he was doing, and he was drunk at 11am. He cussed me out and said he didn't like me or want my pity or my help. I didn't take that too well since I was so sensitive to rejection, so I left and never went back. I have often wondered whatever became of him and have prayed for him.

One night I was at an old house that I used to frequent in New Westminster. It was a party that had never really stopped. There were some new faces, but the main crowd was still there. I got drunk and then realized it was close to 1am and if I didn't want to walk for five miles, I needed to get to the bus stop before the last bus went by. I hoofed it out to the bus stop and when I got there I was shocked to find my old friend Kris Adams sitting there. We didn't exactly part as good friends and I half expected that we were going to get into it. I sat down and figured that if he wants a go then I would give it to him. What he did shocked the hell out of me. He had a Bible in his lap. He told me he was sorry for being so mean to me and that he was praying for me. *"What the heck happened to you?"* I asked him. *"I found Jesus Jon, and he wants me to tell you that He loves you very much and has a wonderful plan for your life."* He had this incredible peace about him and he said he could see that I had grown up quite a bit since the last time we were hanging out together. He was generally freaking me out by how nice he was being. I thought he was faking it. He assured me that he was truly Born Again and that God had the same thing for me, if I would only believe the Gospel. I had no idea what he was talking about and it was as if he was fading out on me because he was talking and I could not hear him. The bus came, and I thought, great, now I'm going to be stuck with him, but he didn't get on. I was like, *"Dude, why were you sitting at the bus stop if you're not getting on?"* He replied, *"Because I was waiting for you."* Confused was the operative word there. I got on the bus and as it pulled away he waved goodbye. I have not seen him since.

Furniture moving pretty much stops in the fall and winter, so I found myself working again for my dad. He had some big jobs on some ocean-going tug boats. They were so big that they had the same engines that are in the diesel locomotives the railroads use. I had gained some maturity and a tiny bit of wisdom and my dad and I were getting along well. He helped me get my driver's license and since I knew how to handle a semi before I even had my license, he trusted me to do the running around for parts. I kind of liked the old guy. He began to open up to me a bit about his childhood and why he was so angry with me when I was younger. I guess he just wanted me to be tough enough to handle this world. He had come up the hard way and didn't have a dad to help him out, so he didn't really know how to be one. Once I turned nineteen, we would go to the bars after work and really got to know each other. He never said he loved me, but I think I had earned a small amount of respect.

My dad and his business partner got a contract to rebuild the generator engines on one of the big dredging ships that were used in the Arctic Ocean to build the islands where drilling rigs were set up to explore for oil. They were frozen in the McKinley Bay sea ice for the winter. He hired me as a Mechanics Assistant. I went up there with Jimmy, my dad's right-hand man, and an old Dutchman named Clem, with his grandson as his helper. It was heavy stuff for a 20-year-old pothead loser. We flew to Edmonton then caught another jet to Inuvik NWT. From there we took a small prop plane out to the ice where there was a runway plowed out on the frozen ocean. There were probably twenty different ships of various sizes frozen in the ice in a big circle. It was the time of year to do maintenance and there was a lot of activity. I couldn't believe it when I saw trucks hauling steel and other supplies there. I had no concept of ice road trucking at all. We got to work and went at it twelve hours a day, seven days a week, for six weeks straight. It was a grueling schedule, but the food was incredible. I ate so much steak and lobster that I got sick of it. To this day, lobster tastes like soap to me.

We were told not to ever go out beyond the boundary of the circle of ships because of the polar bears that were constantly prowling around out there. A couple of the young guys working there asked me if I wanted to come with them to get high one evening after my shift was over. I said sure, but where? Getting caught with any drugs or alcohol was grounds for instant dismissal. They said out on the far side of the ships. They assured me that they had smoked up there all the time and it was close enough to the gangway of a frozen in oil rig. I hesitated and said thanks but I better not. A few hours later, I found out that a couple of polar bears had mauled them. One of them was killed and the other was in bad shape. That is one joint I was glad I passed on.

I came back to Vancouver with money pouring out of my pockets. I promptly started blowing it on useless crap. I was partying it away and was shocked at how fast it was disappearing. I got my first real driving job, working for a small trucking company named Claire Transport, and they sent me out to Sea Island, where the Vancouver International Airport is. As I was coming back from my delivery, I spotted the top corner of a truck cab in a junk yard. I parked and jumped out of the truck. I was a subscriber to Overdrive Magazine and had become hooked on the idea of finding an old truck and restoring it. I was, and still am, hooked on the old Kenworth conventional. I think they were the epitome of what a truck should look like. Well, there it was, an old beat up Kenworth Conventional. I was in love.

I figured that if I didn't buy it, I would soon spend all my money on crap anyway. I made them an offer of $1500.00. The old guy at the scrap yard saw me from a mile away and said, *"If you want the winch too, that will be another $100.00."* Smitten as I was, I paid the man $1600.00 and had it towed to my dad's shop. To say he wasn't pleased would be an understatement. He totally freaked out on me. He said, *"What do you think you're going to do with this old piece of crap!? Are you out of your mind? You paid money for this thing? You are such an idiot!"* I asked him, *"What would you rather me do, rebuild this old truck and put it back to work or just throw my money away?"* He wasn't convinced. When he put a big wrench on the crankshaft and it turned over with no resistance, he blew a gasket. *"It has no compression. It's garbage. You paid how much for this thing?"* Undeterred, and stubborn, I plugged my ears and hummed loudly. I was determined to get the old truck back on the road. I figured it would take a few grand, and a few months.

My dad was not impressed with my after-work project. He was convinced that I was truly the idiot son he thought I was. All that did was make me even more determined to finish the restoration. We had it towed out to a big old industrial site that had once been a huge factory. There were lots of people and businesses renting space there, and my dad decided to move his shop there too. It was perfect because that was where Benson's Shipyards were, and they let me use their sandblaster, if I used my own sand. I stripped the old KW down to the frame rails and began the long slow process of bringing it back from the dead. I used to love to smoke a big fat joint, then sandblast away the layers of paint in a sort of psychedelic experience.

It was an incredible experience, albeit slow. I worked for Claire Transport during the day, but I worked on that old truck every night and weekend. I didn't have much cash, but I learned how to horse trade parts. I had the cab basically finished, with all new switches, gauges, and things. It was quite the motivator to see it there, waiting for the rest of the thing to be ready for it. When it came time to tear into the engine, my dad decided to get involved. That old truck did more to heal the hurt between us than any therapy could have. He found a new cam shaft, which for an engine that old was quite a feat. He had been working on these old Cummins engines for many years and he knew what he was doing, which was good, because I didn't.

My friend, Mark Harvey, was renting a place in New Westminster, across the river from our shop. He was a great guy who liked to party, so I found myself hanging out at his place on the weekends. I was still working for my dad on weekends and one Saturday morning I had to be at a job site, but since I had been up drinking all night at Mark's, I was getting a late start. I had my driver's license suspended for an impaired driving conviction, so I was taking the bus, catching rides or hitchhiking. Since there weren't any buses running to anywhere near that jobsite, I went out to the main street and stuck out my thumb. I was amazed at how quickly I got a ride.

I told the guy where I needed to go, and he said I was in luck because he was going to almost the same place. As we were driving along River Road in Richmond, he started telling me about the hot chick he had in his car the night before and he reached over and grabbed my leg telling me how she enjoyed being touched like that. I told him to stop the car and let me out. He said he was sorry and that he would drive me to where I needed to go. I was already running behind, so I accepted the ride but kept a wary eye on the guy. He dropped me off right at the jobsite and left. I never thought anything more of it.

About a month or so later, Clifford Robert Olsen was arrested for the murder of lots of young men and women. He led the investigators to where he had murdered and dumped the bodies. It was right where "buddy" had grabbed my leg. I'm a bit slow sometimes, but then it hit me. It was Clifford Olsen that had given me that ride that day, and he grabbed my leg right where he had been doing his murdering.

Mark loved the ladies, and most of them loved him. He had been with just about everyone in the building he was renting and it got hectic around there sometimes. One of his "girlfriends" had a boyfriend who was in jail. I guess he was a bit of a jealous type because when he got out, he beat her to a pulp and came looking for Mark. We were having a few beers in his place one Friday night when there was a knock at the door. He went and answered it. A short guy who neither one of us had seen before plunged a knife into Marks stomach and ran away. Mark stood there, kind of stunned. I didn't know what had happened until he turned around to come back in, I saw a lot of blood soaking his shirt. It all happened so fast that he had barely even registered it himself. He looked at the blood. I said, *"We're getting you to the hospital right now!"* He didn't want to go but I basically forced him to. Once he had been admitted, the police were called. They asked him if he was going to press charges and he refused. They were a wee bit mad but couldn't do anything. The doctor told him that it was a miracle that the knife had missed every vital organ. He continued to have "relations" with the stabber's girlfriend. Mark was a good guy, but he was nuts.

About five years into the project, we dropped the engine into the chassis of my old truck. I hooked up a temporary fuel tank, got some batteries and cranked it over. It cranked over easily with the compression release lever pulled out, and when I let it go, she fired right up. I can't begin to tell you how incredible that felt. It was loud without a muffler, it rattled like an old diesel should, and I was one proud puppy. My dad wasn't there when I started it, so he was a bit mad that he wasn't there to see it run the first time, but it fired right up for him as well and we were good.

The rest of it started to come together quickly, at least when I had the money for parts. It wasn't long before I was driving it, without a hood or fenders, around the old industrial building. My driver's seat was just a plastic chair but I was the king of the road in that throne. I put the fenders on and a new air ride driver's seat and took it to my friends' body shop, where it was for the better part of a year. I thought I had the body ready for painting, but he was a perfectionist and I basically had to redo the whole thing. I gained a new appreciation for power sanders. I wanted it painted navy blue with a silver stripe, he said nope, it's going to be black. He loved black. There was no talking him out of it and since he was basically doing it at no cost, he had the final say. It turned out okay in black.

Seven years after I dragged it to my dad's shop, it was running, and I was entering it in parades and antique truck shows. But it was too old to put to work, even with all the work I had done to it. And since we were not a trucking family, I had nothing but horse trading and cash to work with. The frame had more holes that Swiss cheese, and it was geared so low that it's top speed was 42 MPH. It was severely under powered. It was just too old. I kept it as a toy. I worked at various trucking companies while I was restoring the old girl and had a fair bit of 'legitimate' experiences. I joined the local antique truck club, The BC Pioneer Chapter of the American Truck Historical Society. It was while hanging out with a few other fellow old truck enthusiasts that I met some very interesting characters.

My first real truck driving job was for Claire Transport, a very small trucking company that mainly did work for the Savolite Chemical Company. They made cleaning products; from soap flakes to industrial acids. My first truck was a 1956 International Loadstar. It was known to the drivers as *'Dino the Dinosaur.'* It was beat up and well used, but it was my ride and I didn't care. It had some interesting quirks, like a vacuum assisted two speed rear axle and vacuum windshield wipers. As any old timer would tell you, engines only have vacuum when you are applying the gas and almost none when you are coasting or braking. It was quite the challenge to learn how to shift that two-speed axle without destroying it. The windshield wipers were interesting too. If you revved up the engine, they would swing back and forth so hard that the wiper blades would fly off. This was in Vancouver, and it was clean and green there, because it is always raining. I would fling the wiper blades off old Dino more than once. It was probably one of the best introductions to trucking I could have had. I learned how to keep a tool box with me and fix almost anything right when it needed it. The freight box was straight out of the 1930's. It was a wooden thing with metal hoops and a tarped roof. Hauling bags of soap flakes, that couldn't get wet, in the rain, with a leaky old stake rack and tarp was a challenge. After a while, I earned the nick-name, *'Soapy.'*

I met two good friends there, Phil and Bill. We were always together, especially on Friday nights. We would get our pay checks and go straight to the Blue Boy Hotel beer parlor where we cashed our paychecks and drank the whole works away. We were usually too broke to afford breakfast the next day. Don't ask me how but we always managed to make it until the next Friday and we would do it all over again. It wasn't my dream job, but it was building my experience and I knew that one day I would be out on the big road, driving a real truck and making real money.

Chapter Three

My Own Truck, Earl, and Feeding the World

My dad knew a fellow, Earl Collins, who was convinced that he had discovered the simple technology that would feed the world. They met in the bar my dad used to stop in after work. Earl was a smart old guy. He had thought this through very carefully. He had made one attempt to build a prototype, but his investors got greedy as it neared completion and voted him off the board of directors and out of his own company. He was smart enough to have never put the key component in the company's main asset, so when he drove away, he had the key component in the pickup box.

My dad, even though he was a card carrying communist, which we all found out about after he died, was intrigued by the idea of feeding the world, and making a pile of money while helping it happen. So, without consulting mom, he told Earl that it was perfectly fine for him to build his test unit in our backyard.

What was the key component? In WW2 they were known as Buzz Bombs, the V2 Rocket; otherwise known as a Pulse Jet Engine. They have one rather undesirable feature; they are extremely loud. Earl had a friend, Cody, who was his welder, helper, goffer guy. It was quite interesting to me and I found myself spending lots of time hanging around and then eventually helping them.

This thing was huge. It required tons of sand to surround the tank it was mounted in to deaden the noise. It began to grow larger as augers, feed belts, slurry tanks, a cyclone, and other industrial stuff was added to it. My mom hated it, and Earl Collins.

One afternoon, Earl and Cody asked me if I would be interested in coming with them to a meeting they went to every Thursday night. They said it was free, and that his daughter, Shelly, was going to be there. Good enough reason for me to go right there. I had no idea what it was about, other than it had something to do with personal improvement. I knew I could always use more of that, and Shelly was going to be there.

They gave me the address and I met them there. When we arrived, I was a bit shocked to find out it was a church. I wasn't too thrilled, but they assured me that it wasn't religious at all and that they weren't trying to convert me, whatever that meant. It turns out that it had nothing to do with the Bible but was just a big self-help thing. Shelly was there but I was devastated when she told me that her friend and her were going to Thailand for a year. I'm still not sure exactly what it was they were teaching, but since Shelly wasn't going to be there for at least a year, I didn't see the need to keep going. Not sure if it was a cult or what, but they had planted a few ideas in my feeble brain.

Around that time, I discovered that Earl had a 3-ton flatbed truck that he bought for his previous venture, and it was only a couple of years old but had less than 10,000 miles on it. He offered it to me for a fraction of what it was worth, if I wanted it. It didn't take long to think about it and the next thing I knew I was an Owner/Operator. It was a little truck, but it was enough to get me going and soon I was trucking for a hay hauler friend of my sisters, Ed Hensley. He was a Vietnam vet and had a bit of a temper problem but overall, he was a good guy to work for. The price of gas was killing me, and the government had a good subsidy for anyone who was willing to switch to Natural Gas, so I did. My cost for fuel dropped by over 50% right away and the conversion was paid for in very short order.

I had the truck for about three months and I was doing pretty good. I was learning how to track my income versus my expenses. I was getting lots of work and I was fixing the truck up as I went. I saw myself going all the way to the big rigs. Then the rear axle broke. I had money set aside for repairs, but it cost me more in downtime and lost opportunities.

I was up and running again in a couple of days. The next week, the transmission refused to stay in top gear. I had to hold it there with all my might, and it was getting rather hot, which is never a good thing. I knew I needed a new transmission. It turns out that the little truck had lots of proprietary parts that were simply not interchangeable with anything else, and the dealers knew it. The cost of a new transmission was $1400.00, about $1000 more than I could afford. I had no choice but to get it on credit. It was fixed over a long weekend, so all I lost was a hay hauling job, I was right back to work on Tuesday.

My engine had started to burn oil, lots of it. It was from the natural gas not having any lubricating qualities to it. I knew I had to do something because driving around while leaving a big blue cloud of smoke everywhere was not only expensive, but my customers, who were mainly horse people, didn't appreciate being choked by it.

I went to hang out at Bills body shop, where my old '48 KW was, and there was a guy there, George, whose car was getting worked on. I told them of my predicament, and he told me that he worked for an engine repair shop and was always doing jobs on the side. He said he would build me an engine for natural gas for $1500, all he wanted was half down for parts. It was a miracle. He left and said he would have an engine for me in a couple days, all he wanted was for me to pull mine out, so it would be a quick drop in and I would be up and running. I drove it the next week, excited at the thought of not seeing the blue cloud behind me.

That Friday night I pulled into the shop and got to work at ripping the engine out. It required a lot of work, but it was out by midnight. All George had to do was show up, drop the new one in, and I wouldn't lose a day of work. He arrived around 10 in the morning, but there it was, all painted Chevy Orange and looking good. We went to work on installing it and my dad came out to check on the progress. He called me outside and told me he didn't like or trust the guy. What was I supposed to do? I already had mine out and the new one was going in. We hooked everything up and I wanted it to be running before George left, just in case it needed any fine tuning. I poured water in the radiator. As it filled some started to come out of one of the exhaust ports. That was not good. My dad just shook his head, knowing that I was being taken for a ride. George said that was odd, he had no idea why it would do that and he would replace the head with a better one. My dad was not impressed. I was desperate though because I had work lined up first thing Monday morning and I needed my truck. While George was gone, my dad let me have it. He chewed me out for being such an idiot, always being stupid and being taken advantage of. I didn't argue. An hour later, George showed back up with a new head, bolted it on and we tried again. It turned over a few times and fired up. It didn't have the exhaust manifolds on yet, so it was loud, but it ran. George said he had to go and that he would catch up for the rest of the money I owed him by the end of the week. My dad said I was a moron for trusting him.

Dad was a classic pessimist, nothing was ever going to work out right, everything was against him. I don't know why, but I was a born optimist. We had some good arguments over our outlook on life. One day after work, I stopped by his shop. When I walked in he said, *"You know Jon, I've been thinking. I've decided to give this positive thinking thing a try."* I was in shock. He said, *"As a matter of fact, do you see this engine I'm working on?"* I said yes.

He said, *"I'm positive it will never run again!"* He laughed, and I groaned. But looking back, it was funny.

I had landed a job hauling straw bales for a dollar a bale, which was pretty good money back then, considering I could get over 300 bales on per load, and I hired my friend's son to help me. We were doing three to four loads a day around the Fraser Valley and I was able to pay for my new transmission quickly. One afternoon, on my last load of the day, I heard a big CLUNK as I climbed a hill. I checked all my gauges, but everything looked normal. I stopped and had a look around but didn't see any obvious problems, so we took off to finish the load. I dropped my helper off and headed back to dad's shop. I climbed underneath and had a closer look but still couldn't see anything obvious.

It was Saturday the next morning and I had a load of hay to pick up and deliver. I went out and started the truck and it sounded like it was going to explode. I shut it off. I started it again and it sounded terrible. I wasn't doing the hay job that day. I ran it into the shop and climbed under it again, this time I took the oil pan off. Everything looked okay, until I took a pry bar to turn the crankshaft, and only one half was turning. The crankshaft had broken right in the middle. All I knew was that my "new" engine hadn't lasted a week. I was basically screwed. I didn't have the money to replace the engine. Taking it to the shop was out of the question and I was out of business if I didn't get it up and running as soon as I could. I called George but there was no answer. I drove to his house but there was nobody home. I was in a panic, mad at him and mad at myself for being taken. I called the company he worked for and told them what had happened. I said that he told me they let him build engines on the side there. The owner replied that certainly wasn't the case. He asked me if I had any serial numbers and part numbers that I could give him, so I went out, got them then called him back. As I read off the numbers, he was cross referencing them and then he told me that all the parts I had were from the scrap bin. The guy had just cleaned them up, painted them and bolted them together. I felt like an even bigger fool. The guy fired George. I finally got ahold of him and told him that he either owed me $750 or a new engine, and I would prefer my money back. He bellowed that it was a good engine and I still owed him $750. He was caught red handed and he still wanted money from me.

A Real Miracle

I don't remember how I met this couple that owned a small garage, but I did. I told them my problem, and they said that they could fix my old engine and put new heads on it. I had to tell them that I was almost broke. I didn't even have enough to cover the cost of the parts. They said they prayed about it, and God told them to go ahead and repair my engine. I was stunned. I admit that it was like a dream or something because I barely remember anything they said after that.

I was helping them get it done and they had this weird music playing in the background. I couldn't even hear it. I mentioned that to them and they laughed. I thought they were very strange, but they were fixing my engine. I had a very foul mouth. I noticed that none of them swore. I found that odd too, so I tried to keep my mouth under control. A couple of days later, my truck was running and with nothing more than a handshake I was gone. I thought, what a bunch of suckers. I could just drive away and never pay them. I knew I had to pay them and give them a nice tip.

Earl Fires up the Rocket

It was quite exciting to be part of Earl's project. It involved lots of hard work to get it to the point of being ready to test run. A truck came to my parent's place and dropped off four barrels of fish guts that had been shipped all the way from Newfoundland. This was going to be his test product. He was going to extract the complex proteins and amino acids from the stinky mess.

You may have never heard the noise a "buzz bomb" makes. The British knew the sound very well during WW2. The German Air Force would put just enough fuel in the tank so they would run out over England, then fall from the sky randomly and explode upon impact. It must have been a terrifying experience to have one go silent above you.

Even with all the layers of sand used as a sound deadening agent, when Earl fired up that rocket it was heard for miles around Milner BC. Dishes were shaken from the shelves, windows shattered, and animals were spooked, for miles around. Earl was ecstatic. His process was a success. He had done what he set out to do. Earl and Cody were thrilled that they had made history and were well on their way to fame, fortune and acclaim. Then my mom, all five feet of her, came out of the house, enraged. She never did like Earl and his monster in the back yard and this was the last straw. She threatened to call the fire department, the police, and the newspapers if he didn't shut that infernal machine down permanently and get it off her property. She read my dad the riot act when he got home as well.

So, Earl, out of respect, began to disassemble the machine that could feed the world. My mom is basically responsible for the starvation of millions.

Life Lesson Learned

I was offered a job hauling hay out of Eastern Washington back to Langley BC. It was an easy job. I would haul feed down to various feed lots in Washington then go pick up a load of hay and bring it back to BC. But there was one thing that disturbed me about the truck I was driving. It was known in the industry as a *"truck and trailer"* where there was a full body mounted on the truck and a full sized 36ft trailer connected by a draw bar. I had never driven this combination before and it had a *"feature"* that I didn't like. Whenever I was descending a hill, the trailer would swing back and forth quite significantly. It made me nervous to look in the mirrors and see it swaying back and forth!

On my second or third trip I stopped in Ellensburg WA for fuel and a bite to eat. As I sat at the counter having my lunch, a gentleman sat next to me at the counter. He had the look of an old-time driver, with cowboy boots, plaid shirt and cowboy hat. I asked him if he was a driver. He answered yes, so I asked him if he had any experience with truck/trailer combinations. He said yes. I told him about how my trailer was swinging wildly behind me as I descended hills and asked him if that was normal. He didn't say anything, but he took his paper placemat and folded it over and put a crease in it, then he tore the paper off and held it up and asked me, *"Is this about the same size as your mirrors?"* I looked at it and said yes. Then he asked me, *"Do you have any tape in your truck?"* I said I did. Then he said, *"I want you to tape this to your mirror."* His voice got louder as he said, *"Never mind what's going on behind you. Is all your load still on the trailer when you get where you're going?"* I said yes. Then he said something that changed my life, *"Windshields are big, mirrors are small, there's a reason for that. Never mind what's going on behind you, it's what coming at you that counts."* I sat there, feeling a bit foolish, but I knew he was right. In fact, that lesson can easily be applied to our lives. Never mind the past, it's what's coming up next that matters.

Angel Investor

One day I took a load of scrap into the local scrapyard and there it was, a 1953 Freightliner Bubblenose Cabover. I don't blame you if you scratch your heads and wonder why this was so special, it was. There were only a few of them made, relatively speaking, for and by the Consolidated Freightways Corporation, or CF as they were usually known. I asked the scrap dealer how much he wanted for it and he said, '*I just paid $700.00 for scrap, so give me $700.00 and it's yours.*' I had the cash, so I gave him the money. It was still hooked up to the wrecker, so I had him follow me the mile from there to my parents' place. I already had quite a collection of old trucks lined up there beside the driveway, plus a few that a friend from the truck club was storing, so I only had one place to put it. Unfortunately, there was a big gap in the hedge there and it ended up being backed in where the old woman next door could plainly see it. We are talking about a very unattractive truck here, and Anne, the neighbor, had spent a considerable amount of money turning the old farm into her own private English Country Garden. She had spent who knows how much making ponds, one with an island and a little bridge to it, dug out with excavators, a small creek installed, and she even imported swans and ducks. She wasn't impressed with my ugly, rusty old new toy. All she had to do was look up from bird watching in her pond through her binoculars and there it was, the ugliest truck in the world.

About ten minutes after it was dropped there, she came over and with her very proper British accent asked, *"What do you propose to do with this thing then?"* I apologized and told her that it was a collector's item and that, hopefully, it would sell soon, and it wouldn't be there for long. *"A collector's item?"* she asked. *"I'm a bit of an antique collector myself. What did you pay for it and what is it worth?"* I told her how it could be worth four or five times what I paid for it, and there were collectors actively looking for them. She told me about a piece of furniture that she recently bought at an auction for $500,000 and she expected to make 'a small profit' when she sold it.

There we were, talking about antiques and then she asked me, *"If you didn't sell it, what would you do with it?"* Now I had just come back from an 'old timers' threshing bee in the US where a couple of the other old truck collectors had taken their travel trailers and mounted them behind the cabs of their trucks, basically making them into motor homes. I towed my travel trailer behind my old 48 and it used to get beat up badly, so I thought, that's a great idea. With this idea fresh in my memory, I told her that I would like to make a motor home out of it. She had no clue what that was, so I explained it to her but there was an obvious culture gap. She did come to some understanding when I used the term "Caravan." I was thinking on my feet, since I hadn't really given it any detailed thought. It would take a significant sum to do the modification, and I explained it all to her. She had a look of deep contemplation, then shocked me when she said, *"Well, put some numbers on paper and come around and see me about this tomorrow afternoon."* With that she walked back to her house, wearing her wrap around tartan skirt with the giant safety pin and rubber boots, as I stood there, stunned. I couldn't believe what had just happened. In a state of shock, I wandered around a bit and finally had to lay down. I had just been offered dream financing for a dream that I hadn't even fully formed yet. There are people actively hunting for their 'Angel Investor' and I had one come to me, dirty little Jonny, the least qualified businessman possible. I didn't really think I deserved it but why not give it a try.

With no business experience, other than my little flat deck truck, I was about to launch a business. I went into my trailer and sat down to try and *'put some numbers on paper.'* I didn't have a clue where to start but thought, why not just write down everything I had just told her, with a few more details thrown in. So that's what I did. I drew a rough picture of what the old Freightliner would look like as a 'caravan.' I took it all over to her house the next day and we sat down to go over my 'plan.' She thought it was a good idea and said, *"Well, I suppose we'll need to open a bank account then. Do you have a truck in mind to build this on? How much will we need to get started?"* I was still in shock and couldn't believe this was happening to me.

I had spotted my buddies old 1963 Kenworth in the yard when I was walking over to her house, so I thought it would be a good candidate. I figured it would cost $50,000 to stretch the frame and restore the truck to get it ready and $50,000 to build a coach body on it. I told her, and she asked, *"Have you ever formed a corporation?"* To which I had to honestly reply, no. *"Well, it's not that difficult. Find an accountant and tell them that you want to form a corporation. Since I'm putting all the money in, I want to hold the majority of shares, but you will have full signing authority. Have you thought of a name yet?"* Did I mention that I was in shock? I said I hadn't and she told me to think of one quick because it must have a name.

My sister Suzy lived in Prince George with a logging trucker. He drove a logging truck. He drank lots of beer. They came down to our parent's place. I told him what I was proposing to do and showed him a picture of what the old KW would look like when it was converted into a motorhome. He exclaimed, *"That'll have class, eh!"* The name was found, Class Eh Motor Home Manufacturing Inc. I went to the accountant and registered it the next day, before I could change my mind. I have often regretted that impulsive move since it is properly classified as a Class "C" motor home, not a Class "A" motor home.

It was stipulated right from the start that I would not be living off the investment money. I still had to have a job and pay for my own expenses. I didn't want to do long haul trucking simply because I wanted to be close to the motor home project.

I found a job with a container hauling outfit and started hauling containers between Vancouver and Seattle. I was home enough to stay on top of the project and made a little money as well. There was one problem, I was lonely. Years of being rejected by just about everyone left me with zero self-confidence. I was painfully shy around women and of course that is not a desirable trait in a man.

There was a sweet young woman who was driving for the same company I was. We would be driving together, in different trucks, and were just generally good friends. Looking back, it is painfully obvious that she was the one I should have been with, but anyway. So, lonely me didn't know what to do about it. One day, while looking through the local Buy'n'Sell, I found "personal ads" in the middle. Now when did they start putting those in here I wondered? The cost to place an ad? Free. I liked that price, so I put an ad in there, *"Truck Driver. Businessman. Not a bad catch just never in one place long enough to get caught. Looking for life partner to share adventures on the road and maybe start a family someday. Nothing ventured, nothing gained!"*

Shortly after I put the ad in, I was recruited to do a team run for the same company I was hauling containers for, between Vancouver BC and Toronto ON, about 9000 Kilometers or 5500 miles per week. It paid extremely well, and the motor home project was coming along fine with minimal input from me. The next thing you know I am working, and living in this tiny little space with Ken, a stranger, and I wasn't too comfortable with his driving. I found it very hard to sleep in a moving truck as it was, but he managed to make it impossible. I was basically a zombie behind the wheel. But we did it, week after week, back and forth across Canada. We had pretty much given up on the idea of being good friends. Tolerating each other was getting tougher by the day. We weren't going to be best friends, to say the least.

One night, as I was piloting the truck through Saskatchewan in a snow storm, I was bored and started searching for skip. Skip is picking up AM radio stations that are far off because of the way AM radio waves work. As I was slowly turning the radio dial, I found someone yelling at me! *"You, yes you, it's no accident that you are listening to me on the radio right now! God has a message for you and you had better listen!"* Normally I could listen to a cat being disemboweled and Ken would sleep right through it. But not this. He yelled from behind the sleeper curtain, *"Turn that crap off!"* Normally I would have, but I had never heard anything like what this guy was saying before and frankly, I didn't want to, but because it was bothering Kenny, I left it on and turned it up a bit. The guy on the radio continued, *"God sent His only begotten Son that whosoever would believe in Him would receive eternal life. I didn't write those words, GOD DID, AND HE IS TELLING YOU THROUGH ME. BELIEVE, REPENT, AND RECIEVE THE GLORIOUS GIFT OF GOD."* As the skip began to fade he kept preaching hellfire, damnation, and brimstone. I was kind of scared, but I mulled it around and even quietly talked to God. *"Hey God, if you are real, I could probably use You right about now. My life is basically a mess. I have this cool thing going on but I am rather an idiot, I am lonely and I hate being out here on the road. Oh, and I am always tired. If you are real I really need to know."*

Someone answered the ad. It was a long reply letter. She basically said that she was touched by my honesty in the ad and that I should give her a call. She included her phone number. Her name was Sandy. I was as nervous as a long-tailed cat in a room full of rocking chairs, but I called her up. We talked for hours about everything under the sun. We had lots in common and were both just lonely. The only problem was that she lived way off the normal highways that we took. I told her we would try to work out some way to meet and left it at that. One night I got a call from the young lady who drove for the same outfit. Like an idiot, I told her that I was talking to another woman and with that she hung up on me.

Christmas was coming, and the truck needed lots of repairs. It was a nice enough truck, a Peterbilt 377, but it was a lemon. We had lots of problems with it, so getting it fixed was a pretty high priority. That left an entire week to take care of business, party, and maybe go up to meet Sandy. I had money falling out of my pockets. $1400.00 per week and nowhere to spend it can cause it to pile up quickly. The motor home was coming along slowly so there wasn't anything for me to do there but wait. I decided it was time to throw a party, but since I only lived in an old travel trailer beside my parent's barn, I decided that I needed a better place to have it.

I phoned up my old friend, Bill, and asked if he would mind if we had a party at his place. He said, *"As long as you're paying because I'm broke."* I agreed to pay for everything. I stopped at the liquor store and bought about $500.00 worth of booze; beer, whisky, rum, coolers for the girls. Then when I got to Bill's, I gave his girlfriend, Lorri, $300 and told her to get as much weed and hash as that would buy. It didn't take long for people to start showing up and the alcohol flowed. Once the pot arrived and a few others showed up it really got going. Music cranked to ten and we were off, but something was different. As hard as I tried, I couldn't get *'wasted.'* Everyone else was passing out, throwing up or staggering in and out the door, but I felt like I was just a sober observer. I was ticked off. Eventually, around 2am, we were out of everything and whoever wasn't passed out had left. I sat there, feeling almost sober. I noticed that Bill wasn't quite gone, so I went and sat beside him. He pried open one eye and asked me if there was any booze or weed left. I told him no, and he asked me what I was still doing there. I wasn't expecting that, and it hit me hard. I thought, this was one of my best friends. I got up and walked out. I felt sober enough, so I drove the twenty miles to my shabby old trailer. When I got there, I was destroyed. I realized that I didn't have a single friend in the world. I was utterly alone, and waves of loneliness and depression washed over me.

There was a constant battle for an extension cord to get power to my trailer. My sisters would come and take it to use in the barn when I wasn't there. When I got home, it was gone. I didn't care, it seemed appropriate. I was powerless, friendless, hopeless. Even the motor home thing was depressing. It just didn't mean anything to me at that moment.

At the back of most Dell paperbacks, there are lots of ads for useless crap; from do it yourself palm readings to *'special good luck charms'* guaranteed to make you rich and desirable. I was desperate enough to have sent for one of those stupid things a month before and it arrived while I was on the road. It was simple enough. It was a seven-sided card that had each of the things we all crave listed on it. There was also a candle holder and you were to put a candle in the holder and then wrap the seven-sided craving list around it, light the candle and turn it to what you desired most. Since I was desperate to have love, that is where it was pointing when I got back to the trailer, and since it was my only light source, I lit the candle. I sat there, utterly dejected, and lonely, staring at this stupid thing. I was disappointed. I was starting to weep, but I had to pee. I went outside and took care of that, then went back into the trailer. There was one rotten cross member in the floor of my old trailer and it was the one that if you stepped on it, everything on the table would fly off. Of course, I stepped on that cross member and the candle and everything else on the table went flying. I sat down in the dark and thought I couldn't be more of a loser if I tried.

Then I remembered the preacher on the radio. I asked God, *"Hey God, I'm through playing around. If You are real, I really need to know, right now."* The next thing I knew, I felt as if the whole trailer was lit up by lightning. I was instantly sober, and it is hard to describe, but it felt like the light was coming out of me. I was, in that instant, more sober than I had ever been in my life. Suddenly, everything made perfect sense.

Then it was over. Still pitch-black darkness. I sat in stunned silence. I had no way to explain what had just happened, but I knew it was good. I was filled with a peace inside that didn't make sense and is impossible to describe. I had asked God if He was real and He answered. I went to bed and slept like a baby. When I woke up the next day, I had a peace in me that was undeniable. I couldn't wait to share this with someone.

I went to the house and told my mom. She was not happy to hear this news. In fact, she was downright angry. She told me to never bring up that *'garbage'* in her house ever again and if I did, I was out of there for good. I couldn't believe it. This was by far the best thing that had ever happened to me and my own mother wasn't just dismissive of it but was downright hostile. I didn't know how to react or what to say, so I just left saddened that the best thing to happen in my life was a problem for my own mom. I couldn't just stop there so I went and told a few other people. I got the same basic reaction; hostility, and rejection. I was used to rejection, but not hostility. This was new. But I knew there was a God who answered when I asked. Nothing else mattered and I began to feel sorry for anyone who didn't get it. I had a long way to go, but at least I knew there was a WAY to go!

I had arguments with just about all my friends and relatives. One of the biggest ones was how could I not believe in evolution. Since I had basically slept through school I hadn't been paying attention during those classes anyway, all I could say was, *"Hey, I don't know one way or the other and it really doesn't matter to me. All I know is what happened to me and that I feel like a new person. If I'm supposed to know about this, then God will let me know, otherwise I'm not even going to think about it!"* This reply was unacceptable to them, but I really didn't care. Call me ignorant, and they did, but it just didn't matter in the light of what I had experienced.

With this renewed energy, I decided to go meet Sandy. It was a long drive to the Okanagan back then since the Coquihalla Highway wasn't finished yet, at least not all the way to the Okanagan where she lived. When I got there, I was nervous, but once we met in person, I was okay. We went out for dinner and started something we shouldn't have.

I had to get back to the truck since it was just about fixed, and they had a load for us. I couldn't believe it. So off we went, between Christmas and New Year's, heading east to Montreal. We had a few delays, so no matter how hard we drove, we were late getting to our destination and we spent New Year's Eve, day and the whole weekend trapped in the French part of town with only a crappy little diner, closed from 3pm until 7am. It was freezing cold, with blowing snow as well, just to add to the scene. On top of that, the waitresses were surly and mean to us because we didn't speak French. We did eventually get unloaded, but because we missed our deadline we had no return load, so they hooked us up to a flatbed and sent us back to Vancouver. What a nightmare. But we did it.

The regular haul was bringing new clothes and frozen treats for Marks & Spencer's Department stores. They didn't care about anything except us backing up to the dock in Brantford ON at 10am, Ontario time, every Friday. Everything else was just to get us there. We then had to be in Vancouver by 1am Monday morning to drop of a few racks of clothes, then do deliveries to six shopping malls around the metro Vancouver area. Sixty-six hours one way, with very few stops, was brutal. We were tired, hated each other and I was more than ready to quit. But I needed the money and figured that it was just for a short time until the motor home sold, and I could get a return on my labor. The motor home was coming along but it seemed to take forever.

We got a load of apples from the Okanogan, taking us right past Sandy's place. I called her up and asked her if she wanted to come along for the trip. She said, *"You bet!"* We picked her up and away we went. I was thinking life wasn't so bad after all. It was fun to have her along for the ride. She liked travelling and had never seen anywhere east of Alberta. We laughed and came up with great ideas for the motor home company. It was nice.

One morning we were traveling across the Prairies and Ken was driving. I was sound asleep. Sandy woke up and went up into the cab to keep him company. As she came through the sleeper curtain, she was shocked to find him nodding, half asleep at the wheel and heading for the ditch. She shook his shoulder and he woke up just in time to keep it on the road. She didn't tell me because she knew that would be the last straw with me and him. When we got to Vancouver I called the owner of the truck, Gerry, and asked him if he had found a relief driver yet. He had promised us one when we started, and it was six months in with not even a full week off at Christmas. I was burned out. He told me that he didn't have anyone yet and to quit being such a whiner. I was livid. I had gone way above and beyond to keep the wheels rolling for that guy and never complained and now I am a whiner. I hung up on him. That was when Sandy told me about Ken's little sleepy incident. I told Ken to pull the truck over right there on the spot. We were about two blocks from my friend Phil's place and I was done.

I unloaded my stuff out of the truck right on the side of the road and Ken was lucky I didn't hit him. I had Sandy stand by my stuff as I went to find a payphone to call Phil. Well, you sure find out who your real friends are in an emergency. Phil wasn't too enthusiastic about helping me out. Granted, I shouldn't have expected him to but I had helped him out many times and thought that driving me out to my parent's place wasn't too big of a deal. I was paying for the gas and I would buy him a case of beer. He still put up a big fuss.

Now I had a bit of a problem. Sandy didn't live there, and I had no job. I did have some money saved, so I drove her back up to the Okanogan. Since I was working under the table I hadn't banked any hours with UI, therefore I couldn't claim anything either. The motor home project was nearing completion, but it was still way too slow. I went and did some one-time trips for some guys I knew and kept my finger on the project.

All this time I was feeling like I was ignoring God. He had made Himself very real to me and I was just barely acknowledging Him. I knew that deep down I needed Him, way more than just a flash of light in a dark trailer. Some people have the perfect born again experience. I didn't. I knew that I believed in God. I knew that I believed that Jesus was His Son. I knew that He had a wonderful Plan for my life. I knew I didn't have a clue how to make it mine.

I asked Sandy to move in with me. She agreed. I got a job driving part time for a company that delivered newspaper flyer inserts and the owner agreed to let me use his truck to go get her and her stuff. I wrangled Phil into helping me and away we went. When we got to the Laidlaw Scale, near Hope BC, I was called in. He said, *"That truck doesn't have insurance to go any farther than Hope, so you aren't going past there, are you?"* I was going a lot farther, but I lied and said I was only going to Hope. Once we were past Hope I had my doubts about whether this was the right thing to do. I was driving a truck that had no insurance once it got beyond the town of Hope. I was going to move a woman that I barely knew into my trailer beside a barn. I didn't have a real job and even if the motor home thing took off, I knew I was probably not smart enough to run it. Then I remembered that there was another scale near Penticton, and we would have to cross it since it was open 24/7. There was only one solution. take the backroads. I guess I should mention that it was snowing heavily. When we got to Princeton, we went into a gas station to see if there was a local map we could look at. There was a backroads guide book and we bought it. It showed that the roads connected and would bring us out at Summerland, just north of Penticton. I decided to go for it.

God looks after fools, children, and apparently crazy truck drivers. We were flying along at a good clip for a one lane snow covered bush road. We were basically on the old Kettle Valley Railroad roadbed. It was like a one lane freeway with gentle corners and no steep grades. There were a few spots where it had washed out and we had some fun negotiating those spots. We made it though and were loading Sandy's stuff and on our way back. We came back the same way and got back to Langley around 10pm. We blew Sandy's stuff into a storage unit and dropped Phil off. We then proceeded to start the biggest mistakes of our lives.

I guess I should have asked, why would a girl answer an ad like mine in the first place. Maybe I shouldn't have been so quick to jump at the first one to come along. Why didn't I go with the one I drove with? I was still a very old-fashioned guy. I figured that we would get married, love would conquer all and we would have lots of money once the motor home thing took off.

Living with someone is different from being married. There is always the 'out clause' since there is no real commitment. We were both given to partying, lying and generally being irresponsible. I was still trucking part time, but the motor home was nearing completion and I had to get with the program. I bought a suit. That should be a shocker right there. We attempted to do something that was out of both of our elements; run a small business selling a high-end product. Neither one of us had a clue. We had one enquiry from a very wealthy owner of a trailer manufacturing company who came to see the unit. Within ten minutes of meeting us, he, his wife, and their friends left, angry. I guess I shouldn't have offered them a beer at 10am on a Sunday.

I couldn't sell the thing. As cool as it was, I wasn't in the right league. No one wanted to be the first to fork over $200,000 to some hay seed hick who lived in a trailer with his loud, obnoxious girlfriend. I knew what I had was a winner product, but I wasn't the right guy to sell it. I knew that I needed someone else to help with that, and someone who knew how to run a business, because you need to go to school for that. It was funny how my dad and Sandy got along so well. They were like best friends or something. I just didn't get it. They liked each other. Sandy had some rich taste, for more than I could provide. She was getting impatient at the lack of sale of the motor home. My own sisters hated her. They took me off to the side one day and really let me have it, *"She's a gold digger Jon. Dump her now Jon. She's nothing but trouble Jon."* Since I knew better, I didn't listen to them.

Anne wanted to know why I hadn't sold the unit yet. I told her it was because most people out there didn't know how to drive a manual truck transmission and it was built on an old truck. Even if it was restored, it was still twenty-seven years old at the time. I figured that if we built one on a brand-new truck that had an automatic transmission, then sales would be almost guaranteed. Anne was a bit dubious but asked how much would that cost. I had done a little bit of figuring and came up with $120,000.00; $70,000 for the truck and $50,000 for the coach. She shocked me again and said, *"Go order the truck."* I mean, how many people does this happen to? I would say one in a billion. So, I had to get to work.

I tried Kenworth and the salesman was really into the idea of specking it out for me. He worked out all the details and had a quote for me of $75,000. I said do it. He got back to me a couple of days later and told me that Kenworth's legal team had gotten wind of the project and said there was no way that Kenworth Trucks was going to build a personal vehicle. They were in the commercial truck building business and just couldn't expose the company to that kind of risk. Well that sucked. I had my heart set on an aerodynamic Kenworth T-600 for a cab and chassis and now I can't even try from another angle because my name is all over it.

So, down the road I went to Peterbilt Trucks Pacific. It turned out that the salesman who we found was the cousin of the neighbor who had the huge dairy farm across the street from my parent's place. I told him about the problem at Kenworth and he specked out the same basic drivetrain but not an aerodynamic truck. He lied to the lawyers at Peterbilt and they agreed to build it, if I put down a hefty deposit, just in case I backed out of the deal. So, with the deposit in hand they put in the order and we simply had to wait.

I was feeling over confident and Sandy hated the crampy old trailer, so we started looking at new ones. We came across a new 35feet, 5th wheel and she said, *"I love it"* with a squeal. Like the lamb lead to the slaughter, I used our old trailer as a down payment and signed on the dotted line, for $40,000.00. I guess writing all those big checks got to me and I felt invincible.

We pulled the old trailer out and slid the new one in, beside the barn. My dad came home from work and he was pissed when he saw it. He said, *"I work my ass off all my life and you just buy one of these things? There's no way I can afford one. What the hell makes you think you can?"* He was torqued. He went into his shop and proceeded to get rip roaring drunk. I knew what that meant. He grabbed a shovel, took a scoop of dirt and rocks, and flung it at the trailer. I didn't see that coming. That was it, we were moving out.

I got the old 48 Kenworth fired up, hooked on to it and an hour later we drove away. My dad was standing in the driveway, totally angry, but with tears in his eyes. We found a campground not too far away and parked there for the night and then proceeded to try and find a place to put the thing. In our haste, we didn't think about the details, just getting away from the mad drunk who threw dirt at our new trailer was all we could think about.

We found a private campground that was only $200.00 per month, with everything included, and moved in. We had some interesting neighbors. Lots of transients with big bank accounts. We met our potential customers and really got to know more about what we needed to do to market them properly. The problem was that neither of us had a clue how to do it.

Although Sandy said she believed in God, when it came right down to it, she didn't. I asked her to pray with me for someone to help us with the business and she was quite hostile to the idea. I was beginning to think that I had made a terrible mistake with her.

One Sunday we went for a long drive with no destination in mind. We ended up on the north side of the Fraser River east of Mission. When we got to Harrison Mills, we turned up the road that goes to the west side of Harrison Lake. We didn't get too far before we saw a sign that said, *"Tapedera Estates, Strata Title RV. Lots for Sale!"* We drove in and it was obvious that it was a brand-new development. The roads and services were in, but there wasn't anyone there yet. It was pouring rain and we drove around a bit. As we were heading towards the exit, a gentleman in a suit came running out of the trailer and said, *"Hey folks, see anything you like?"* I rolled down the window and said, *"Not really, but I do like the idea of owning a lot."*

He introduced himself, *"I'm Richard Furrer, sales director for the project. Come on inside and let's discuss it."* We went inside. A good salesman is going to qualify a potential customer right away, just to see if they are worth pursuing, *"So, Jon, what do you do?"* I said, *"I own a small manufacturing company."* He asked, *"What do you manufacture?"* I responded, *"Well surprisingly enough, motor homes."* We laughed. He rubbed his hands together. He asked me, *"So, who is selling these units for you?"* I replied, *"I am and it is hard to do everything by myself. I sure could use a good salesman."* He said, *"Really? I'm a pretty good salesman!"* We laughed some more. Could this guy be the answer to my prayers? I left him with my card and a brochure and we headed back to our trailer.

By the time we got home, the phone rang. It was our new friend Richard and he wanted to meet me to discuss the possibility of working for me to sell our motorhomes. I was ecstatic. I played it cool though and said, *"I'll have to check my schedule and get back to you, but sure, it doesn't hurt to try."* We laughed some more.

Sandy had a miscarriage. It was a surprise to me. Obviously, she knew she was pregnant. I found out afterwards that she wasn't going to tell me.

I met Richard for coffee and we had a good chat. I tried to keep up appearances, but I think he figured out that I was a rank amateur rather quickly. Nevertheless, he said he thought this was the opportunity that he and his wife had been praying for when they left Australia and he wanted to work with me to make it happen. Wait a minute. Prayed? *"Do you believe in God?"* I asked. *"Absolutely,"* he said. And with that we were in business together.

He invited Sandy and me to the Harrison Hot Springs Hotel to meet him and his wife, Janelle. She was charming, and a true Christian woman as well. She was far more religious than Richard. It was Janelle who really shared the love of Christ with me for the first time. Because of her, I made the biggest decision of my life and fully committed my life to God in Christ Jesus. My dad hated that. He yelled at me and said there is no God. The peace that had been eluding me was back and I knew deep down inside this was right.

Janelle and Sandy didn't really hit it off, but that didn't matter to me since I now had my salesman. We plotted and strategized and planned. We developed a few ideas on napkins. We had some big ideas. He said we needed to manufacture 300 to 500 units per year, get one on every RV dealers lot and storm the market place. Wait a minute. That's not my plan. I want to build one at a time, custom, high end, nothing but the best for exclusive customers, not mass produce them. Our first disagreement. He said either we do it his way or he would walk. I should have called his bluff, but I was a neophyte businessman and capitulated all too easily. I agreed to his plan. Of course, we would need gobs of startup capital, not to mention a team of people to make it all come together. This was getting way over my head fast.

He arranged to get us into the strata RV property with no money down. We moved the 5th wheel trailer out there and began our new journey. He assured me that it was all going to be fine. *"Get used to nice things Jon because you're going to be able to afford them."* My old Chevy pickup was getting rather tired looking. It was a great truck, but it just didn't represent the company well. Richard got on the phone to one of his old friends, who happened to be the owner of a huge car dealership in the Okanogan and arranged for us to go and pick up our brand new '91 Silver Anniversary Ford Bronco. *"Wait a minute, how is this being paid for?"* we asked. *"Don't you worry Jon, as soon as one of these units sell, you can pay for it outright. It's a short-term lease and we will have the first motor home sold within a month. Go, get your new ride!"*

We drove up to Vernon and were driving home in a nice new truck later that day. Now, deep down inside I was having serious doubts about how fast this was all going. Anne was still wanting to get her investment back; the second motor home was almost finished, and we still hadn't sold the first one. Sandy decided that she hated the Furrer family and refused to be nice to them. I was still seriously lacking self-confidence and my new friends and neighbors secretly hated my guts. Richard and I had a meeting and I laid all this out on the table. Bad move. He appeared to be sympathetic but, I had just given him the green light to steam roll right over me. He drew up some documents and told me that it was best if I signed them, just in case anything bad happened to either of us. It seemed like a good idea. In my naivety, I signed my business over to him while retaining the debts. Lesson here, READ THE FREAKING CONTRACT. I was still struggling with alcohol and pot, which didn't make things any easier. Sandy was turning into a total bitch from hell. Then she got pregnant again. My life was spinning out of control.

Then we got a call from someone at the Washington State RV Dealers Association. They wanted to know if we were interested in having our motor homes as the feature products for that years' 1991 Washington State RV Show. We had to drive them down to Seattle for some promo shots and some filming down at the piers. We were on KOMO News 4 and it was all quite heady stuff. It looked like we were going to make it after all. It was still a couple of months away, but we felt confident that God was finally going to bless us. Around a month later my dad was diagnosed with pancreatic cancer. There is no surviving that one. The good thing is that it was over quickly. The bad thing is that it was over quickly. He was getting sicker and sicker, just a shell of a man on his death bed.

I was scheduled to be at the RV show and was torn between going or being with my dad when he died. We might not have had the best relationship, but he was my father. I stopped by their house where my dad had been sent, since there was nothing they could do for him. My mom was in the kitchen acting as if nothing was wrong. My sisters were out in the barn acting as if nothing was wrong. I went in to see my dad. He was a pale-yellow skeleton laying on his death bed. I didn't know what to say, so I said, *"Hey dad, how's it going?" "I've been better,"* he said. It was very awkward. Here was this man who terrified me as a child, dying. This man that I had grown to love as an adult, dying. I tried to make small talk. *"I have a big RV show this weekend,"* I said. *"I'm proud of you son."* He had never said that he was proud of me, ever. I choked up and told him, *"I love you dad."* He said, *"I love you too son."* That was the first time my father ever told me he loved me. I said, *"So when I get back, maybe we can go fishing or something?"* He said, *"I would like that."* Silence. We both knew that wasn't going to happen. I said, *"Look, I'll just cancel the show and stay here and look after you." "No, you go. You've worked hard for this. I am proud of you son."* More silence. He then told me that I might as well have all his tools, his boat, and the camper since he wasn't going to need them anymore, but I said I didn't really want to talk about that. He asked me to look after mom and I promised him that I would. I told him that I loved him again and turned to walk out of the room. When I got to the door he called me. I turned around. He asked me, *"Do you really believe in Jesus?" "Yes, I do dad, with all my heart."* He just sighed, smiled a bit, and said, *"OK, that's all I wanted to know."* I took one more look at him, said good-bye, turned, and walked out. I drove my shiny 1963 Kenworth motor home away from there slowly. It was with a very heavy heart and yet a strange hope that everything was going to be all right.

I drove to the border where I met Richard, who had the Peterbilt motor home. We crossed the border and were on our way. We arrived at the RV show and got everything set up. We simply waited for the customers to arrive, write big checks and we would be on our way. The first day was slow. Lots of people came in and checked the units out and quite a few commented on how much they loved them. The most frequently heard comment was, *"When I win the lottery, this is what I'm getting!"* It was a bit depressing that there were no takers, but we consoled ourselves by looking forward to Saturday, the day when the serious buyers would be there.

We awoke to a rainy, cloudy Saturday. It wasn't a total washout, but it rained just enough to dampen the crowds for the outdoor show. As we tried to keep the units clean after all the muddy shoes had trudged through, I was getting depressed. All this and it didn't look promising. We were expecting a couple from Oregon who had called and wanted a private showing of the Peterbilt, so there was hope there. But otherwise the rain was killing us. I asked God why He was allowing this and all I heard was, *"There's a good reason, just keep trusting."* I still smoked at that time and went outside in the dark rainy evening to have a cigarette.

As I was standing there under my umbrella, looking down the dark corridors of the empty cattle barns across from me, I heard my dad's voice! He said, *'JON!'* quite loudly. I was shocked as I looked down the corridors to where it sounded like the voice came from. I heard it again, this time much quieter, *'Jon.'* I knew that my dad had just died.

About half an hour later, some Washington State Troopers came and found me and told me that I needed to call home right away. Our couple from Oregon wanted to talk to me specifically, since I was the builder of the units, but I wasn't at my best at that moment. I tried to separate the two incidents but I had a hard time being all upbeat and positive. I guess that was one of the reasons why the Oregon couple left. The show was over. We didn't sell anything, or even get any potential good leads. It was, as far as I was concerned, a disaster.

Richard suggested going out and getting dinner and having a few drinks. I was up for that. We found ourselves at an after the show party and I admit to having more than enough to drink. I was dancing with strange women and Richard was trying to keep a positive spin on the show to all the other attendees. It kept hitting me that my dad had just died. He had asked me if I believed in Jesus, and that gave me hope that he made his peace with God before he went, but I guess I won't know until I get to Heaven myself. I more than likely made a fool of myself, trying to keep a smile on, then losing it when I would think about my dad. I called it an early night and took a cab back to the hotel.

Chapter Four

A New Chapter

I woke up, sat on the edge of the bed with a big hangover and prayed. I can't remember exactly what it was but I am sure it was about dad, my mom, sisters, and family. I don't know why, but I opened the night stand drawer, and there it was, a Bible. I was surprised to find it in there, since I had never heard of the Gideons. I picked it up and randomly opened it. It opened to Philemon. I began to read:

> *Grace to you, and peace, from God our Father and the Lord Jesus Christ. I thank my God, making mention of thee always in my prayers, hearing of thy love and faith, which thou hast toward the Lord Jesus, and toward all saints; that the communication of thy faith may become effectual by the acknowledging of every good thing which is in you in Christ Jesus. For we have great joy and consolation in thy love, because the hearts of the saints are refreshed by thee, brother...*

At that last verse, tears filled my eyes as I was overcome with emotion. I felt a heavy burden lifted from me. I began to cry, some tears for my father and some of joy. But I was confused, so

I called Janelle to ask her what had just happened. She was joyful as she exclaimed in her charming Australian accent, *"That was the Holy Spirit Jon! God just spoke to you through His Word!"* This was new to me. I admit that it was nice, but I had no idea how it worked. She then prayed for me and I thanked her and hung up. I had to leave right away for home. It was all a blur.

My mom was upset. My parents didn't get along at all before he died, but after he was gone she was a mess. We had the funeral a few days later and my dad's side of the family wouldn't even come to mom's house. The big family split had reached its conclusion. Around that time, Janelle bought me my first Bible. I tried to do as my dad asked me, to look after mom. He had tools, some of them very expensive, all over the place. I thought since he had given them to me, I would sell whatever I couldn't use and give the money to mom.

He had a big bench lathe at his shop on the Fraser River where he worked for Weldwood. It was probably worth $50,000. I had no use for it and thought that mom could use the money. I was in the process of lifting it off the barge that his workshop was on with a crane when I was called into the office. My mom was on the line and she said, *"If you touch one more thing of your fathers, I'm calling the police and having you charged with theft."* I was stunned. I may not have been the nicest person before I was saved, but all I wanted to do was honor my father's death bed request. I ordered the crane operator to lower it back on to the barge and I left.

I tried to talk to my mom, but she had lost it and kept threatening to call the police on me if I so much as went into our shop at home where a lot of my tools were. I had to sneak in when she wasn't home and get my own tools. When I drove away, I was heartbroken. Not only had I lost my dad, but my mom as well. I simply decided that none of these material things were worth it, so I didn't see or talk to my mom for almost five years after that.

Mom and Jack knew each other from the local pub that dad and her frequented. I wasn't around then but the story is that Jack moved in on my mom, and her property, within weeks of my dad passing. I heard about it from my sister Suzy and I smelled a rat. It was obvious that he was there for what he could get, not for my mom. I could do nothing about it, so I left it in God's hands and carried on with my strange life. One of the stranger things that happened there was how Jack took mom camping and fishing almost every weekend. That's not the strange part. He says he put an ad in the Buy'n'Sell to sell some of my dad's tools. He said that a guy was interested in them but couldn't come until Saturday to look at them, but Jack and mom wouldn't be there. He said he gave the address to the guy, a stranger and told him to come by and check it out. He even left it unlocked for him. Upon returning on Sunday evening, they found the shop had been pretty much cleaned out, virtually everything stolen. So, who did they blame? I hadn't even been in the area and would not have done anything like that, but Jack convinced my mom that I had stolen all my dad's tools. I will let you draw your own conclusions.

With all of this going on, Anne turned off the tap and I had to get back to work and fast. There was a character by the name of Billy Jay Leger, who fancied himself as a new up and coming country music star. He had seen the old KW motor home and wanted to use it in his next music video. That never did happen, but he did get me a driving job where he was working until he hit the big time. The next thing you know, I'm working for the same company as Billy Jay, a plywood wholesaler and distributor we called Big Plywood. I was back driving trucks, super B-trains at that. It paid well enough, and there was an expense account which made living on the road a whole lot easier on the bank account. It was a relatively easy job, delivering plywood to all the little lumber yards around BC. Once I figured it all out, I could make some decent money, plus there was a full dental plan, so I was in the dentist chair every Saturday.

It was while working for Big Plywood that I discovered the Transport for Christ Chapel in Abbotsford. I wandered in there one day and met the Chaplin, Don Hannah. He was a nice older gentleman and he calmly explained the full gospel to me. I had heard it all before but this time it was different. This time it was very real, and I knelt on the floor, confessed my sins, and accepted Jesus as my Saviour. I already believed but that act of obedience was like getting a *"Paid in Full receipt."* I couldn't wait to tell Sandy. She was less than thrilled. I said, *"Hey, I thought you believed in God?"* She said, *"Not that one."* I was confused, more than usual, and asked her which god she believed in. She said, *"I don't have to tell you anything."* With that, the real split began.

Sandy discovered how easy it was to apply for new credit cards. She had so many and they were all maxed out in short order. She seemed to believe that happiness came from the mass accumulation of stuff. I was expected to pay for it all and I had a hard time saying no because I didn't like facing her wrath, which was formidable. She once pulled the knife drawer out of the cabinet and threw the whole thing at me. Praise God that even though there were knives sticking into everything around me, not one hit me. We were facing bankruptcy. All our hopes and dreams were dying.

Furrer had managed to put me in a position that left me powerless and penniless even though I had never worked so hard in my life. Sandy was mad that her caviar dreams were not going to come true. I just wanted to die.

Sandy and I were still pretty involved with the antique truck club. The few friends we had came from that group. We met some interesting characters there. One was John, a Jewish guy who loved old B Model Macks. Then there was Ted Hough, a true gentleman trucker. He was the part owner of a huge trucking company, Bobell Transport, and had a bunch of cool old trucks that he took to the shows. There was Norm and Evelyn Thompson. They were the President and Secretary of our chapter. They were grooming me to take over when they retired from it. It was around that time that Sandy and I decided to get married, mainly to *"do the right thing."* She was pregnant, and I didn't want the child to be a bastard. We went through the motions, but I knew she didn't really love me, at least it didn't feel like it.

I had a good job but there was never enough money to cover our debt. When your expenses exceed your income, your upkeep becomes your downfall, as some wise man once said. We were there. We didn't even have the $1000 needed to declare bankruptcy. It was sad and pathetic. We scraped it together and went to meet one of the nastiest people I have ever met. The bankruptcy trustee. He told us that we were basically toast. We had to live on $1100 per month. Anything that I made over and above that was to be split amongst the creditors. If I didn't follow the plan to a tee, I would be thrown to the wolves. On September 4th, 1991, our son, Brandon, was born.

I started to notice a certain number, 63, appearing in odd places regularly. I had no idea what it meant but it was noted. I kept this to myself because I thought people would think I was crazy if I mentioned it.

I know I was far from the perfect catch, but all I ever wanted was to be a blessing to others. I didn't need to be rich. I just didn't want to be poor any more. As I was spiraling down, I once again cried out to God for help. But it seemed like it was too late. There was no stopping this and it was going to hurt. Why can't we just sell those stupid motor homes!

Going through bankruptcy ended any chance of buying the lots at Tapedera. Humiliated, we had to abandon the trailer and find somewhere to rent that we could afford. The good thing was that as a truck driver, I could live just about anywhere along one of the main highways and be home regularly. We choose Hope since all the highways split off from there. We found a decent house that we could afford and settled in. One problem though, I needed to put my old 48 Kenworth somewhere since the guy whose place I was storing it at sold his house. There was a guy I knew, a truck driver I worked with at an earlier job, who lived in Hope. He said I could store it at his place. I agreed. I had already lost all my other stuff and there was no way that I was going to declare the truck I had worked on for seven years to the bankruptcy trustee. I was afraid of losing that too, so I wrote up a 'Bill of Sale' with my friend who was going to store it and he agreed to buy it, on paper. But the idea was that if anyone came looking for it, it would be sold before the bankruptcy. Admittedly, not a smart move on my part but I was scared, desperate and didn't have much time to deal with these things since I was on the road all week.

Sandy and I stopped by their house regularly. We all went out to dinner and had a few beers. We weren't super good friends, but we got along. One Saturday morning we dropped by because we forgot something from the night before. They were still in bed and called us up to their bedroom. It was obvious that they were still quite naked under the blankets, and it was very awkward. I said that we had to get going and that is when they invited us to join them in the bed. Shock isn't even close enough of a word to describe my feelings. I must have turned twenty shades of red and apologized for intruding as we backed out of the room slowly. It was just too weird.

About a week or two later, we drove by to check on the truck, and it wasn't there. I went to ask him where it was, and he told me to get off his property or he would call the cops. Once again, I had been suckered. I found out from his brother that he had sold it to some guy in Ontario who was passing through with an empty lowbed trailer. Seven years of my life, and the thing that healed the relationship with my father was gone.

They moved to a smaller house. When I found them, I took a couple of my bigger friends to the house and told him to come outside. He blocked the door and threatened to call the police. We stood outside, and I yelled at him through the closed door, but I was getting nowhere. Not wanting to meet the police, we left. It was shortly after that I realized I had a copy of the contract that he had signed, agreeing to pay me $3000.00. So, I sued him in a small claims court. It took a while but when we got to court, I won. The judge told him to pay me right away. He said that he did not have money and asked if he could pay in installments.

The judge asked me if I was okay with that to which I said yes. He gave me $300.00 right there and was ordered to pay me $300.00 per month until it was paid off. It didn't get my truck back, but it was better than nothing. One problem though. He declared bankruptcy the next day. Not only that but he told the trustee that I had committed fraud by 'selling' him the truck while I was going through bankruptcy myself. Nice. So, I got a letter informing me that I was in a lot of trouble and that I now owed $3000.00 to my trustee. Being a fool sure is painful.

One afternoon when I stopped in at the trucker's chapel, which had become a regular thing, Don gave me a big JESUS IS LORD bumper sticker. It was blue with white reflective letters, so it stood out. I put it on the back of my trailer for all the world to see. I wasn't ashamed of the Lord so why not. I was waved at by quite a few people as they passed me on the highway, but quite a few had some fingers missing. Sandy thought it was horrible and wanted me to get rid of it. I guess I am funny that way, but the more I was pushed in a direction I didn't want to go, the harder I would push back. I refused to remove it. I remember one trucker calling me on the CB and saying, *"Boy you sure have guts to put THAT sticker on your wagon!"* I didn't understand what he meant. I thought everyone knew that Jesus is Lord. Ignorance can be such bliss.

There it was again. A truck with trailer unit #63 passing me. What was it about that number? One Friday evening when I pulled into "Big Plywood's" yard, the owner, Alan, was waiting in the office for me. He told me to follow him, so I did. We walked along beside my trailers and when we got to the back, he pointed at the bumper sticker and said, *"Get that off my trailer, NOW."* I was shocked. I pointed out some of the other one on the other trailers, like, *"Party Naked"* and *"Leg Inspection, 75 Ft Ahead."* He said, *"Those don't bother me, that one does! Get it off my trailer or you're fired!"* I had no idea that people hated the name of Jesus. My real Christian education had begun. I told him I would remove it when I got home, and he agreed but warned me that if it was still there when I got back, I was toast. When I got home, I was indignant. I knew I wouldn't get any sympathy from Sandy, but I told her how I felt anyway. She said, *"It's his trailer, so you have to do what he wants with it."* I didn't want to hear that, but I knew it was true, so I went out with a scraper and pealed it off. I apologized to the Lord while I did it, and promised Him that I would make it up to Him. Boy was that an understated promise.

Angels Entertainment

It was Thursday October 22, 1992. I was supposed to load plywood from a mill north of Kamloops that afternoon but didn't get there in time, so I had to wait overnight. I dropped my trailers at the mill and bobtailed to a pub that wasn't too far away. I went inside, and the place was packed. Not being a big sports fan, I had forgotten that the Toronto Blue Jays were battling the Atlanta Braves for the World Series. It was the first time a Canadian team was in the World Series. Oddly enough, even though there was standing room only, there was a big horseshoe shaped seat and table right in the front with one guy sitting there. It was the only table available, so I asked if he was waiting for anyone. He looked at me and said, *"You, apparently."* I laughed and said, *"Seriously, you must be holding the table for someone."* He repeated, *"I'm the only one here and if you want to sit here that's cool with me."* So, I did. We struck up a conversation and it turned out that he wasn't there for the game. He said he just hated cooking for himself and they served good food there. I ordered a coffee and something to eat. As we were talking, I opened up a bit about some of the things going on in my life, especially about God. I was shocked when he told me that he was a Christian too. We started to have fellowship in a pub where the rest of the crowd was only there for the ball game and the beer. He asked me where I went to church. I admitted that I hadn't been in a church since I was around five. He said, *"If you're a Christian, you should go to church."* I had to agree, although in my foggy mind I barely put Jesus, the Bible and church together. It was just a personal thing to me at that point. I asked him where he went to church. He said he didn't go. Wait a minute! He said he married a pastor's daughter and she had divorced him, and that the entire congregation was against him.

I asked him why she divorced him. He said because he was calling her out for being a spoiled rotten feminist brat and that she took her revenge on him by telling everyone that he was abusive. I have no idea if it was even true, but I had no reason to doubt him. He seemed rather bitter about the whole thing and didn't want to talk about it anymore. But I couldn't let it go. So, I said, *"I have a plan, why don't we both go to church somewhere this Sunday? We'll exchange phone numbers and check up on each other next week."* He thought it was crazy, but he eventually agreed. The Blue Jays lost that game, but eventually did become the first Canadian team to win the World Series. There was a car passing me on the freeway, it had 63 in the license plate number.

The Hand of God

I got home early on Friday and informed Sandy that I was going to church on Sunday. I asked her if she wanted to come with me. She replied, *"Not in a million years!"* The rest of that day and all-day Saturday she was acting strange. She said she wanted to go to Chilliwack on Sunday to get something from the store. I said fine. She said, *"I'm taking the car."* I said no problem.

She started to lose it on Saturday night saying she thought she was coming down with something and I had to stay home on Sunday. I said, *"I'll only be gone for a couple of hours. You will be fine."* She then started accusing me of all kinds of strange things and wanted to start a fight. I simply refused to engage, and she went into a frenzy. She was throwing things at me and cussing me out for no apparent reason. I had no idea what demons were at the time but looking back I can see how they were manifesting through her. They hated me.

The next morning, I got dressed and started heading to the door. She practically begged me not to go. I had no idea what had gotten into her, but I made a promise and I was going to keep it. I said, *"Look, it's just this one time. If I don't like it, I won't go again."* That seemed to placate her, but she repeated that there was no way I was taking the car. *"No problem,"* I said, as I walked out the door. I tucked my Bible under my arm and walked the few blocks to the storefront church I had seen as I drove through town. I got some funny looks from people, but I was used to that. I didn't acquaint it with the Bible under my arm. As I got closer to the little church, it sounded like angels were singing. I had never heard such heavenly sounding music before. There was a sign hanging over the sidewalk, *"NORTHWEST HARVEST."*

As I opened the door, the sound of angels disappeared. It sounded horrible. There were some old folks up front. One was singing and banging a tambourine. He sounded like a cat being tortured. There was an old guy trying to cut a violin in half, and almost succeeding. There was another old guy playing a guitar out of tune. But they all had great big smiles on their faces and were singing about Jesus. I had never seen, or heard, anything like it. I was right by the door, ready to make my escape, when suddenly, this young guy was standing in front of me offering his hand for a handshake. I shook his hand and he introduced himself as the Pastor, Steve. He said, *"Welcome! So glad you could join us! Please come in and make yourself at home!"* I was honest and told him, *"I'm only here on a dare. I believe in Jesus but if it wasn't for this stranger and me meeting in a pub the other night, I probably wouldn't be here."* He smiled but didn't seem surprised and then he asked me if he could pray for me. I said, *"Sure, why not?"* So, he put his hand on my shoulder and started to pray. Now, I wasn't used to being touched, especially by strangers, so I stood there and watched him as he prayed. I guess I decided that he wasn't a threat, so I closed my eyes as he prayed. The song ended, and he had stopped praying a few minutes before, but I could still feel his warm hand on my shoulder. It was starting to creep me out, so I opened my eyes, only to see him back up front, getting ready to sing another song. Wait a minute, who had their hand on my shoulder then. It was then that I felt that God was in that place and He had just welcomed me home. I closed my eyes again and the sound of angels once again filled my ears. I found a place to sit and felt right at home. I knew I would be coming back.

There was a car in the parking lot with a 63 on a sticker in the window. When I got home, I must have been glowing or something because Sandy asked me, *"What's the matter with you?"* I didn't understand why she was so hostile towards God, but I just said, *"God touched me in that place. I know I said I might not go back, but I'm definitely going back!"* She was less than thrilled and said, *"Fine, just don't ever expect me to go with you."* I was saddened by her response but at that moment it didn't matter. I truly wanted her to know the peace I finally had inside; the joy that was overflowing within me and the truth that had set me free.

It wasn't long after that she told me she was pregnant with our second child. The old guy who owned our house informed us that he was selling it, so we had to move. We had avoided Chilliwack for as long as we could, but it was looking like that was where we were going to end up. We needed a house with a fenced yard for Brandon and our new child.

I was informed by my company dispatcher, that beginning immediately I was going on vacation. I protested that I hadn't asked for it and wasn't ready, but they said, too bad, it starts now. Today. Clean out your truck. I got ahead of myself there.

While working for Big Plywood, I discovered a few things about the plywood business. There are different grades of plywood; from de-lam (short for delamination), where the veneers didn't glue together properly, to D Grade, C grade, etc. Big Plywood would buy loads of de-lam, probably five or six a week from the various plywood mills. They would have a big D, written with a grease pencil on the sides of the bundles.

When I get to the yard, one of the warehouse guys would fire up the pressure washer and blast off the big "D" that was written with a grease pencil. He would set it aside to dry, then run an ink roller up the side of the bundle that said D GRADE. Not being an expert at this, I asked him what they were doing. I was told that it was just part of the job and not to worry about it. I didn't give it much thought, until I read a newspaper article about how there were suspicions of members of the Forest Council who were not playing by the rules. They intended to stop things like changing the grades of various wood products. They spelled out how much extra a company could make by simply doing what I had plainly seen my employer doing. My conscience was bothering me about it, but I didn't know what to do. I knew if I said anything, I would be fired if they found out, and I needed that job.

One afternoon, I simply took a few pictures of them changing the grade. It was for insurance in case they decided to play nasty, which I had every reason to believe they would, since the owner hated the fact that I was a Christian.

I had forgotten about it, when one day after work, a week or so later, Al, the owner, asked me if I had a camera. I said, I did. He said, *"Great! Follow me. I need you to take some pictures for me, since mine is broken."* I thought it was an odd request, but I went and got my camera out of the truck and I followed him to the warehouse. We walked around the big stacks of plywood and went through a door. It led into the famed *"sex room"* that I had heard rumors about. We walked through that room and ended up in his office. My dispatcher, Brian, was sitting in the office and he didn't look happy. Al went behind his desk and sat down and glared at me. He said, *"Look, I think you have some pictures on your camera and if you just give me the roll of film, I'll take them in and get them developed for you. I'll keep the pictures I want and give you the rest."* I stood there, pondering my options. Then I played dumb, which wasn't too hard. I said, *"I don't know what you're talking about. All I have on there are some pictures of my truck, some of a forest fire I drove through and of my sons 1st birthday party."* He was visibly ticked right off. He said, *"Don't play games with me. You know what I'm talking about. I know where you live, take that any way you want."* I still played dumb. *"What is it that's so important?"* I asked. The dispatcher came unglued on me, stood up and started yelling. I said, *"Well, whatever it is it must be important!"* Feigning shock, I said, *"I'll tell you what, we got lots of other pictures of my son's birthday and none of the other pictures mean that much to me, so why don't*

I just expose the film and then whatever it is that you're so upset about will be gone." They growled.

I popped open the back of the camera without hitting the rewind button. There wasn't any film in it. They went crazy. They said that if those pictures ever surfaced that I was as good as dead. So, I left his office, pretty much knowing that my days there were numbered. I went home and asked Sandy if she knew where the film from my camera was. She told me that she took the last few on the roll and took it to London Drugs for developing. In fact, they should be ready. I drove the half an hour back to Chilliwack, to London Drugs, just to retrieve the pictures and film. They told me that they had already been picked up and there was no other film under our name. It is a mystery to this day.

I was out of a job. We had a new rental house on a lease for $950.00 per month, utilities not included. It would take at least a month before my first unemployment check came and we were broke. I went to pick up my last check and the cowards didn't even have the guts to have me come there. The dispatcher said it would be in his mailbox at his house in Abbotsford. I was a little nervous going there after they had threatened me with murder. I prayed and went, taking Sandy and Brandon. I got to his mailbox and it was in there as he said. I opened it up and there was my layoff notice. It said I was fired for insubordination. I guess not wanting to be part of committing fraud is insubordinate.

Now Sandy was ticked, as if she wasn't mad enough all the time anyway. I told her not to worry. Just trust God and He would get us through. I would find a job soon enough. She wasn't comfortable with that idea at all and let loose a stream of profanity, trying to pick a fight with me. I simply refused to engage with her and that drove her even more crazy.

Hammer Down

I met Will, a super nice guy, at a church I had attended in Chilliwack. The next Sunday he told me about Marshall, owner of CB Transport. He introduced me after the service and he said he did have an opening, but he emphasized that *"this was hardcore trucking."* If I couldn't cut it, don't even bother applying. Not one to back down from a challenge, I said, *"No problem, I can handle anything."* I went and met him the next week. He explained the job and he wasn't kidding when he said hardcore. The first thing he said was, *"Around here we operate by grace, not the law."* That sounded sort of Biblical. *"We do switches. Two trucks will travel together, one driver in each truck. You go empty to one of two places. Both are about 11 hours from Chilliwack. You load yourself at one, they load you at the other. You then turn around and head straight back, 14 hours loaded, to Chilliwack where you'll drop the loaded trailers and your switch driver will hook up to an empty set and do what you just did. I pay $600.00 per rounder and you should be able to do 10 trips per month."* I quickly did the math and that added up to $6000.00 per month. I was calculating the hours involved. At a minimum, it would be 27 hours without sleep, every other day, so I had a question, *"What do I do if I get tired?"* The response was, *"If you stop for anything other than fuel and to load, you're fired."* Yep, one tough run, but $6000 a month.

My first trip was on the weekend. In trucking, no matter how much experience you have, you are always a rookie when you start at a new outfit. There wasn't anyone running with me, so I was on my own for my first trip. I was given an old Western Star cabover, and did what I was paid to do, drive. That truck was a challenge to drive in a lot of ways but that thing had power.

With a decked-up set of Magnum Ultralight Super B's, I flew up the hills. I drove non-stop all night to my destination. It took me 11 hours on the dot. I arrived in Burns Lake BC on Saturday morning, just as they were opening the gates at 7am. The old native guy on the forklift was nice but once he started loading, he was scary. We had to set our own dunnage, since it wasn't strapped to the lifts of specialty grade lumber. If you didn't do it quickly and jump out of the guy's way, he would gladly crush you with the lifts of lumber. Maybe it wasn't that bad, but you had to be careful around the guy. After loading and tarping, that took about an hour and a half, it was time to head back. Of course, being loaded is a lot different than being empty and I wasn't flying up the hills now. It still pulled great though. What it lacked in looks, it made up for in power, so I made it back to Prince George in good time, where I fueled up, got a coffee and a burger to go and down the road I went. It was just after 2pm when I left PG and I had an 8-hour drive ahead of me after getting no sleep at all the night before. You had to be tough.

It is hard to describe, but being on the road for years at a time made it impossible to participate in church activities, and some Sundays I simply had to leave early in the morning if I wanted to be on a customer's doorstep first thing Monday morning. That made it hard to relate to my brothers and sisters in Christ, since 99% of them had never seen the inside of a truck, let alone had any understanding of the dynamics of life on the road. Explaining to my new Christian family that it was hard to maintain my good Christian civility when someone in a car would almost get themselves, and maybe others as well, killed from some stupid move on their part, and that it's a regular occurrence, was never very well received. I asked God if I had to forgive all the morons driving their little bumper cars all around me. He said yes of course, and this is where amazing grace enters the story.

I knew BC Hwy. 97 very well since I had been up and down it for Big Plywood regularly for the last year. I was feeling good. The sun was shining, traffic wasn't bad, and I had my second, or was it my third, wind. I knew that the other driver, my switch driver, was going to be ready to head out as soon as I got back to Chilliwack and I didn't want to let him down. It started to get dark around 5pm, since winter was coming. I rolled into Cache Creek around 7pm. I needed to go, plus I was basically starving, so I said if a guy can't grab a burger and have a pee then who needs this. Fifteen minutes later I was off. It's a three-hour drive in a loaded truck, from Cache Creek to Chilliwack, down through the historic Thompson and Fraser Canyons. It's not a bad road if the traffic is light and if you know it, it's actually a rush, but when you are tired it's a different story. I had both windows down and the cold air from the open windows was helping keep me alert. A couple of hours later I had to stop in the little town of Yale to call my switch driver and let him know to get ready. Even though I was only fifteen minutes behind, he was ticked off at getting a late start. I drilled it into Chilliwack where my switch was waiting. He wasn't too mad but we had to fly at peeling off the tarps and switching wagons. If you knew all that was involved, you would be impressed.

I drove the car the couple of miles home. When I got home, I was asleep before my head hit the pillow. Sandy was upset about something and wanted to talk. I was dead to the world. She started to hit me to wake me up. I said, "I'm sorry honey but I have been awake for close to forty hours straight. I need to sleep." Undeterred, she kept harping at me about something. I was barely coherent, and I did try to listen, but I just passed out.

The next day, Sunday, I woke up around 10am. I was still groggy but tried to see what was so important the night before. She said, "Nothing." Nothing never means nothing for a woman. I tried to pry it out of her. She was pregnant. Some women go insane when they are pregnant. I was experiencing this first hand. She started yelling at me again, about what, I didn't know. She had a temper. She kept pushing me and even said I was a wimp because I wouldn't hit her. I was stunned. I had a pretty messed up childhood, but I had never, and would never hit a woman, no matter how much she deserved it. She started to hit me and yelling for me to hit her. Now the media would have you believe that men are always the aggressors. I can tell you from personal experience that we are not.

It's funny how what you think you are going to be doing isn't always what you end up doing. After a week of working for Marshall, my switch driver had enough and quit. Marshall said,

"Don't worry, I'll have another driver in a couple of days." Famous last words. So, I ran harder.

Since I was the only one on the truck, I could grab an hour sleep here and an hour there. There are rules in trucking. Lots of rules. One of the biggest for drivers is the daily log book. In Canada, a driver can drive for thirteen hours a day, in a sixteen-hour window, and not be on duty any longer than fourteen hours in a twenty-four hour period. The old split sleeper rules would let you balance rest and work time better. You are also not allowed to accumulate more than 70 hours in a week. If you have the kind of job where you can make a good living within those parameters, then good for you. Most don't. Virtually every driver is paid on a per mile, per ton or piece work basis. So, the faster you go and the longer you work, the more you make, and vice versa.

Marshall's operation was bending the rules. I was getting very tired, fast. Between driving, tying down and tarping, my poor body was pushed to the max. I was expected to do the work of two drivers. I was running three logbooks. I was running out of hours on the third. I found out that there are 168 hours in a week, because one week I worked every single one of them. I called Marshall and said, *"I'm out of hours on my logbook again."* To which he replied, *"Logbooks are $1.39. Go get yourself 70 more hours!"* I was on a treadmill and I couldn't get off. I would stop at a bank machine to take out $100.00 for road money and it would say, *"Insufficient Funds."* I called Sandy and asked her, *"Honey, did you put my check in the bank yet?"* She freaked out at me and said, *"Why, don't you trust me? You are such a jerk!"* I managed to get $20.00 out so I could buy some garbage that passes as food. I was never the biggest guy, but I was losing weight and feeling sick all the time. Being up, working for 160 hours a week will do that to you. But we never seemed to have any money in the bank. Sandy said she was paying off credit cards, but since the bankruptcy we only had a couple.

Death on the Highway

One of the unpleasant things about trucking is the fact that people die on the road, and sometimes we are there to witness it happening. I have seen two people die from traffic accidents. There were no grief counsellors to talk to. In one instance, I almost lost my job. I was late due to being held up because someone died.

The first accident where I witnessed a death was when I drove for Big Plywood. I was west bound on Hwy 3, just west of Fernie BC. It was a nice sunny fall day and I had just dropped some plywood at a Fernie lumber yard and was heading back to Cranbrook. As I came around a long sweeping corner, traffic was coming to a stop, but I didn't know why yet. There were about six cars stopped in front of me, and I could see smoke coming from the bushes up ahead and to my left. I got out of the truck and ran towards the accident scene, just in time to see a small pickup engulfed in flames while the driver, who was pinned under a flipped over semi-trailer, screamed the most blood curdling scream. It was incredible how fast the fire spread through the pickup. As it reached the victim, he threw his head back so hard that he smashed the back window out. His screams stopped shortly after that as he succumbed to the flames. The other travelers and I stood there in stunned silence on the road, trying to process what we just saw. It was gruesome to say the least.

The accident was caused by an older couple in a small car going the other way. The old guy who was driving fell asleep at the wheel and drifted across the center line, right into the path of the oncoming tractor-trailer. As the front of the car went under the left side of the truck, it sheared off the U-bolts holding the steering axle, causing the truck to suddenly go to the left, across the road and into the brush. As it crossed the road, the guy in the pickup, who was following the old couple, was swept under the trailer, and pinned under it. It occurred a few minutes before I arrived on the scene, but the fire started just as I got there. Watching someone burn to death, with the screams that just stopped as he died, is one of those memories that is indelibly imprinted on the soul.

The second accident where I witnessed someone die was on Hwy 16, between Houston and Burns Lake, just east of the summit of Six Mile Hill. It was while I was driving for Marshall. It was a Saturday morning and I had just finished loading at Houston Forest Products. As I was almost at the crest of Six Mile Hill, I was passed by an American flatbed with a small load of lumber on. Obviously, with a fraction of the weight, compared to my truck, he flew past me at the top of the hill. I remember thinking that he better take it easy on this road since there was fresh frost on it that hadn't melted off yet.

About 2kms from there, as I started rounding a long sweeping right curve, I saw dust flying in the air ahead of me. I instantly got on the brakes, not knowing what I was about to encounter. It was a good thing I did, because the buddy in the American truck had almost flipped his truck. The only reason he didn't was because the lifts of lumber on the back of his trailer broke free and launched directly in front of a west bound pickup truck. One of the lifts hit the pickup squarely in the driver's side. This caused it to crumple and pushed the entire side of the pickup into the cab. The pickup sailed down over the bank and came to a stop in the weeds, directly below where I was forced to stop. I looked down at the steaming pickup and saw the driver, an older guy, with the steering wheel and dash pushed right up against his chest. I thought he was dead. There was lumber scattered all over the road and the driver of the other semi got out of his truck, looking stunned. There was another pickup stopped in the middle of the westbound lane that had a few 2x10's balanced between the windshield and back window, with two very shocked people in the cab.

I looked back down at the mangled pickup just to see the driver move. I couldn't believe it, he was alive. I was in a rental truck and didn't have a warm jacket, or any of my tools, but I ran down the bank to the driver. His horn was stuck on, blaring loudly. I went up to talk to the driver.

"Are you okay?" Stupid question, but what else are you going to say.

"I've had better days," was his reply.

I didn't know what to say. I realized that he wasn't going to live for long and said, *"I guess you know you're going to die today?"* He looked at me and said, *"Yeah, it looks like it, doesn't it?"* I asked him what his name was. *"Charlie, Charlie Goodwin." "Hi Charlie, I'm Jon."* More silence as the horn still blared. I didn't know what else to say so I asked him if I could pray with him. He said that would be a good idea. So, I began to pray, *"Heavenly Father, here's Charlie. He's going to be seeing you very soon. I wish I knew how to pray right now. Anyway, Lord, Charlie is coming to meet you today and…"*

Just then, the two guys who were in the other pickup came running down the hill. It turned out that they were his sons. One of them pushed me out of the way, obviously very angry, while the other pulled the battery terminal off, shutting off the horn and possibly preventing a fire. I wanted to talk to Charlie some more, but the son who was with him growled at me, *"Haven't you done enough already?"* I understand their reaction, so I went back up to my truck to warm up and wait for the police.

When the young female RCMP constable arrived, I gave her my statement. A lane had been cleared, and she wanted me to get going to let traffic start moving. There was a flurry of activity down where Charlie was, with EMT's and Charlie's two sons working to extract him from the wreckage. As I pulled away, I felt numb. I knew that Charlie was going to die the instant they took the pressure of the steering wheel from his chest.

Sure enough, as I scanned the radio for information later that day, there was a news report on the CBC about the accident and Charlie did die at the scene. I called Marshall when I got to Prince George a few hours later. He was mad because I was an hour behind schedule. I tried to explain why, but he went into a rage on the phone, yelling at me for not moving the lumber off the road and get going. My dislike for the man was solidified and calling him a Christian brother became difficult.

I was in shock, traumatized and mad. I had no one to share this with, except God. Now, He's a great listener, but as for PTSD therapy, it would have been nice to have another person to talk to. Here I am, all these years later, and I still relive the scene, wishing there was something else I could have done.

My Amazing, Beautiful Baby Girl

Our daughter was born, July 19th, 1993. Christina Alicia Los was such an angel. I was in love with her but because I was constantly on the road, and only slept when I got home, I never had a chance to do more than see her sleeping in her crib. I was burning out. My left hand started to go numb, but it hurt above where it was numb. You can't just let go of the steering wheel and rest it, so I hung on. I would switch arms on the wheel, but after a while my right arm was going numb too. Pretty soon both my arms were numb, and my shoulders were aching. I literally had to steer with my elbows because I had no strength and almost no feeling in my hands. I was falling apart physically, mentally, and emotionally. I was driving down the road, crying out to God asking, *"Why is this all happening to me? I just can't do this anymore."* I remember coming home at one of the rare times that Christina was awake. I bounced her on my knee and she giggled and laughed. I loved my children so much that I would do anything for them, but I wasn't going to die to pay the rent. The last straw came when I was sent to the new and improved Hinton Saw Mill. It used to be great there. The forklift drivers would help you tie down and tarp. That was unheard of, but the powers that be decided to build a bigger saw mill. It was horrible. It was the exact opposite of the old mill. They had the tarping area in a wind tunnel. No one would lift a finger to help you there. You were on your own, just like all the rest of the mills.

It was warm and raining when I rolled up my tarps in a puddle in Vancouver about nine hours earlier. It was -25c and the wind was howling, and the snow was blowing sideways when I got to Hinton at midnight. I knew this wasn't going to be fun. I went to the shipping office and was told that they were no longer allowed to thaw our tarps in the drying kiln, a practice that has been done at lumber mills, everywhere, forever. My tarps were basically 200lb. solid blocks of ice with some tarp in there somewhere. I protested and asked them why not. I was told, *"New policy. If you don't like it driver, go somewhere else."* I said, *"Okay, let me at least get to Jasper Park where it's a bit warmer. I can tarp it there."* Not a chance. So, I went out into the bitter cold and wind to load.

I had done this hundreds of times in conditions just as bad, but not letting us thaw our tarps and belts was just cruel. I had a few belts in the cab that weren't frozen. but the ones that were rolled up in a rain storm and in the belt box on the trailer were frozen solid. It was brutal work and my arms and shoulders ached and were pretty much numb from the pain. My snipe bar came loose as I was pulling to tighten a strap and I landed hard on my backside on the frozen ground. I was done. I went up to the shipping office and tried to explain my predicament. The shipper's grabbed a two-way radio and called the forklift driver, telling him *"to start unloading that truck since the driver obviously can't handle the job!"* I was so mad at this jerk, sitting in his nice warm office gloating at his ability to destroy what was left of my pathetic life. I asked, *"Can I use the phone?"*

Normally, Marshall would take the call anytime, day or night, but his wife Patty, who didn't seem to like me, answered at 2:30am. *"Hi Patty, sorry to call at this hour but is Marshal there?"* She replied, *"No, he had to do an emergency run. Where are you and why are you calling?"* I said, *"I'm at the Hyatha Mill in Hinton, my arms are numb, they won't let us thaw our tarps in the kilns and the shipper is threatening to pull the load off the truck!"* I didn't want to talk to her, but she was the only one there, *"Listen Jon, if you cause us to lose that account you will be fired. I've about had enough of you and your excuses anyway, so when Marshall gets in I'm going to tell him about this. You are through here as far as I'm concerned."* Well, that took a bit of pressure off. It didn't matter what I did now since I was being fired anyway. So, I told the shipper that I would tarp it, but I was going to take my sweet time doing it. He said if any trucks came I would have to move, to which I replied. *I don't think so.*

I bundled back up and went out in the snowstorm and proceeded to tarp my load. It took almost three hours and there was a lineup of trucks by the time I was done, and I simply didn't care. A couple of the other drivers helped, and we were all mad that we couldn't thaw our out tarps there. I went in and got my bills signed then told the shipper that he had better get right with God because he was building up a huge pile of penalty points. I know, that's not how it works, but I still wanted to maintain some dignity, even though everything inside me was yearning to say something I would regret. With my bills signed, I sauntered out of the mill, drove to a wide spot beside the highway, pulled over and went to sleep. I slept for hours then got up and took my time heading back to the yard.

As I was coming into the Fraser Canyon, I saw one of our other drivers heading the other way and he called me on the VHF radio and said, *"Hey Jon, you're going to be in trouble for being late."* To which I replied, *"I was already fired so who cares."* He couldn't believe it. I pulled into the yard in Chilliwack around 5pm. I parked and went around to where Marshall was greasing a set of trailers. He wouldn't talk to me. I walked over to the shop, picked up the phone and called Sandy and told her to come and pick me up. She was instantly mad, *"What happened, it's only the middle of the week, did you get fired?"* I said, *"I did. Just come and get me please."* I went and unloaded my stuff out of the truck and waited. Marshall was still avoiding me. I knew Patty wore the pants.

Sandy showed up and was in a royal fit. She was yelling at me for being such a loser, berating me and cussing me out. I didn't care. I was so burned out, beaten down and tired that I just couldn't be bothered to put up a defense. To his credit, Marshall did say, *"Sorry, man. I'll do the Compo thing for you."* And that was it. I said semi-sarcastically, *"See you at church on Sunday."*

I was confused. I thought they were Christians. How could they just use a brother in the Lord up and throw him in the gutter the instant things got tough? Why God? I have bills. I have a young family. I am so gimped that I can barely hold a pencil, let alone go back driving. My wife is perpetually mad at me. My business is as good as gone. I trust you Jesus, but it is tough out there. I know it's almost a cliché but it's still true, someone said that God never gives us more than we can handle. I had no idea I could handle that much. I tried to assure Sandy that everything would be okay. She didn't think so. I had no idea how, but I knew I had to trust God. Humans will let you down, but He never will and honestly, I am extremely grateful to live in a country where I could recover and eventually get back on my feet. God will always make a way.

I started to lean on God. I had a long way to go, but I had seen him come through for me in so many small ways that I knew he would come through in the big things too. *"Lean not on your own understanding, but in all your ways acknowledge Him and He will direct your paths."* I didn't know what to expect but He was breaking me down so that He could rebuild me. I understood that from my restoration of the old 48 KW. If something is broken, you must take it apart, fix what's wrong, and put it back together. It didn't make it easy, but I did understand.

Sandy was threatening to leave me. She said she had enough of being married to a loser. I was just beginning to spend time with my precious daughter Christina and my three-year-old son, Brandon. He was a blast, a typical energetic little boy, and was fun to hang out with at the park. My doctor told me that I was almost dead. His exact words were, *"You look like you just went fifteen rounds with Mike Tyson!"* I said, *"No, I just worked six months for Marshall. It was worse."*

The Highway to Hell

I had a dream that I was on a multi lane freeway. I was in the second from the curb lane. I couldn't see how many lanes there were to my left but there had to be at least twenty. The freeway was full of vehicles of every type you could imagine. Since I was in a semi, I had a good view over most of them, except for other trucks. There were horses and chariots. There were lawnmowers. There were cars and trucks. There were bicycles. There were Conestoga wagons. There were children on tricycles. It was pure mayhem. The drivers were all yelling at each other. The guys in the chariots were the worst because they were whipping the people around them when they weren't whipping the horses. I saw a child on a tricycle get run over by a car as if it wasn't even there. Not only was there no remorse from the driver but it only seemed to make him angrier and more determined to get in front. There were drivers shooting at each other.

As I looked towards the horizon, I could see a beautiful sunset. It was red, yellow and orange and quite pretty. At least it didn't look like everyone was heading to somewhere bad.

I looked over at the lane to my right and there was no one in it. I couldn't figure out why. In all the other lanes it was an all-out war. Then I saw a sign, *"ETERNAL LIFE RIGHT LANE ONLY."* I was getting passed by a guy on a chariot and as he came up beside me he started cursing me and then he snapped his whip only inches from my face. I saw another sign, *"SALVATION RIGHT LANE ONLY."* I passed a car in the right lane. The driver was smiling as he was poking along. There was a glow coming from him. That really struck me as I looked at the rest of the people out there fighting, yelling, and cursing each other. I saw one more sign, *"SALVATION AND ETERNAL LIFE EXIT 1 MILE."* I knew that I had to decide, and quickly. I thought, *"I'm certainly in the right place to do this. It's as easy as moving over one lane."* I saw one more sign, *"RIGHT LANE MUST EXIT 1/2 MILE."* I couldn't see where the exit lead to, but it had to be better than the pandemonium to the left of me. I put on my turn signal and started to move over.

Suddenly, I saw in my mirror that there were cars trying to block me from changing lanes. The ramp was getting closer and I only had a few seconds to move over, so I used the size of my rig and forced my way into the right lane. As soon as I was in that lane, people started to shoot at me. I hit the brakes and slowed down for the ramp. The ramp had a bit of a tilt to it and as I swung to the right I glanced over my left shoulder to see where the rest of the traffic was going.

That wasn't a pretty sunset. The road ended abruptly at a huge cliff and all the traffic flew off into a huge abyss. What looked like a sunset was a huge fire pit. I slowed down as I came into a peaceful little town. Then I woke up.

Chapter Five

One Marriage Down

It was a typical Sunday. I rode my bike to church because Sandy wanted the car. I went with a heavy heart because I had a feeling that she was leaving. Honestly, I wasn't going to miss her temper tantrums, accusing attitude, spending money we didn't have ways. But I was sure going to miss my children. I asked her if she was going to be there when I got back. She said, *"We'll see."*

I wasn't too thrilled to see Marshall and Patty at church, but I went up to them and said, *"I forgive you."* He mumbled something about how *"it's just business."* I secretly hoped that it rang as hollow in his ears as it did in mine. Sorry God. I was trying to get into worship and I did a little as I praised God through my tears. I don't remember the sermon at all. I remember feeling lost, adrift, like I was the only one there. I hung around for a little while, hoping that someone would ask me out to lunch. No one did. I rode back to the house. I could see as soon as I turned the corner that she was gone. She had cleaned the place out good. The only things left were the furniture that I still owed rent-to-own for, and the plastic lawn furniture in the back yard. There was no note. No anything, and it was deathly quiet. I sat down on the couch and wept. I had given my life to God and it was getting tougher and becoming a very lonely walk.

I called Richard and Janelle. They had just returned home from church and were very sad to hear about what had happened. Well, Janelle was anyway. Richard was happy for me to not have *'the bitch around to drag me down.'* I can't begin to describe the agony of losing my family. First my own mother and now my wife and children. I had worked so hard only to find myself all alone, again. Not only that, but I had absolutely no income. Sandy had cleaned out the bank account and left me with all the bills. I finally realized that the only reason there was never enough money in the bank was because she was stashing it away for when she did leave me. It had been coming for months, but I was always on the road, working too hard and being too trusting to see it.

All I had left was the motor home business, such as it was. Richard was still working on it, and he had been keeping in touch. He said I would be perfect in the design department and I agreed. I knew I didn't have what it took to run a business like that anyway. He met, and was in meetings with, Dionne Warwick, the once famous singer. She owned a company called DW Design and did expensive interiors for movie stars, the wealthy, etc. She loved the motor homes and Richard was negotiating with her and her company to do the interior designs. Janelle and I were mortified. This was also the same Dionne Warwick who owned most of the occult 900 number business. We wanted nothing to do with her, but Richard was enamored with the thought of having someone famous as a friend. He thought we were fighting him when all we wanted was to prevent the company, which we had dedicated to the glory of God, to not be unequally yoked with unbelievers.

Ramen Noodles for Breakfast, Lunch, and Dinner

I didn't have much success with the Workers Compensation Board. Their initial reaction to just about every claim is to deny that there is a problem with you, that *'it's all in your head.'* I wasn't going to take that for an answer because it was a real problem. Unless there is a visible physical trauma, they will make your life very difficult. I don't blame them. There is no shortage of fakers out there. They had me going to different doctors for tests, and even when the tests showed that there was something wrong, they said they needed more tests. What a racket.

It got rather lean while waiting for the compo to be approved. One day I was at the grocery store and they were having a sale on Ramen Noodles; $2.00 for 24 packages. All I had was $10.00 and I knew it was going to be a while before I saw any money, so I bought five boxes. Now, I am not a big fan of those things. They are full of MSG and they give me heartburn. I didn't have much choice though. So, I had Mr. Noodles for breakfast, lunch, and dinner, for almost a month. When I finally had some money to buy some real food, I noticed that my finger nails had a thin line across every one of them. A sure sign that there was no nutrition in that stuff at all.

I lost count of all the times the number 63 would just randomly pop up. I still had no idea what its significance was, but now that I knew God, I could ask Him. He was very quiet about it.

My landlord, Victor Fong, was an economic immigrant from Hong Kong. He had a pile of money and bought his way into Canada. This was not long before Hong Kong was going to revert to Chinese control and there were thousands of Hong Kong residents who were buying property in Canada, and elsewhere. He wasn't a believer, but he was a decent man. I was honest about my situation and he allowed me to continue living in the house, instead of evicting me. He phoned me one night and asked if I had ever heard of Feng Shui. Oddly enough, I had just heard about it on the radio not long before, but had concluded that it wasn't Biblical at all, if not downright occult, so I had rejected it. He went on about it for some time and I wanted to be polite, after all, he was letting me live in his house without paying rent. I thanked him and said goodnight.

A few nights later, I looked out the window as he pulled up in his Lincoln Town Car. He got out and went around to the other side and helped a little old man out of the car. I went to the front door to greet them and Victor introduced me to Uncle Yo. He was here to help me with my feng shui problem. I went inside, quietly rebuked the demons, and let them in. Victor said that Uncle Yo was a feng shui expert and he would go through my house to tell me what to do to get my good luck back. Luck is the abbreviated version of Lucifer. I didn't want any luck, good or bad. Not wanting to cause an offence, and because he was sincere in his concern for me, I allowed Uncle Yo to do his thing. He slowly went from room to room, into the back yard then around the house to the front. He stood there, silent, for about ten minutes, looking. It was kind of creepy, but they meant well. Then Uncle Yo took Victor aside and began to tell him something in mandarin. Victor nodded knowingly then came up to me to explain what Uncle Yo said. He said, *"Your feng shui is not that bad. But there are a few things that must be addressed. The hedge in your front yard has holes in it and your bedroom is in the wrong place. You should move it to the room in the back of the house."* He then offered to pay me to find and replant the bad and missing hedging cedars. I owed him over $2000.00 with no income in sight and he was going to pay me. I was floored. So, He and Uncle Yo got in his car and drove off.

It took ten months, but the WCB eventually accepted my claim. They paid me retroactively from when I first submitted my claim. Richard, Janelle, and family had moved to Bellingham WA and were struggling financially. He was a good talker, could negotiate, and knew a lot of people, but if God doesn't want something to happen, it won't. I felt like the Lord was telling me to help them out, so I gave them $3000.00. I paid my landlord, Victor Fong, in full.

Shortly after Sandy took off with the children, I met a wonderful couple, Chad, and Linda, at church. They told me how they had been divorced and how God had restored their marriage. That gave me so much hope. They gave me a car too. They blessed me as they prayed for my wife, children, and me. Chad was a driver for a local hardwood company.

The Guilty Flee When No One Pursues

One morning, as I was starting my day reading the Word, I came across this in Proverbs, *"The guilty flee when no man pursues, but the righteous are bold as a lion."* I pondered it for a while, said my morning prayers, and went about to wherever it was I was going. I was sitting at a traffic light, waiting to turn left, when I noticed a very nervous looking young guy sitting at the bus stop where I was. An RCMP cruiser turned right and drove past the guy. As soon as the cruiser was by him, he got up and ran as fast as he could the other way. The cop kept right on going and never paid any attention to him but that didn't stop him from running. Less than ten minutes after reading *"The guilty flee when no one pursues,"* I saw it happen for real. *"...But the righteous are bold as a lion."* (Proverbs 28:1).

Faith For Your Needs, Not Your Greeds

Richard had found a building in an industrial area just north of Bellingham, in a little town called Ferndale, in Washington State, USA. He had secured the deposit and all we needed was the capital to start tooling up. That didn't happen as we hoped and we were flat broke once again. We prayed and trusted God, but it was getting extremely tight.

It was a Friday morning, around 9:30, near the end of the month, and we were deep in the hole. Richard called me that morning and told me that if we didn't have $200,000.00 by the end of the day, we were out of business. No electricity, no phone, no business, and back then, when cell phones were starting to appear, international calls were very expensive. I was the one who wanted to build one or two a year. Between the overdue promissory notes and all the other bills, we were up against the wall. Janelle got on the other line and we all prayed, *"Dear Lord, You know our needs. We only look to You to provide for us. If this business is supposed to be a success, then we know You can provide all we need and more. We humbly pray in Jesus name, amen."* All we could do was wait and trust as God moved on our behalf.

It was about 2:30 in the afternoon when Richard called me. He was laughing and yelling *"Praise the Lord"* which, if you knew him, was out of character. Not only did we have the money, but we had $250,000.00 and a new CFO. Ward was a son of one of the founders of Consolidated Freightways, or *CF*, one of the largest trucking companies in the world at the time. He had become very successful in his own right and was the Vice President of Key Bank of Washington when they were bought out by a competitor, Washington State Bank. He was close to retirement anyway and they gave him a huge severance package. He had heard about our motor homes from a friend of his, and since he had a trucking background, he looked us up to find out more. He called Richard about half an hour after we had prayed, they met for lunch and it was done. Once again, let go and let God, a lesson I still needed to learn.

Richard's Big Faith Adventure

We still needed money. Richard hadn't sold either motor home and we had debt that was piling up again. We needed to liquidate one of the RV's, and we decided to let the Peterbilt go. There was an exclusive auto auction coming in Las Vegas, at Barret-Jackson, and we decided to take it there and see what we could get. We had hopes of at least $150,000.00. Richard scraped every penny he could find together and, after a prayer was offered up to the Lord, away he went. He drove all the way from Bellingham to Las Vegas, where he set a minimum reserve bid of $100,000.00. We were all quite excited and hopeful that we might even hit the $200,000 mark. On the morning of the auction, Richard, Janelle and I had a conference call and we prayed that the Lord would open the hearts, and wallets, of the buyers. He said it was starting and he would get back to us as soon as it was over. About three hours later he called, and he was spitting nails mad. He said that the auctioneers were buttering up all the other vehicles, speaking in glowing terms about them, but when our motor home came up the ramp, they laughed at it. They were saying things like, *"What the heck is this thing?"* I was ticked off too. Who are these jerks and why would they be so negative? Richard said the bidding got to $75,000.00, not even close to what it cost to build, or the minimum reserve, so he pulled it. He had spent every penny he had to get there. He maxed out his credit cards and had almost no time left on his cell phone. But now he had to get home and the fuel tanks were almost empty. It did not look good.

He didn't have much choice, so he started heading north. Then he remembered an old business acquaintance who lived in Monterey, up the California coast. He thought that if he could at least get there and show him the unit, that maybe he could help somehow. Maybe even buy it. As he was just around Malibu, he started having electrical problems. He called me collect from a payphone, *"Jon! What is wrong with this thing? The lights don't work. The radio doesn't work. the blinkers don't work. Nothing works."* All I could say was that I was 2000 kilometers away and couldn't do anything from there, and it sounded like the alternator was shot. I asked him if he had tipped the hood to check and he said that even if he did, he wouldn't have a clue what to look for. He said that the gas station he stopped at said that they would look, after they ran his credit card first. He knew that it would decline so he just hung up on me and said he would call back. I got down on my knees and prayed. I called Janelle and she prayed. There was nothing else we could do.

About an hour later, he called. He was excited and said he had just seen his first bona fide miracle. He went to pull out of the gas station but could only turn right. He was on a boulevard and he couldn't turn around for quite some distance. When he finally found a place to turn around, he saw a cement truck parked with his four-way flashers going. He pulled up behind him, hoping for something, not knowing what. He walked up to the cab where the driver was sitting and told him about his problem. The driver said he might be in luck because he was broken down and was waiting for the company mechanic's truck to arrive himself. Richard gave him the tour of the motor home while they waited and when the mechanic arrived he gave him the tour too. The mechanic tipped the hood and noticed right away that the alternator belt was missing. No belt, no alternator, no electrics. He said that their fleet had a bunch of those same engines in their older trucks, but they had sold all of them and didn't stock any parts for them anymore. *"But,"* he said, *"Let's go look in the shop truck and see if we have something, but I doubt it."* They opened the door and he moved a box of rags, and there it was, the exact belt that was needed. He said that he had just put that box of rags in the truck that morning and that belt wasn't there when he did. The mechanic put it on for him and gave him a jump start and everything worked. Is our God good or what? So, with fumes for fuel but a working electrical system, Richard headed to Monterey.

When he got to Monterey, he found his old business associate. He said that he had never met such a mean, miserable old man in his life. Not only was he miserable but he cussed Richard out for bothering him and kicked him out. Richard didn't have a choice but to leave. Amazingly, he had made it that far and the fuel gauge was still just above the empty mark. If God wasn't miraculously providing fuel, then the gauge must have been broken, or it got 100 miles to the gallon. I wish I could have done something myself, but I was just as broke as he was. He kept heading north, hoping that if he ran out of fuel, it would be in a safe spot. We simply prayed and trusted God.

Teresa

Raised by her single mom, Teresa had a real problem with men. Nothing obvious, she did want to get married and have a family, but you could tell there was no way she was going to let any man lead her. I liked her. She was funny, and she knew scripture. She would come and hang out at my place occasionally. She had met Richard and one night she came over to my house, furious at him about something. I wasn't exactly thrilled with him either, but I didn't think it was any of her business. As fate, or God, would have it, Richard called while she was there. He had something to tell me and then Teresa insisted that she talk to him. I said, *"Richard, hang on, someone wants to tell you something."* She ripped into him good. I could almost feel his shock and anguish through the phone. She was in the middle of tearing a strip off him, when I got another call. She asked what the beeping was, and I told her there was another call coming through. She said, *"Richard, don't you go anywhere, I'm not finished with you yet."* She handed me the phone. I apologized to Richard and hit the button.

It was Senator Edward Lawson. He said, *"You keep calling this number and leaving messages for my wife. Who are you and what do you want?"* I was in shock. The strangest part is I knew his daughter from Buckingham Elementary school. I assured him that I wasn't trying to call him and that there must have been a mistake. Then it hit me, I had been trying to call Ken Ericson and he wasn't returning my calls. I asked the senator what his number was as I looked at Ericson's number. Dyslexia had struck again. I had switched two numbers when I tried to call Ken and had dialed the senator by mistake. To top it off, both of their wives were named Bev. We laughed, and he accepted my apology. Then he asked me about this business venture I had mentioned on his answering machine. He said it sounded very interesting. I told him a bit about it and then I told him that I had met him many years before when he lived on Burris St. in Burnaby and that I went to school with his daughter, Lisa. He was shocked but thought it was quite funny. So, there I was talking with a Canadian Senator, one who I even knew, while Richard is still on hold, waiting to get the rest of the tongue lashing from Teresa. What a strange life. He said, *"Well you have my number. Give me a call sometime to keep me updated with your project. It sounds fascinating and I can't wait to hear more about it. I'll tell Lisa that you said hi. Thank you, good bye."* With that, I hit the button and handed the phone, and Richard, back to Teresa. She picked up where she left off.

One of my part time driving gigs was for JDT, a reefer outfit that mainly served one customer, doing the Vancouver, Toronto, LA circle route. I was working with one of his owner/operators as a second driver on a team run and occasionally doing solo runs to California and back. We would bring tropical plants or citrus fruits back to Vancouver or Toronto. One afternoon I was on the *"peddle pick up"* run, heading through the San Joaquin valley, stopping at every little orange packing plant along the way. I was cutting it close to get all of them loaded before quitting time at my last stop. When I got there, at exactly 5pm, the shipper was saying I might have to spend the night and load in the morning. This was for two totes of oranges, and it was not a good plan. I asked to speak to a supervisor and he led me through the plant to his office. As we walked through, I noticed that every single worker has "JESUS" as a name tag on their coveralls. So, I started thanking Jesus for getting those last two totes on my truck right away. The supervisor was glad to get me loaded and out of there, and I was glad too. Goodbye California.

One Knight in Rusty Armor Coming Up

One day I got a frantic phone call from Teresa, saying that all her possessions were being held *"hostage"* at a small moving company's warehouse in Toronto. She had decided she was moving there to be closer to her father, but he told her to get lost, leaving her out in the cold with nowhere to go. So, as she was on a plane back to BC, her furniture and belongings were in a moving van headed to Toronto. Since they had nowhere to deliver it, they put it in their warehouse and started charging her for storage.

I told the owner of JDT about her problem, and how, if there was room in the trailer, I could get her stuff and bring it back for her. Amazingly enough, he agreed to do it even leaving a small portion of a payload behind to make room for it. Frank, the truck owner, was not impressed. I tried to explain why we were rescuing Teresa's stuff, and all he was concerned about was lost revenue and time, which I honestly can't blame him for.

We called the moving company, based in Milton Ontario, and a long way from where we had loaded frozen meat destined for Vancouver. These guys didn't seem happy that we were coming to get her stuff. Once we found the place, I went inside the office. I'm not kidding, every single one of these guys, obviously of middle eastern descent, had a big Freemason ring on their finger. I paid the balance that she owed, expecting her to cover it when we finished the rescue mission. We had to back the rig into a small gravel lot and pack all her stuff into the back ten feet of the trailer.

I called her repeatedly, explaining that since we were on an incredibly tight schedule to get the load of frozen meat delivered in Vancouver, that the only way we could do it was if she showed up at a pre-determined meeting place, so we could blow the stuff into a couple of pickups. For some reason, she couldn't grasp the importance of doing it my way, and she kept trying to get us to take it all to a storage unit. I explained, again, that we were not able to dictate how and where it was unloaded and that the only way it would work was if she did as we required. She just didn't seem to get it. As we got closer to the border, my patience was wearing thin. She had it in her pretty little head that we were going to do it her way, no matter how much it made an already inconvenient and difficult situation worse. Of course, all of this was done on my cell phone, and the bill for those calls was insane.

I gave her an ultimatum, *"We are dropping this stuff on the side of the road if you don't do as we require, simple as that."* Now I'm the bad guy. I called Roy, hoping that he had an idea how to help. He suggested his friend in South Surrey could store her stuff. We didn't have much choice since we were literally down to minutes before we crossed the border and the receiver closed for the weekend in two hours. With Teresa mad and not talking to me, I got the address from Roy and told Frank that is where we were dumping her stuff. We started driving into a very fancy neighborhood, looking for the address. It didn't exist. I called Roy and he had no idea.

Well, that was it for Frank. He was beyond mad, he was livid. If he didn't get the meat off his trailer, he would lose an entire trip. Finally, I spotted a vacant lot with a big gravel berm. I told him that we are going to drop it right there. He must have thought we were all nuts. We backed up to the wide spot, opened the back doors, and proceeded to unload her stuff on the side of the road!

While we were doing this, a woman came up to us and asked us what we were doing. She lived across the street and the sight of a couple of guys unloading furniture from a truck in her fancy neighborhood was a bit *"suspicious."* We never slowed down, while I explained how trying to help someone had turned into a nightmare, and that after Frank left, I would be staying with the stuff until someone came to get it, and me. She calmed down and felt sorry for us, offering to go back to her house and get us some refreshments.

It took us about twenty minutes to unload her stuff, and, after apologizing to Frank and shaking his hand, he was off to Vancouver to unload, cutting it very close. As he pulled away, I was left sitting there, on her chair, having a nice time with the woman from across the street. She even went and made me a couple of hotdogs. It was about two hours later when Roy arrived with a pickup and we loaded it up and took it to his friend's house, exactly one block over. Roy had given us the right address but on the wrong street. When I finally talked to Teresa again, she was mad at me. I guess all that didn't count since I didn't go the extra miles to deliver it to her storage unit. I never did get reimbursed for my paying for her storage fees, or for the insane cell phone bill that came a month later. Oh, and JDT wanted to be paid for the trailer space left behind because of having to leave a portion of the load of meat behind. That was another few hundred bucks, and it came off my paycheck.

There are some people you just can't please. After sitting in my house with my plastic lawn furniture and my empty, unpaid for, entertainment unit for a few months, I got my tax return. It was for $2200.00. I needed that. I paid one month's rent to Victor, and a few bills and had $1100 left. I was so tired of listening to the clock radio and I missed my good Christian rock. I asked God if I could please take this remaining money and buy myself a nice stereo. I had suffered quite a lot and just wanted something nice for myself. Selfish as it might have been, that's what I did. I started going to stereo shops and was shocked at the cost of the things. my $1100 would barely buy me a speaker, let alone a whole stereo system. I didn't want to settle for an expensive ghetto blaster either, I was believing for a nice stereo.

Keep in mind that this is happening while Richard is doing the auction thing in LA. I walked to the gas station that was a few doors down to get a few things. While I was standing there, I saw it. On the little newsstand at the counter were Buy & Sell's and on the front cover it said, 'HOME ENTERTAINMENT SYSTEMS INSIDE.' I bought one and went home to check it out. When I opened it to the stereo section, it was almost all ads from stereo stores. I was kind of disappointed and out $1.25. But, there it was, near the bottom of the column, 'Owner leaving country, must sell everything. Receivers, tape decks, CD players, speakers. No offer refused.' It looked suspicious but since it was the only ad in there that wasn't a commercial, I gave him a call.

A East Indian voice answered the phone, with dogs barking in the background. *"Hello, this is (unintelligible), how can I help you?"* Due to previous bad experiences I said, *"I'm sorry I made a mistake, sorry to bother you."* I was just about to hang up when he said, *"You are calling about stereo? Please, don't hang up, I am Christian man."* Well, that got me. *"What do you mean by Christian man?"* He said, *"It is a very long story, but I believe that Jesus died for my sins. Do you know Jesus?"* I wasn't expecting that, so I thought, maybe this guy is legit. *"When you say you believe in Jesus, what does that mean?"* I pressed him. *"Do you not know Him? He loves you and died for your sins. Please, don't hang up, let me tell you about Him."* Ok, so the guy didn't sound like he was faking it. Sorry for my judgement God. I told him that I was also a believer and that I appreciated his boldness in sharing his faith. He said, *"Please, come to see me about stereos. I have many and must sell them because I am being kicked out of Canada."* Kicked out of Canada? It couldn't hurt to go check it out.

I got in my car with $500.00 in one pocket, $200.00 in another and the rest in my wallet. I had the prototype model and all our promotional material in the back seat just in case. It was a good 45-minute drive there. I saw a 63 on a license tag. When I found the address, it was unkempt. The lawn hadn't been cut in ages and the whole place looked very run down. It looked creepy, but I felt like the Lord wanted me to go in, so I pulled into the driveway. Before I got to the front door, it opened and there was a big tall smiling brown guy standing there in his pajamas at three in the afternoon, with a mobile phone hanging from his waistband and puppies in his arms. He tried to wave without dropping a puppy.

I got out of the car and he came up and asked if I was the one who called about the stereo, and if I would like to buy a pit bull puppy very cheap. They were cute, but I said no thanks. He took me into the house and to the living room. The smell of dog poo was overwhelming, and I said, *"I'm sorry, I made a mistake, I need to go."* He apologized profusely for the smell and assured me that he was an honest man. I said, *"You said you are a Christian on the phone?"* He said, *"Oh yes, I love Jesus very much. I only wish I had met Him sooner."* He did have quite the stereo collection and that was what I had come for. *"Why are you selling this stereo equipment?"* I asked. He began to explain in his broken English, *"It is a very long story. I don't want to bother you with it. Please, pick the pieces that you want, and we will work out a good deal."* I was more curious about his circumstances than the stereo at that moment, so I told him I didn't mind hearing his story. He asked if I was sure and I said yes, so he began, *"I was born into the royal family of Indonesia. I was very far from the throne, but I was still a close enough relative to the king that we could live on the royal grounds. My family worked with the horses and we lived near the stables. There was a revolution when I was young man, about twenty-five, and I was forced to leave the country. I was* given a check for fifty million dollars and I chose to come to Canada. I have spent the money over the last twenty years and I am very sad to say that I have almost no money left, and I never did finish my immigration application, so they are kicking me out of the country. This is why I must sell all my things. Would you like to buy a Lamborghini?" There are only two conclusions and only one right one, either that was all true or this guy was a con artist supreme. He didn't strike me as dishonest though, so I gave him the benefit of the doubt and told him I would buy some stereo equipment from him. He had lots to choose from. He took me to his garage and showed me his Lamborghini. It was covered in dust and mouse crap, but it was authentic. He wanted $10,000.00. It was probably worth a lot more to somebody, but I didn't have that kind of money. We went back into the house and I started looking closer at the stereo components. I found an older tube amp, a five CD carousel, a double cassette tape player but no speakers. He said, *"Come into my back room, I have speakers still in the box."* We went in the room and it was filled with stuff but there they were, two brand new Sony tower speakers, still in the box. I said okay, I would take them as well, so we hauled them out. I had my system picked out and asked him *"How much?"* He asked, *"How much do you think it is worth?"* I said I would give him $700.00. He looked sad and said, *"But I thought you were such a nice man?. How about $900.00?"* I told him my top price would be $750. He thought about it then said, *"I thought you were such a nice man but okay, $750.00."* I told him that I didn't have all of it on me and that I would need to go to a bank machine, but I gave him the $200.00 I had in one pocket. I drove around for a while wondering if I was doing the right thing. Wondering if he was who he said he was. Wondering why I kept meeting these weird people. I pulled back into his driveway and handed him the rest of the money. He helped me move the components out to the car. Then he saw the prototype motor home model in the back seat. He asked, *"What is that? It is beautiful!"* I got it out of the car and set it on the hood and explained the concept we were trying to develop and hopefully, build. He said, *"Oh! Why do I not have money now? I would certainly give you all that I had to help you build this."* Yeah, Lord, why is that, I wondered. *"Well, it is what it is, and the Lord must* have a different plan. I'm not worried though; God knows and that's good enough for me." He said, "Wait a minute, I know a man who can help you." He unhooked his phone from his pajama bottoms and dialed. I could hear someone answer. "Yes Ken, it is Cresno Widjojo. I have a man here with a great idea and he wants to talk to you." He shoved the phone at me. I took it and the other guy said, "Who is this, what do you want, and how do you know Cris?" I was a bit taken aback but I composed myself and explained, "I just came to buy a stereo and he saw a prototype and some of our literature from our company and that without any announcement he dialed your number and now I'm talking to you. I'm very sorry to disturb you!" He laughed and said, "No, that's Cris for you. What kind of company do you have and how much are you looking for?" I hadn't even mentioned money, but he had it figured out quickly. He said, "Look, I'm pretty busy, but I can probably spare fifteen minutes this afternoon. I assume you're at Cris' so if you leave now you can be here in fifteen minutes. He knows the way. Let me talk to him." I handed Cris the phone and he said, "Yes, yes Ken. I will pay you the money. Please be patient." Now I'm thinking, what did I just get into? He was going to go in his PJ's, but I said no, I don't think so. He quickly got dressed and we were on our way. When we pulled up to Ken's place, he was out lunging a horse in an arena. He was a big man. He came over and introduced himself. *"Hi, I'm Ken Ericson, and you are...?"* I shook his hand and introduced myself, *"Jon Los, sir, Chief of Design and one of the Directors of Pedigree Motorhomes. Pleased to meet you."* I showed him the prototype model and some of our literature. He invited me in to meet his wife, Bev. They seemed like down to earth folks. They asked me if I was a Christian to which I replied, *"Praise the Lord!"* He announced that he didn't like to do business with unbelievers because they can't be trusted. Then he said, *"Let's pray."* With that, we began to pray. *"Dear Lord, thank you for bringing Jon here today. If we are to do business together I pray that You would be at the center of whatever it is we do, In Jesus name, Amen."* I didn't know this guy, but the prayer was a nice touch. This day had become much more than just buying a stereo. He explained to me how he was also in the middle of trying to raise capital for a new venture he was working on. He explained that he had developed a process where his system could extract up to 5% of the mineral values left behind from the traditional precious metal smelting process. I did some quick math and realized the potential of this, if it was true. He suggested that maybe we could explore the possibility of doing a joint venture. If we could raise money for his project, he would be willing to fully fund the motor home company.

When I got home, it was quite late. I knew that Richard should have been arriving home, assuming he didn't run out of fuel, anytime. I called their house and Janelle answered. I told her that I might have met someone who can help us finance the business. She was excited, and said, *"Richard is just backing into the driveway now, I'll take the phone out to him."* She handed him the phone. He took the phone and said, *"Jon, do you have any idea what I've just been through? I am not in the mood for talking right now. I want to spend time with my family. Goodnight."* He hung up. Oh, Richard, why are you so short tempered?

Dennis H

Brother Roy introduced me to Dennis regarding raising capital for the motor home business. He didn't invest, but he did invite me to study the Bible with him every Friday morning from 7 to 9am. I rather enjoyed our time together studying the Word. I had been going to his little Bible study every Friday for almost a year. The morning after my meeting with Ken Ericson was one such Friday.

I told him everything that happened the day before and he got very excited. He was jumping up and down in his chair exclaiming, *"It Is The LORD, It Is The LORD."* He told me to wait right there and he took off out of his *'prayer closet.'* About ten minutes later, he came back in and handed me a check for $50,000.00. It had no name on it, and he said he would trust me to make sure it was used to start the ball rolling. I was stunned. He insisted that we use the money as seed capital for the precious metals extraction process.

It Worked

It was an amazing process, extracting precious metals from used ores, getting up to 5% of the recoverable mineral values. On a large scale, that is a lot of gold, as well as things like iridium, platinum and every other mineral available.

Obviously, when something looks this good, you should be skeptical. We all wanted to believe that it worked, but we needed proof. Mr. Ericson was ahead of us as he pulled out two recent engineers reports, who both said it worked as claimed. It was a simple process, it just required money to set it up on a large enough scale to be profitable. The offer was simple as well. If we work with him and raise capital for his company, he will fund Pedigree Motor Homes once his operation is up and running. We didn't have anything to lose and after all, two engineering reports. We did the deal.

It was a whirlwind of activity as the few of us who were made directors of the new company, FACT Group, FACT Gold Technologies Inc. could offer shares in the venture to friends and family to raise capital.

I was a complete business neophyte who was aware of my shortcomings. It was quite the learning experience. The minimum buy in was US$25,000, and if you didn't have it to lose, you didn't play. I was concerned about people who couldn't afford to invest, since if it did go south, it would be a major hit to them financially. The first thing I would ask them is, *"Can you afford to lose this money?"* If the answer was yes, then we would go forward. If not, I felt bad for them but there was no way I could, in good conscience, take their money.

One older couple of German descent wasn't about to be persuaded. They told me that they had no problem if the investment failed; they win some they lose some. Something wasn't right, but they insisted, so I let them invest. They put in US$40,000.

Dennis put in another US$60,000. A friend of mine put in US$350,000. Another friend put in US$25,000. Overall, I raised just under US $600,000.00. From that I was awarded 10%, so it was a very heady time with all that money flying around suddenly. We were all told that this was nothing, it was all about to become very lucrative. Frankly, I was nervous. There were a lot of Christians from around the region who were attracted to the investment, and once they had a little bit in the kitty, they all started to fight with each other. It wasn't what I expected from these people at all. I was disgusted with their pettiness and greed, and these were my Christian brothers, sisters, and elders. Not all were like that of course, but the few that were made it challenging.

In the Beginning, God

One of the investors, a missionary family, said that they understood the risks and it was all the Lord's money anyway. They were glad to be a part of it no matter what happened. I was visiting them for dinner one evening when they asked me if I had ever heard of Dr. Carl Baugh. I hadn't, so I asked them why. They told me how they had been praying for the Lord to show them, finally, if Biblical Creationism was scientific, or not. Then someone gave them some video tapes of some lectures by Dr. Baugh. What he taught blew them away. He proved, mathematically, archeologically, logically, and scientifically, that evolution was not only impossible, but that it required more faith to believe in it, than to believe in a loving God who created all things. They loaned me the videos and I sat fascinated as Dr. Baugh blew the evolutionary *"theory"* out of the water. My prayer from all those years before had been answered as God showed me that His truth was not only scientific, but it was the same source that my salvation came from, Him.

The combined total investment in FACT GT and James Metallurgical was over $3M, raised in under five months. There is an industrial park in Abbotsford that was started with some of that money. James Metallurgical occupied three full sized industrial bays. The main components didn't take up a lot of room, but the lab was huge, and the ore handling area needed some space as well. There were some very educated and high paid people working there. But investors were getting anxious, they expected a faster return, and while not the most complicated system, it still took time to build. At the six-month mark, Ken announced that he was ready to give a full demonstration by pouring gold. That got everyone's attention.

There were probably forty people there for the big day. My old neighbor, Senator Ed Lawson was there, and a few other local politicians. One of the engineers who had signed off on it was there, Susan, as well as all the investors and principals. We were given a tour of the facility, and then split into groups of ten each, so we could fit comfortably in the lab were the gold was being poured. There were a couple of big smelting kilns in the lab and they gave off some serious heat when the doors were opened.

So, we watched gold getting poured into bars. They also poured some silver. There were pictures taken and handshakes all around, but there were a few who still weren't convinced, even though they had just seen it with their own eyes. I could explain the process since it is so simple. I saw that it worked, and that was good enough for me. But the investors wanted their ROI, asap.

Fundamentalist, Bigoted, Rightwing Christian

Around ten months after Sandy left, and after a few attempts to find them by driving up to the Princeton BC area, without success, I got a knock at the door. I was being served divorce papers. Well, the one good thing was that I knew they were still alive. I had cried so many times for my lost family that I even told God that it would have been better if they had died in a car crash or something, because I could grieve, and it would eventually be over. The uncertainty of not knowing was such torment that it was pushing my faith to its limit. Anyway, I signed for them and read them.

On the paper that stated the reason for her divorcing me was, and I quote: *"Due to his fundamentalist, bigoted, rightwing Christian beliefs."* End of quote. There it was, in black and white, my soon to be ex-wife had channeled Rosanne Barr.

I applied to see Brandon and Christina as soon as possible. Sandy wanted to prevent me from seeing them, but the courts forced her to allow me. I drove up to Princeton, to her parents' house, who obviously didn't like me, since they never made any attempts to even let me know that my children were okay. When I got there, they had both grown so much. Christina had learned how to walk, and she came running up to me and gave me a hug that I remember to this day. Brandon acted like it was no big deal as he said, *"Hi Daddy, I got a new Spiderman."* It was all I could do to stop from breaking down. I knelt on the grass and hugged them both telling them how much I loved them and missed them. Christina asked me, *"Daddy, are you coming to live with us now?"* I wanted to die. I wanted to say yes. All I could tell her was that I was praying for it to happen, but it wasn't up to me. She didn't understand, but she hugged me and said, *"That's okay Daddy, I love you."* It was one of the hardest days of my life.

I was still going to Church on the Southside, the church I had started attending when Sandy left. It was a Pentecostal church that had been an offshoot of a bigger church that had out grown its capacity. It was rather liberal in its form of worship but lots of folks seemed to like that, so it kept growing. I had been listening to Christian radio in the truck for a few years and was well versed from teachers like Charles Stanley, John McArthur, and many others, but as a believer I was still new to the church experience. I like to think I had a solid grasp of basic Christian tenets.

I knew that I loved God. I knew that Jesus died for me. I knew that the Word of God was amazing and powerful and the bedrock of truth. What I didn't get was how Christians could be so mean to each other. The backstabbing, gossiping, cheating and just plain old nastiness toward each other was a real turn off. I found myself digging in the Word to see what it said, rather than taking the word of others. I found out that a lot of what others said it said was just wrong. Nowhere in the Bible does it say that God helps those who help themselves. In fact, it says God helps those who cannot help themselves. There are many more examples of people putting words in God's mouth.

I started to question some of the things I was being taught and was met with hostility instead of an earnest desire for searching of the scriptures to *'see if it was so.'* I was seriously beginning to doubt that we were being truly faithful in worship as well. I didn't know why, but some things didn't feel right. I had time, so I volunteered for a couple of different jobs at the church, one being to drive the church van, taking the youth to functions and things like that. This was during the *"Toronto Blessing"* which was being pushed on the church as the latest and greatest *"move of the Spirit."* I was still relatively ignorant of church history and the number of charlatans that had blown through, fleecing the flocks as they blew through town. I started to see what was going on at these meetings and was shocked from watching people going into convulsions, barking like dogs, rolling on the floor, clucking like chickens and even one well-dressed businessman rocking back and forth on the ground peeing himself. They called it *"Revival."* I called it a mass hypnosis freak show.

I drove the church youth to one of these so-called revival meetings where I was witnessing madness, all done in the name of Jesus. They had a guy with a guitar on stage and all he played was one so called worship song, *"Freefalling,"* by Tom Petty and the Heart Breakers. It was played over and repeatedly, like a mantra, for hours. I was highly uncomfortable and disgusted with what I was seeing, and I prayed and asked the Lord to reveal the source of it all. I was concerned for the youth I had brought there.

I went back to my seat, grabbed my Bible, and opened it to Galatians 5:22,23, the fruits of the spirit. *"But the fruit of the*

Spirit is love, joy, peace, longsuffering, gentleness, goodness, faith, meekness, self-control. Against such there is no law."* That's not what I was witnessing at those so called *'revival meetings.'*

I attempted to ask one of the leaders of the meeting to help me reconcile my doubts with scripture and he said I *"didn't have enough faith"* and I *"just wasn't ready yet."* Ready or not, it was just wrong. I knew it deep down in my heart that these poor brothers and sisters were being led astray, but no one wanted to hear it. I remembered seeing a couple dressed completely in black from head to toe, each wearing a great big pentagram necklace as they walked through a *"service."* Our eyes locked, and they knew I was one there who could see who they really were, full on Satanists. The guy grinned at me. I rebuked them in the name of Jesus and they laughed and walked out the door. But what troubled me the most was that none of the other two hundred or so Christians there noticed them. It grieved me, big time.

The 63 Thing

I am not trying make it into any kind of doctrine or some special thing for Jesus Freaks. It was simply something that happened in my life that God used. Now that I have made myself clear about that, let me tell you the story.

As I mentioned earlier, and have sprinkled lightly so far in this book, the number 63 kept showing up all over the place. Why? I had no idea. I would see it on license plates, in a phone number, the unit number on a trailer, just all over the place. I started seeing it before I was saved and had no idea what the significance was. Before I was born again I considered numerology, no answers. I considered mathematics, but still no answers. I didn't go out of my way to try and spot it, it was just there, usually when I wasn't looking for it. I remember thinking, *"This is how people go crazy."* I thought I was losing my mind. It was starting to become irritating. I tried to avoid it, but it was just there, regularly. I remember being assigned to a truck once and when I looked at the odometer to write it down on my pre-trip report, it was 636363. I jumped out of the truck and yelled *"What the heck is it with this stupid number?"* The other drivers must have thought I had lost my mind, and I wasn't too sure that I hadn't.

Years later, I'm going to the Church on the Southside and watching as the congregation is getting bamboozled by the Toronto blessing. I tried to talk to the leadership but was met with, *"It's a new move of the Spirit Jon,"* or *"You should talk to your home group leader about it."* I was concerned since nobody seemed to see what was going on and the leadership was nonexistent on the matter. The last straw came when one Sunday service started with country music. I am not against all country music, I have heard nice country worship music, but this was different. This was the same crap that was being played in the local bars, not worshiping God at all. Not only that, but the pastors' wife came up and announced that a woman, not even a Christian, was going to be leading worship that morning. She announced that we would be line-dancing for worship. My jaw hit the floor. Some of you might not think that was a bad thing. You need to check your theology. There they were, 90% of the congregation heel-toe doe-see-doeing. There were a few of us who just sat there, mortified, confused, and disgusted. We looked at each other and at the madness that had descended on our congregation and rolled our eyes. I knew my days were numbered there. I prayed and asked the Lord to please release me from that place.

I didn't want to just bolt for the exit. Maybe God was going to do something that would shake them out of their stupor, and maybe He wanted me to stay as a witness against the madness. Maybe I was missing something. I didn't feel led to leave yet. I stayed for a few more Sunday services, none as bad as the line dancing one, but it was just uncomfortable there. Then there was one of the women who led worship. She obviously had a crush on me because she sang to me pretty much through the whole worship service. It was obvious. I was very uncomfortable, and I was still trusting God to restore my marriage. I wanted nothing to do with another woman until I had an all clear from the Lord. Then the sermon began. The pastor sounded very effeminate, I knew he wasn't, but he had such a wispy, wimpy voice. I don't need my pastor to sound like a gravel crusher but lisping? Really? He got up to begin his sermon but before he did he made a few extra announcements. He said, *"We got the new computers in the church office last week. In fact, they have these new things called CD-ROM's. Now when I prepare my sermon, instead of taking three or four days I can do them in a couple of hours."* I'm thinking, *"Yep, bet you agonized over every minute."* Then he said, *"There's trivia too. For instance, did you know that it says FEAR NOT **63** times in the Bible?"* I said, *"What?"* Now that was the answer from the Lord I had been waiting for. I stood up and shouted, *"That's it. That's what I've been waiting for. Thank you, Jesus."*

It was then that I noticed everyone was staring at me. But I didn't care, God had taken years to get me to this point of understanding. FEAR NOT! DO NOT FEAR! STOP BEING AFRAID! TRUST GOD AND QUIT BEING A BIG CHICKEN! WHATEVER ISN'T FAITH IS FEAR, NOW STOP IT! He really drove that one home. I was released from that church. I had the answer I was seeking for all those years, FEAR NOT... 63.

The System

As the divorce proceedings went forward, I resisted as much as I could, but the divorce industry system is stacked against fathers and husbands and I was helpless to stop the system from destroying my marriage. Sandra was as obstinate as ever, even more so. She said that she didn't want anything from me, but the welfare people had told her that if she didn't initiate the divorce and sue me for child support that they would take the children, charge her with neglect, and make her pay back every penny of the money that they had already given her. What an evil system.

I tried to get a lawyer, but I had no money. I left a message for one and he called me back and said there was no way that I could afford him, but he did give me some free advice. He said that due to a legal precedent, no one on Workers Compensation could be forced to pay alimony or child support. That was great, but I ended up with a lawyer from Legal Aid, and I got what I paid for. He really didn't care one way or another. It was something he was forced to do, and it was obvious.

I told him about my not having to pay because I was on WCB and he said he would consider it. He never did. On the day we went to court, he said that if I want to try to get out of paying based on the WCB claim, that I was on my own. Nice guy. I told him that I needed to be alone and pray about it. He found a vacant room for me and I prayed. *"Dear Lord, I don't know what to do. I want my family to stay together more than anything but that's not looking like it's going to happen. I know I don't have to give Sandy a penny, but I love my children and I want to support them. Please, Lord, tell me what to do."* I didn't get the still small voice, but I knew I had to do the right thing. In court, I was surprised by my lawyer when he told the judge that technically I couldn't be ordered to pay anything because I was on Workers Comp. Where did that come from? The judge asked if I knew that and I said yes. But, I told the judge that even though I didn't have to pay, I wanted to. He asked me how much I could afford and at the time I wasn't sure how long I would be on it, so I said $200.00 per month per child. He asked Sandra if that was okay with her and she said sure. So, the order was made to pay child support. Honestly, I would have paid more if I could.

The big surprise came a few days later when I received a letter from the Family Maintenance Enforcement Program. FMEP wasn't a nice bunch, right away they made threats and demanded that the payments be made on time and in full. I found out that they kept some of the money that I was sending my children and I realized that I had made a terrible mistake.

God Has a Plan

I met Roy at the Church on the Southside when it was still very small. After the service was over, I saw this long-haired guy standing at the front of the auditorium, hands raised in worship, head tilted back and with a great big smile on his face. I was intrigued by this brother, so I hung around and introduced myself after he came down. We decided to go for a coffee and have some fellowship. He was married to Brenda, an attractive half Korean and half Hawaiian woman from Idaho. They were certainly an odd couple, but they both seemed to love the Lord so that was good enough for me. I had found a friend who was a simple and down to earth guy. We were spending lots of time hanging out together and he introduced me to quite a few of the locals. One day, one of these locals came up to me and told me how Roy owed him a huge amount of money and to never lend him anything because I would never get it back. I didn't know Roy that well yet, but it did seem like I was the one paying for everything. I guess I overlooked it, but I never forgot that guys advice and tightened up the purse around Roy.

One Sunday after church, on a late August afternoon, he pulled into my driveway, in an older Toyota pickup truck that I had never seen before, while I was mowing the lawn. It was heaping over with plywood, lumber, and other building materials. He asked me if I wanted to go to camp. He had mentioned camp a few times before, but never asked him about it. This time I did. He explained that it was a brother's place about two hours from there and that God would bless me there. I said I had a meeting at 8:00am the next morning, so if I went we needed to be back by midnight at the latest. *'No problem,'* he said. I grabbed a jacket and away we went.

As we were heading up there, I remember feeling like it was all somehow familiar, a few times, even though I had never been up there before. We turned at Boston Bar and crossed over the bridge to North Bend, then on up the logging road until way after the pavement ended. The road got smaller and tighter and soon it was just a couple of trails with grass growing in the middle. It was quite cool in the forest and, as we rounded a small bend, we came upon a beautiful little flooded meadow. *"That's the beaver pond,"* he declared, as he kept heading back into the dark woods.

It was quite the adventure, if nothing else. It certainly was not what I thought I would be doing that day.

We turned down an even narrower trail and soon we were driving through a creek. After that, it was a bit muddy and he kept his foot on the throttle as we spun our way through the mud to where I saw big crosses carved into the giant cottonwood trees that lined the trail. We took a run at a short hill, where I started noticing lots of out of place stuff; big steel frames, pieces of pipe of different sizes and lengths, old dead cars and just lots of other junk. I remember asking him why someone would bring a dump to paradise. He assured me that those things were simply building materials that had yet to be repurposed.' He swung the little truck around and backed up to a big plastic covered shed and parked. *"Where are we?"* I asked. He said, *"This is Tranquility Station."*

We got out and started walking up the trail. There was smoke coming from a small gathering place that had a carved sign over it at the back, *"SUMMER KITCHEN."* There were a few men sitting around the fire pit made from a stack of old 18-wheeler brake drums, and they seemed very happy to see us. A tall older and very scruffy looking fellow stood up. Roy introduced me to David Lillos for the first time. He had tears in his eyes when he met me and told me that he had been waiting for me for a very long time. I was a bit taken aback but thought, hey, I guess the guy doesn't get that many visitors.

I also met Richard and his two children, Dana, a boy about seven, and Ashton, a little girl around five. There were a couple of others there whose names I don't recall.

As we sat around the fire, I was offered some coffee, but since I had quit drinking coffee and was only drinking tea, they made me some mint tea from the wild mint that was growing everywhere around there. It was very nice. I began to realize that these men were more than just some guys who lived in the bush.

As we were talking, it was obvious that they were all Christians and they seemed to have a much deeper knowledge of the scriptures than I did. As we were fellowshipping, I began to discuss my childhood and how difficult it was. It wasn't long after that, the floodgates of tears that I had held inside for so many years finally burst forth, and I cried tears of sweet release as all of those hurts from my childhood, and my present with my children being taken from me by my wife who hated the God she claimed didn't exist, were finally all washed away by the love of God. There was no condemnation or judgement from these guys and I felt completely free to share all the trauma from my past. As I did, it was as if the Lord was washing me from the inside out. I had never felt so free and alive as I did that Sunday afternoon in that bush camp, Tranquility Station. We sat up for hours just sharing what the Lord had done in each of our lives and how good it was to finally let all the pain that the devil had inflicted on us wash away. I lost track of time when I noticed that it was starting to get light out. I looked at my watch it was 4:00am. I had a meeting in four hours and it was a two-hour drive from there. I freaked out and an hour later we finally left after unloading the *"building materials" f*rom the truck.

It was daylight as we headed out and the lack of sleep hit me hard. I tried to get a nap in, but it was just too cramped and uncomfortable. When I finally got home, I jumped in the shower and got ready for my meeting. I must have looked like a zombie because the meeting wasn't successful. I went back home and promptly fell asleep on the couch.

Another funny, and trying, incident happened one day after church. It was a warm sunny day and I was out in the front yard cutting the grass. The house was right across the street from the Chilliwack City Hall and when I glanced over that way. There were four very attractive young women wearing nothing but skimpy bikini's walking directly towards me. Now, self-control is one of the fruits of the spirit and I was silently praying for more of that as they approached me. One of them spoke up and asked if I knew anything about cars because theirs had just died and they had coasted into the City Hall parking lot. It turned out that it was a Hyundai Pony, the same as the one my dad had, and I had a pretty good idea what was wrong. I helped them push it into my driveway where I could look at it. I went into the house and turned on the stereo with some nice Christian rock on, then prayed to be able to effectively share the Gospel with them. It was a very simple fix after all, a blown fuse for the ignition system. As I was repairing the car they all put on some clothes. Thank God! I then shared the Gospel with them and they all agreed that they needed to hear that. One of their phones rang and it was the girl's father. She tried to explain the situation but couldn't, so she handed the phone to me. I told him all was under control and that as soon as I found a fuse they were good to go. I also told him that I was a Christian and that they were safe. He said, *"Praise God! I was praying for those girls. A couple of them are pretty messed up and my daughter has been hanging around with them. We have been so worried."* I dug around in my shop and found the right fuse, got their car going and even prayed with them before they left. Once again, God arranged the whole thing and He gets all the glory. As they drove off, and waved goodbye, I couldn't help but feel a huge sense of relief and victory over the temptations of the enemy.

It was Halloween evening. I had just come from a meeting in Abbotsford, where my car had been pelted with eggs from a bunch of East Indian punks. As I was driving towards Chilliwack, I felt the Holy Spirit telling me that I needed to stop at Dennis' house and we needed to pray. I pulled into his driveway at around 11:00pm and since they were all sound asleep, I went to his bedroom window and called for him. He came to the window and as soon as I told him why I was there, he said he would be right down.

I went into the Prayer Closet and turned on the heater while I was waiting. He came in about five minutes later and we got right down to the business of prayer. We didn't know what to pray for specifically, but we were aware of what night it was and what kinds of things were probably taking place. As we prayed, we both felt the need to pray against any satanic sacrifices that would be attempted, not knowing of anything specific but feeling that we were winning a battle in the heavenlies. We prayed until about 1am and I went home. Nothing more was said about that.

During this time, 1994/96 I was taking computer and IT lessons in preparation for what I believed I would be doing very soon. I could see that the internet was going to be huge, and I wanted to be on the forefront when it happened. I knew that I would need to learn AutoCAD to be able to collaborate with others in the design of the motor homes. My teacher was Emile Farrah, a Coptic Christian who had fled Egypt because of the persecution he and his family were experiencing there. He was an awesome teacher.

In the fall of '95, Dennis Hammer asked me if I wanted to go to Israel with the Chilliwack Alliance Church in February. I wasn't expecting that. I didn't have much success raising anymore capital as I had run out of friends and relatives, so money was a little tight. Workers Comp had cut me off about four months before and it was sink or swim time for me. The money I did receive from FACT was enough to cover my bills, but there wasn't much left over. I just didn't have the money for something like that. I had submitted an appeal of the compo decision but had no hope of it being accepted. I told Dennis that I would pray about it, but it would take a miracle because I couldn't afford it. The next day I received a call from WCB informing me that my appeal had been granted and that I was going to receive my last four months retroactively. At $2900.00 per month, that paid for my trip to Israel. Before I could change my mind, I took a cashier's check to the church and reserved my spot on the tour.

As the business of raising capital was becoming increasingly difficult because I had run out of friends and relatives who I could legally approach to invest, I found myself delving deeper into spiritual matters. One of the most important ones to me at the time had to do with the State of Israel. As most of Christendom had been taught, we were to venerate Israel because it said so in the Bible. So, like all good obedient Christians I unquestioningly did so. One of my Christian friends at the time was very heavily into John Hagee and we were constantly listening to his sermons extolling the Christians duty to support Israel, no matter what, because *"it says so in the Bible."* So, when the opportunity to go to Israel was presented to me, I couldn't wait to go.

This trip was ostensibly an *"archeological study"* which basically meant that we were going to be seeing the archeological evidences of Biblical history. Not a lot of tourist stuff for this bunch, we were going to get some meat. The leader of our tour was the head Pastor of the Chilliwack Alliance Church, Ken Schmoon. He was a nice enough fellow and was ex-Canadian Military. There were seventeen of us and most were the wealthier members of the church. There were four of us who were single, but the rest were married couples.

One of the strangest members of our group was Bob Lee. He and his live-in girlfriend were quite the controversial pair. He claimed to be a Christian but was a very vocal Freemason and a Shriner. I asked Pastor Schmoon about this and he didn't see anything wrong with it, which began my questioning of his ability to discern good and evil.

There were the other couples as well, and these were accomplished, well-traveled retirees. I don't remember their names, but I certainly remember their snobbiness. I was fully aware that I wasn't *"one of them"* and they re-enforced that regularly, so once again, I was the outcast of the group.

The Hammer family was there, and I wouldn't have been on the trip if it hadn't been for Dennis inviting me in the first place. Dennis and his wife were nice folks who had made their fortune by hard work and frugal spending. They had been taking worldwide vacations for years, so this was just another one to them. Their children, Keith and Marla, were a bit strange but then again, the whole family was. Keith was a natural born tinkerer. Working in the family welding business had made him quite proficient at designing and fabricating anything you could think of from metal. He was quite happy to do nothing else but weld all day, but Dennis was determined to find him a wife.

Marla was a very sweet young girl who knew how to weld anything. She had the typical, very attractive German face and I thought she was one of the prettiest girls I had ever seen. She was so far from my reality that I never thought there was any kind of a chance with her. I remember that as we were flying over the great expanse of Greenland, on our way to London, I asked the stewardess if she could ask the captain if I could sit up front in the cockpit. I had done this years before as a child and loved the experience. I was granted permission and I asked Marla if she would like to come. She was thrilled to. We sat in the navigator's seat, pressed tightly together, and chatted with the pilot and co-pilot. The sun was just about to break over the horizon when we all saw a bright green and blue light, that looked like a meteorite or something, flash by the front of the plane. The pilot estimated that it couldn't have been more than a mile in front of us when it streaked by. That was close. We were excitedly talking about it when the navigator returned to the cockpit. He was curious at first and then became agitated that he had not only missed it but it was his job to deal with it. We were asked to return to our seats. As we were going back to our seats one of the stewardesses asked us if we would like to sit in first class, since there was a vacancy there. Of course, we agreed. So, there I was, sitting with Marla, the prettiest girl in the world, in first class on our way to Israel. She laid her head on my shoulder and fell asleep while I was trying to figure out how to talk to Dennis, her father, and my Christian brother, about this new development. I drifted off to sleep as well.

We landed in London and since we had nine hours between flights, someone arranged for us to have a quickie tour. We visited Buckingham Palace, St. Paul's Cathedral, and the City of London, among other stops, then back to Heathrow for the flight to Israel.

Marla and I sat together and some of the women on our tour were pointing and tittering about it. They seemed to think it was a wonderful development but one look at the scowl on Dennis' face told me that he wasn't happy about it at all.

We landed in Tel Aviv. After clearing customs, we went to meet our tour guide and bus driver. As soon as we got to where they were, Bob Lee started handing out his business cards that had Masonic and Shriner symbols all over them, as well as cans of water that he had brought from his bottled water company in Canada. Our tour leader was aghast. She thought she was going to be leading a group of Christians, not Freemasons, so she went to talk to the pastor about it. She was seriously ready to walk away from us over it. After Ken assured her that Bob and his girlfriend were the only Masons in the group, she agreed to remain as our tour guide. It was funny to me, but I seemed to be the only one who got the joke. I was appalled at the lack of discernment by my brethren, which only served to alienate me even further from the rest of them.

Here we were, in The Holy land. We started in Joppa and we made a stop at the traditional home of Peter the Tanner right on the Mediterranean Coast. Then off to Jerusalem we went, up the narrow winding back way, where we ended up at a Carmelite monastery for our first night's rest. It was the middle of the day there, but we needed to adjust our sleep to the local time. We all awoke around 3pm on Friday, and since this was Israel, Shabbat was about to start at sunset, so we all dashed out to the streets. The sound of roll shutters closing everywhere was ubiquitous as we stood in the Jaffa Gate.

Out of nowhere this greasy looking fellow came up to us and greeted us. He asked us if we were tourists and where we were from. When we told him British Columbia he said that he has relatives that lived there and asked us if we knew them. We didn't. He then said, *"I own a small store here and haven't closed for Shabbat yet. Please, come to my store and let me rip you off."* We were shocked by his forwardness and declined his offer.

The next morning, we were off to our first official landing spot. It was a kibbutz on Lake Gennesaret, also known as the Sea of Galilee. It had, like most kibbutzim, a dual purpose. It was a summer camp on the lake and an ostrich farm. Since it was the off season, being that it was February, the kibbutz was very quiet. We did some sightseeing that day but it was Shabbat, so most things were closed.

We went to bed early since our internal clocks still hadn't transitioned to the local time and I found myself wide awake at 4am Israel time. It was still dark out when I decided to go for a walk. I walked down to the beach where there was a jetty that went quite some ways out. I was thanking the Lord for bringing me to that special place as I walked out to the end. It was closed for the season so only the metal frameworks of the summer umbrellas were standing, and I sat on a bench and began to pray. It was surreal to be sitting there, out on the Sea of Galilee where Jesus had walked on the water, talking to God. I could see Tiberius on the other side of the lake with its lights reflecting on the water that was as still as glass. There was such an incredible peace to that place.

Then I heard it. Off in the distance there was a loud explosion. Then another. And another. It was then that I realized that the Golan Heights was just behind us. I thought, *'Great, they are bombing each other.'* But I was wrong. As the dawn was just starting to break to the east, I saw the most incredible sight. Coming up the Jordan Valley to the south was a big black cloud. The sky was perfectly clear everywhere else, but this black cloud was slowly making its way towards me, shooting out lightning bolts and deafening thunder claps. I was mesmerized by this spectacle as it moved closer. Then the wind picked up and within a minute the peaceful lake had 3 to 4-foot waves crashing against the little jetty where I was sitting. I had seen firsthand how fast storms could develop on the Sea of Galilee. Lightning bolts and thunder were still shooting out of this black cloud as my view of Tiberius was obliterated. I'm a bit slow, but I realized I was sitting under a metal framework sticking out in the lake as a lightning storm was only a mile away, so I ran away from it and sat on a rock on the north side of the jetty as the storm rolled northward. Then it started to rain, then pour. I was soaked right through within a few minutes so there was no point in running back to the kibbutz. I sat there on the jetty as the storm went up the lake and seemed to lose its power at the north end and then just vaporized. Once again it was completely calm, and the sun was just beginning to shine on Tiberius on the other side.

God had just given me a personal welcome to one of His favorite spots. I was so blessed to have had such a wonderful and powerful introduction.

I went back to my cabana and changed into some dry clothes then took my Bible and went for another walk. The biggest thing on my mind though was Marla Hammer. As much as I tried not to, I couldn't help but think about her. I prayed and asked God what I was supposed to do. I knew that it was going to be a touchy subject with Dennis and I didn't want to cause any friction, but at the same time there was a mutual attraction between us and I wanted to do the right thing. I felt like it was my duty to ask Dennis if I could court his daughter.

The next morning after breakfast I asked Dennis if I could talk to him privately. We went for a short walk and sat on the patio of the restaurant that was closed for the season. We made some small talk and then I told him that I had a very important question to ask him. I thought he already knew what my question was going to be, but I asked him anyway.

"Dennis, I can't tell you how much I appreciate you as a brother and a mentor in my walk with Christ. I know that the Lord has put us together and I feel like I am part of your family." He was silent, so I continued, *"I don't know if you have noticed but Marla and I have been spending a lot of time together and we really like each other."* His eyes narrowed. *"Therefore sir, I would like to ask your permission to court her, if that is okay with you."* He was silent for a few more seconds and then he bellowed at the top of his lungs, *"A DIVORCED MAN AND A VIRGIN? NEVER. I don't want you anywhere near her, do you hear me."*

I was devastated. I didn't know what to say. I certainly didn't expect that response. I thought maybe a gentle no but to be so thoroughly humiliated because of my situation made me feel like a total loser. It was surreal, again. I had the most intimate and wonderful time with the Lord, our Lord and Saviour Jesus, only the day before and now I was forbidden to even talk to Marla. I knew it was his prerogative as her father, but I honestly didn't like him at that moment. So, for the rest of the trip Marla and I could only look at each other sadly, knowing that it just wasn't going to happen. She was a very obedient and faithful daughter who would never question her father's authority, so it was simply over. I look back now and am very thankful that the Lord protected me from having Dennis as my father in law.

As it slowly sank in that I was in the same places that Jesus had walked, preached, done miracles, had been crucified and raised from the dead, it was becoming very clear to me that my view of The Way was very limited. We in the west live in such an insulated environment, cut off from the realities that are common to the rest of the world. The poverty, even in relatively prosperous Israel, was heart wrenching. We were warned before we left Canada to beware of the scam artists there, but my heart went out to the Bedouin people. They were living in tents and shacks beside the roads and we were told that they were constantly harassed by the police and soldiers and forced to move, even though they were already a nomadic people.

One afternoon we stopped at a wadi to take some pictures. It wasn't anything spectacular and the historic reference has disappeared from my memory. As I was aiming to take a picture, a young Bedouin boy, maybe seven years old, jumped in front of my camera just as I snapped the picture. This was before the days of digital photography, so he had just ruined a frame of my film. As if that wasn't bad enough, he started to demand that I give him $5.00 for taking his picture. I told him that he could forget that since it was obvious that he was trying to extort the money for something I had not agreed to. Well there was no reasoning with this little tyrant and he started to make verbal threats against me. It was very strange to be told that he was going to kill me for *"stealing"* his picture. A crowd of other Bedouins started to come towards us and our tour bus driver, Mahmood, told us all to get back on the bus quickly. We all got on the bus and as he was pulling away, the Bedouins all started to throw rocks at the bus. It was unreal. Mahmood explained that this was very common there and that more than one tourist had been killed over the same thing. Nice place you have there.

As we toured the rest of Israel, it became a blur. We went to all the regular tourist spots plus a few archeological sites as well. I saw a T-shirt that I regret not getting that said, *"I RAN WHERE JESUS WALKED."* It was so true. It was a very full schedule as we went from place to place. I won't even bother to tell all the little stops along the way. There was one stop that was very significant for me.

At the beginning of the Jordan River, where it drains from the Sea of Galilee, there is a Baptism Park. I had been baptized once at Cultus Lake, in BC, but I had been told that unless you were baptized in the name of The Father, Son and the Holy Spirit, it wasn't a proper baptism. I don't worry about such hair splitting now but back then it was important to me. So, I requested that I be baptized there in the Jordan River, just like Jesus was. Pastor Schmoon didn't seem to object but a few others on the tour did. It became a bit of a topic as the ones who plainly didn't like me were opposed to it, but there were the few others who thought it was a good idea. Then one of the other members suggested that they wanted to be re-baptized as well and since this was a respected member of the group, the opponents all conceded, and we made our way there.

Once we arrived we were warned that since the river was so polluted that we needed to take extra-long showers after getting into, and being submerged in, what was basically an open sewer. That didn't sound too inviting. They highly recommended that women not be baptized there due to the parasites and other nasties in the water. Well, I was there and since I had been the one who started all this I felt like I had to go through with it. As we walked up to the river, the smell was rank. We waded down in and Pastor Schmoon, God bless him, waded in as well. Despite the nasty smell, I totally felt like I was in the center of God's will right there and was excited to go through with it. Pastor

Schmoon baptized the both of us and we couldn't get out of there fast enough. We hit the showers and washed all that crap off. But there it was. I had been Baptized in the Jordan River.

We eventually arrived back in Jerusalem and were put up at the St. Georges Monastery on Nablus Road, just a few hundred feet from the Damascus Gate. In between there was Gordon's Calvary. This is a controversial spot in Israel since the traditional Christian denominations all call the Church of the Holy Sepulcher in the old city the place where Jesus was buried in Joseph's Tomb and rose from the dead, but the archeological evidence doesn't support it. Gordon's Calvary not only has an empty tomb, but the hill called Golgotha is only a few hundred yards away. It is heavily guarded with a high wall to prevent vandals from desecrating it, whereas the Church of the Holy Sepulcher was guarded by Muslims, since the seven denominations that claimed it couldn't be trusted with the keys. I found myself spending a lot of time there, seeking the Lord. I was still hurting from the rejection by Dennis and was pretty much an outcast from the rest of the tour group. Let's just say I was struggling big time with feelings that weren't Christian.

We were nearing the end of the tour and we had some free days to do whatever we wanted. I had convinced Dennis that I wasn't going to pursue Marla, so he let me hang out with her, if brother Keith was there. I had gotten over it all by then and we had decided that on our next free day we were going to go explore modern downtown Jerusalem.

It was around 6am and I was just waking up, still lying in bed, when I heard a huge BOOM. Dust fell from the ceiling and I was sure that I had just heard a bomb go off. Keith, my roommate, slept right through it, but I was up now. I went to the communal dining hall and there was only the wait staff there. They were Palestinian and were visibly anxious. I asked them if they heard the big explosion and they all heard it. The one who spoke English said that it was never a good thing when this happened and that they might not be able to make and serve us breakfast if they had to go and report to the local authorities. I had no idea what he was talking about.

As the other tour members arrived, I asked if any of them had heard the explosion. One of the old codgers that didn't like me said that it was probably a car backfiring. None of the others had heard it. As the news began to filter in, we found out that it was indeed a bomb that had gone off. It was on a bus in downtown Jerusalem, full of young Israeli army recruits, and at least twenty-four had been killed. As the shock began to sink in, and I had been vindicated, we were told that due to the blast, downtown Jerusalem was closed for the day. There went our plans for the day but the fact that an explosion had just taken twenty-four innocent victims weighed heavily on me.

Keith, Marla, and I decided to go back into the Old City and just wander around, since our plans had been scuttled to go downtown. As we were walking towards the Damascus Gate, we ran across some others we had met during the tour. We exchanged small talk and told them how our plans were changed when they suggested that we take a taxi to the Jerusalem Mall. Of course, there had to be a mall. So, we stood on the corner at the Damascus gate and tried to flag down a taxi.

During our pre-tour briefing, we were told to avoid anything Palestinian. That included taxis. The Palestinians have white license plates, while the Israelis have yellow ones, so we were only trying to flag down the ones with yellow plates. They simply ignored us and wouldn't stop, but there was one taxi with white plates that kept circling around and waving at us. We stood there for almost half an hour, until finally we decided *"How bad could it be?"* We trust God anyway. So, we waved at the Palestinian taxi and he pulled over at once. We all climbed into the back seat and told him our destination. Once we were underway, I noticed a cross hanging from his rearview mirror, so I asked him if he was a Christian. To which he replied, *"Of course! My whole family are Christians. We live in the Holy Land; how can we not be."* Well, this came as a surprise since we had been told that all Palestinians are Muslims and would probably kidnap and/or murder us. As we talked, I asked him a lot of questions about the Arab/Israeli conflict, and specifically, the explosion that morning. He said something that forever changed my mind about the social and political dynamic of the region. He said, *"Politicians from both sides are always fighting, but it is the people at the bottom who always suffer. Yes, there are many Muslim Arabs, but there are just as many Christians like me who the world never talks about. We love everyone, just as Jesus told us to, but we are completely ignored by both sides, and never mentioned in the media."* It was quite a revelation to us and before we knew it, we were at the Jerusalem Mall. When we tried to pay him, he refused any payment. From that moment on, I have been praying for our Palestinian Christian brethren. As for the Jerusalem Mall, if you have seen one mall, you have seen them all.

As the tour was ending, our last day was another free day where we could do whatever we wanted. After breakfast, I went for a short walk down to Gordon's Calvary and sat down to pray and ask the Lord what to do that day. As I was sitting there, the guy in front of me turned around and asked, *"How would you like a personal tour of Jerusalem?"* He introduced himself, John was his name. I was taken aback but as I talked, it became obvious that he was a brother in Christ, so, as far as I could tell, I had no reason not to trust him. As we started on our tour, he told me that he had to be back at Gordon's Calvary by 4:30 that afternoon. He had been asked if he could minister to a tour group that was having some serious problems, but he didn't go into detail.

He showed me around the old city and shared about how he came with a tour group a year earlier himself but never left. I can't remember all the things he showed me, but he asked me if I wanted to go with him to his apartment. I remember thinking, *"he doesn't look gay"* but I figured why not, I have nothing to fear. His apartment was on top of the Mount of Olives, in fact, it was on the top floor of the tallest building there. We stopped at the Garden of Gethsemane and prayed, then continued up to his place. We had to go through another family's apartment to get to his, but once we were there, it was incredible. The view was unreal. Then he asked if I wanted to go up to the roof where we could see all of Israel.

When I stood on the roof, I could see the entire country, aside from the haze in the air. I could see the Mediterranean to the west, the Jordan River to the east, the mountains to the north and the Dead Sea to the south. It was breathtaking. Then it hit me, I was standing in the very place that Jesus ascended into Heaven, and where he said he was coming back to. I was truly humbled that the Lord had led me to this place.

Time was ticking, and we needed to get back to Gordon's Calvary for his meeting, so we took a *"sherut"* (a private taxi) down to his church. It was a small church made of stone, but the thing that stood out was how it had all of Acts Chapter 2:4 written in the tile around the inside near the ceiling. I wish I could remember the name of it. He introduced me to many of the saints there and we had a nice time of fellowship and prayer. Then it was off to Gordon's Calvary for his meeting.

As we walked, he explained what was going on. There was a tour group from the US South, a black church, and a white church together. And, during their trip, old animosities had resurfaced, resulting in much tension and disagreement. He was asked to see if he could help heal the rift. When we arrived, I immediately recognized them from crossing paths with them on many occasions. It was obvious that there was a serious problem because all the white folks were sitting on one side of the seats and all the black folks on the other. First, my new friend John got up and led us all in prayer, then the white congregations pastor spoke, and then the black pastor spoke, but the tension was still there. Suddenly, I felt like the Lord was prompting me to share a scripture, Hebrews 12:22-29. I asked if it was okay and all agreed. I stood up and read from my new Bible,

> *"But ye are come unto mount Sion, and unto the city of the living God, the heavenly Jerusalem, and to an innumerable company of angels, To the general assembly and church of*

the firstborn, which are written in heaven, and to God the Judge of all, and to the spirits of just men made perfect, And to Jesus the mediator of the new covenant, and to the blood of sprinkling, that speaketh better things than that of Abel. See that ye refuse not him that speaketh. For if they escaped not who refused him that spake on earth, much more shall not we escape, if we turn away from him that speaketh from heaven: Whose voice then shook the earth: but now he hath promised, saying, yet once more I shake not the earth only, but also heaven. And this word, yet once more, signifieth the removing of those things that are shaken, as of things that are made, that those things which cannot be shaken may remain. Wherefore we are receiving a kingdom which cannot be moved, let us have grace, whereby we may serve God acceptably with reverence and godly fear: For our God is a consuming fire."

When I finished reading, it was very quiet as there was a healing taking place. Then, an old black woman and an old white man stood up and moved towards each other. They both were crying as they hugged and forgave each other, for what I don't know, and it was beautiful to watch as the spirit of division was broken. Then everyone was hugging and crying as the power that the enemy had over these precious saints was removed. All I did was read a few verses of scripture. I was, and still am, humbled by how God had me go all the way to Israel to be a part of that. That was the last experience of my last day in the Holy Land. We were ushered to the airport in Tel Aviv at 5am the next morning and one of the most amazing experiences I ever had ended.

Back To The Grind

Once I was back in Chilliwack, it was time to knuckle down and get back to work. We were still waiting on Ken Ericson to finish the metallurgy lab, and it was getting a bit tense with the investors. I needed to make some money, but it was becoming increasingly difficult to find investors.

I was also in the process of ordering a new Land Rover Discovery. They were the ultimate 4 x 4 as far as I could tell at the time. The house I was renting was huge. I was sharing it with Roy and Brenda, but I was paying virtually all the expenses. It was one of the oldest homes in Chilliwack that once belonged to the most prominent veterinarian in the Upper Valley. It had a pool and about four acres of lawn, with a pond and a creek that meandered through it. I was totally looking forward to having some real wealth.

One morning, as I was rushing out the door for a meeting, I grabbed my Bible, flipped it open to a random page and read, *"Seek ye first the Kingdom of God, and all these things will be added unto you"* (Matthew 6:33). I remember thinking as I was running out the door, *"Well, that's backwards."* Then it hit me, if I think that is backwards, then it must be me and my heart that's backwards. I shuddered at the implications. I tried not to think about it, but I just couldn't shake it. When I got home later that day, I read all of Matthew chapter 6, You can't serve two masters. But lay up for yourselves treasures in Heaven, where neither moth nor rust doth corrupt and where thieves do not break in and steal. My priorities were totally backwards. I pleaded with God to have mercy on my wicked heart, but I felt no peace.

A few days later, at about 7am, Janelle called. This was out of character for her. They never get out of bed until 8:30am at the earliest. She was frantic as she told me, *"Jon, I've just woken from a horrible dream. I dreamt that Ken Ericson has stolen everybody's money and fled the country."* I tried to calm her down and told her that it was just the devil trying to steal her peace and not to worry about it. We had all kinds of protections in place and he was a Christian man. I had just seen him at my church just the Sunday before. She seemed to calm down, but she repeated that it seemed so real. Frankly, with the way the investors were starting to attack each other, with the greed that I had seen in Furrer and all the other little signs, I was seriously starting to wonder myself, but I kept that to myself so that I didn't panic anyone. I was praying to God though, *"Lord, what is going on?"*

This seems like a good time to share a little lesson that a brother shared with me. We were discussing wealth, and all the responsibilities that go with it, when he said, *"Hold out your hand, palm up."* I did as he said. He picked up a small rock from the ground and placed it in my hand. He said that the rock represented a gift from God and it was my responsibility to look after it, and even enjoy it while I had it. As I stood there holding the rock, he went to grab it suddenly. I instinctively closed my fingers to protect it and he said, *"It's not your rock, so why are you so protective of it?"* I didn't have an answer. He said to open my hand again, so I did. He then reached over and took the rock. Now, even though it was just a rock, it seemed like I had lost something. He then said, *"You never owned that rock Jon. It was given to you to care for, but it was never yours. Keep your hand open though because God wants to teach you something."* He then reached down and picked up a much larger stone and placed it in my hand, saying, *"When we allow God to place things in our lives, we must also be prepared for Him to remove them at His pleasure. Once we learn to do that, He can, and usually will, place a bigger thing in our hand."* I have always remembered that lesson.

That week seemed off. I didn't know what to think, but I was having doubts. I called Richard and tried to talk to him about it, but he basically said, *"You better not be saying anything like this to the investors. That's all we need is to have them lose confidence and start demanding their money back. Nothing is wrong. And never mind your paranoid delusions."* He was known to be rather blunt, but this seemed downright demonic. After all the outbursts I had seen from him, this was by far the most intense. One week later, almost to the hour, I was awakened by the phone. It was Janelle. She reminded me of the dream she had shared with me the week before. She came right out with it, *"Ken Ericson has fled the country with all of our money. There's nothing left. He cleaned everything right out. He even left his wife Beverly, with all the bills in her name. My God Jon, what are we going to do."* My first reaction was that there must be some mistake, but she assured me that there was no mistake, that she had been on the phone with Bev for the last hour. She woke up in the middle of the night and he was just gone. She was frantic, thinking something bad had happened to him. He called her from the airport just before he got on the plane and dumped it on her. I couldn't believe it. I told Janelle to hold on because I was coming over after I stopped by the facility.

I drove straight to the building and got there around noon. It was locked, but there were a few of the other investors standing around outside. Word had travelled fast. They wanted to know what was going on and all I could tell them was that I just found out myself less than an hour before and was going to do everything I could to figure this out. I thought a couple of them were going to lynch me right there. They were furious at Richard and I, but a couple of the other more experienced investors knew that it wasn't my fault and calmed them down. I took off, heading to Richard and Janelle's, about forty-five minutes away. When I got there, they were in full panic mode. Janelle had been on the phone with Bev all morning and the story was starting to become clearer. Richard was at the bank and confirmed that all the accounts had been completely cleaned out the day before, right before closing time. We figured that he must have been planning it for quite some time and we couldn't believe what suckers we had been. Poor Bev was almost having a stroke. The jerk left anything that wasn't paid for in her name. So, just like that, we were all flat broke, in worse shape than we had ever been. I had huge bills to pay every month and there just didn't seem to be any way out.

Chapter Six

Despise Not Small Beginnings

I was getting the occasional call from guys who I had driven for, asking me if I was interested in doing a run here and there. Of course, I was so engrossed in the business that I could almost never go. I had done a trip here and there, but only a couple. I was now calling these same guys asking if they had any work. It was humbling, but I was desperate. Not one of them had anything. "Sorry Jon, I have all the drivers I need." "Sorry Jon, don't need anyone right now. Call back in a month." "Sorry Jon, I just found someone to do a run for me yesterday. Try back in a month or two."

I didn't know what to do. This wasn't supposed to be happening. I had no contingency plans. I drove up to Tranquility Station to try and sort it out. Just get away for a day or two to put it all in perspective. When I got up there, it was like David had some kind of hotline because he seemed to know all about it. Since there was no electricity and especially no phones, it was kind of freaky. He said that I was welcome to stay there, that there was always room. The thought of moving there was not comforting at all. I was planning to build a nice house on a mountain someday, but I had no intention of starting from complete scratch. I told him I would pray about it, secretly hoping that by some miracle all would be well, and everything would be back to normal when I got back to the city.

Later that night, as I was lying in a hammock behind the Summer Kitchen, starring up at the stars, I asked God, *"Lord, this was so unexpected, what do You want me to do?"* I heard that still, small voice as clear as anything, *"I want you to rest here a while Jon."*

Now when you hear God talk to you, you sit up and take notice. I rolled out of the hammock and walked back to the Summer Kitchen. It was pitch black out as I made my way behind everyone. As I was almost there, I saw David stroking his beard as he said, *"I feel like God is telling Jon that He wants him to rest here a while."* I said, *"What did you just say?"* He repeated, *"Oh hey Jon, I feel like God wants you to rest here for a while."* You could have knocked me out with a feather. Not what I wanted to hear, but there it was. I wasn't going to argue with God anymore. My striving after the things of this world had worn me out and I knew deep down inside that this was the right thing for me to do. It was time to seek first the Kingdom of God.

Once I had made the decision, on the one hand everything was just falling into place. On the other, the enemy was working through believers who were weak in the faith, or whatever it was, and they were saying I was crazy, that I would be killed by wild animals, that I would starve to death, that Sasquatch would get me, that it was illegal to walk in the woods, that I was just running away from my problems. I'm sure there were more, but you get the picture.

I told my circle of friends what I was doing and that I had no need for furniture in the forest. Come and get it. I gave everything away. My bed to Roy because his wife, Brenda, had a bad back. My furniture to my other brother Phil because his was worn right out. My stereo, the one from Cresno, to another brother, but there were two of them that wanted it. I watched in disgust as they fought over it. Roy had a line on some 30-gallon food grade resealable barrels for $1 each. I bought ten or so of them and filled then with the few possessions that would fit and that had meaning to me. I bought some roof racks for my Oldsmobile, which I had kept to restore, but now was my only car, and began to build a load. Phil, one of my closer Christian brothers, came by on his motorcycle one afternoon and said, *"I know that everyone is saying you're crazy, but I want you to know that I really believe that you're doing the right thing. My prayer for you is that God would grow you into the man of God that He has planned for you to be. God speed brother."* With that blessing, it was settled, there was no turning back. I remember how depressed I was. Shortly after I arrived, to stay, David came up to me one day and said, *"It looks like the end of the road, doesn't it?"* "Yep," I replied. *"Well turn around and it's the beginning of the next one."* I was so blessed by his encouragement and wisdom, *"The Lord doesn't despise small beginnings."*

During all this time, and virtually every waking moment, I was thinking about my children. My dream had been to gain enough wealth to find them and have a relationship again. I would pray, *"Lord, I lift my daughter, Christina, up to you. I know You know where she is and I'm sure she misses me as much as I miss her. If there's some way You can comfort her and bring us back together, I'd sure appreciate that."* But God had a different plan. I didn't understand it, but I trusted Him.

I was moving loads from Chilliwack to Tranquility every other day. The next time I went up to Tranquility, I didn't arrive until late at night. As I was setting up my tent beside David and Heidi's place, I heard something come crashing through the woods towards me. I shone my flashlight towards the noise and this guy yelled, *"Get that light out of my eyes! Who are you and what do you think you're doing?"* I yelled right back, *"I am a friend of David's and who do you think you are? I rebuke you in the name of Jesus! I command you to be quiet, NOW!"* He backed right down and mumbled something about something. I told him, or rather the demon in him, that I had commanded him to be quiet. He did as he was told. I finished setting up my tent and walked over to the Summer Kitchen where Heidi and this big guy were sitting. I said Hi to Heidi and nodded towards the tough guy. He started to say something again and I said, *"You don't listen, do you? I said shut up in the name of Jesus!"* I found out his name was Rick and he lived in an old bus down at the bottom of the hill.

It was three weeks until the end of the month when we were hit with the news of Ericson fleeing the country. I had a few days until I knew I couldn't pay the rent. Roy and Brenda were staying but I knew they wouldn't be able to afford it. They were mad at me for abandoning them. I felt a little guilty, but God assured me that He would look after them and that my priority was me at that time. I built a few big loads on the Oldsmobile and found out that a great, cheap way to make any car a lowrider was to put a ton of stuff on the roof.

I was concerned about meeting the police up there. The last thing I wanted was to meet them on the wrong footing. I was an upstanding Christian citizen, not some lowlife from the woods and I wanted to make a good impression on them. I prayed for just that. I had taken all my loads up to Tranquility at night up to that point, but one day I had no choice but to go during the day. It must have been quite the sight, as I measured it and it was almost eleven feet tall.

I got to Boston Bar and as I was crossing the bridge between there and North Bend, I saw a young woman sitting on the railing. That was the Fraser River below her, a boiling whirlpool filled muddy mess that had swallowed lots of people over the years. The natives had great respect for it for good reason. I stopped where she was, rolled down the window on the passenger side and asked her, *"Are you all right?" "Do I look alright to you?"* she yelled back.

I put the car in park, shut it off and got out. As I walked closer she screamed, *"Don't get any closer or I'm going to jump!"* I stopped. I told her whatever it was, it wasn't worth dying over and that Jesus loved her very much. She screamed at me, *"Where was He last night?"* I said He was right there with her, suffering whatever it was that she was going through. I didn't want to pry, but I asked her if she could tell me what happened the night before. She told me that she had been gang raped, that her boyfriend basically gave her to all his friends. I started to really feel her pain and started to weep for her. She said, *"Why are you crying? It didn't happen to you!"* All I could say was that God was there and He felt her pain and was sharing a little of it with me.

I stepped over the no post barrier. She flung herself to the other side of the railing, hanging on with only her hands. All she had to do was let go and she was as good as dead. I said I was sorry, that I didn't mean to scare her more than she was already. I kept trying to calm her down and assure her that God really did love her, so much that He gave Jesus to die for her. While I was talking, an RCMP cruiser pulled up. As he got out of the car, she freaked out and I told him to wait there, that I had it under control. He waited by his car. Then a scruffy native guy came running down the bridge yelling, *"Natasha, Natasha, what are you doing?"* As he got closer, she told him to stop or she was jumping. I guessed that this was her boyfriend. Then an old woman drove by. She had a demonic look of hatred in her eyes. She stopped, got out of the car, and said, *"Why don't you just jump you bitch!"* I was filled with righteous indignation as I spun around and yelled, *"I rebuke you in the name of Jesus. I command you to shut up."* She dropped to her knees and hissed. In all the confusion, Natasha let go. Her boyfriend lunged after her and grabbed her, pulling her back on to the sidewalk. She was kicking and screaming and the RCMP member came and subdued her. He had to handcuff her to prevent her from lashing out as she was flailing around. He put her in the back of the police car and came up to me with his hand outstretched. I shook his hand as he said, *"Thank you for what you did there."* I replied that anyone could have done what I did, to which he replied, *"No one else did though. I want you to know how much I appreciate what you did here today. Can you come back tomorrow and give us a statement?"* I said sure. Then he looked at the insane load on my roof racks and asked where I was going. I told him Tranquility Station. He just smiled and said, *"Well, you drive carefully!"* As I drove across the railroad tracks a little farther up the road, my roof racks collapsed. I pulled over and tightened everything down again then made my way up to camp.

One of the biggest things that was trying to hold me back from making the move to Tranquility was the child support order. $400.00 per month wasn't a big deal when the money was coming in, but it was a huge deal when it wasn't. I had paid Sandy cash, bought her a car, and kept up with the children's needs as best I could. I considered getting the order changed to reflect on my lowered income but there was no legal aid available and I couldn't afford a lawyer. As I prayed about *'letting go and letting God'* I felt Him telling me to simply trust Him. I knew He could take care of it, it was up to me to have enough faith to LET Him take care of it.

Once it was clear to me that God wanted me there, I knew that a tent wasn't a good idea, so I went for a walk in the woods. Right on the upper edge of the rain forest and the arid interior around Lytton, there was a nice mix of old growth and second growth, stinging nettle, devils club and debris and deadfall. I just walked along the ridge beside the creek and came upon a large ravine, that had a huge old fir tree, dead, and laying across the length of it, like a bridge. I love cool bridges, so I made my way around the dead roots and across. As I got to the crown, I looked up the other side of the ravine and saw a beautiful, thick bed of moss, with the sunlight shining on it. Then it hit me, or God did, this is the spot.

From that moment on, I was determined to get to work. This wasn't a game anymore and if I was going to be there a while, I better come up with some home improvements. With my tent, cot, army sleeping bag and my Bible, it was going to be a lot of work.

I build a crude platform to get the tent off the ground, then I made a cover for the tent out of bits of tarp and plastic that I found around camp, and it wasn't too bad. But you know what, winter comes quickly in the mountains sometimes. Right up from my tent were four almost perfectly squared off trees on the side of the bank. It was a no brainer, I was building a treehouse.

I didn't want to touch any of the live standing trees, but that was no problem because there were lots of dead fall and snags that were still solid. I had some of my dad's tools, like an old short pull six ton come-along, which sure came in handy. I had cables strung across the ravine, and with the log suspended from snatch blocks on the cable, I simply took my logs for a walk and basically to right where I wanted them. My framework needed to be flexible because trees move, especially in the wind. I needed single spikes at all main beam intersects to allow for that. As I was building, I was amazed at how the little things that I needed always seem to find their way to me. Nails, logs that were nearby and all kinds of other things that I needed. I had come to appreciate how Roy had described the *'junk'* in the woods as building materials. But there came a day when I ran out of everything. I didn't have anything to eat, and nothing to build with. I knew winter was coming and felt an urgency to get my shelter finished, but there was nothing to work with and I was having big doubts about my chosen path. I prayed and asked the Lord for a sign to let me know if I was still supposed to be there. I said, *"Lord, I give You 48 hours from now to show me what You want me to do. If You don't give me a definite sign, then I'll chalk this up to being a good experience and head back down to the Valley."* That was around 4pm on a Wednesday afternoon.

I managed to keep myself occupied for the rest of that day and the day after, by helping the others around the camp. On Friday, David came and asked me if I could give them a ride into town and offered me $10.00 for gas. I didn't have anything else to do, so I said sure why not. As we got closer to the local dump, they asked if I would pull in. I said, *"Why? You don't have any garbage."* David replied, *"We're not dropping off, we're picking up."* Now here was a reality that I hadn't faced yet. The memory of going to the dump with my dad when I was young and finding a perfectly good Tonka dump truck there, only to have my dad angrily yank it from my hands, throw it in the trash pile and yell, *"We throw things away here, we do not pick things up"* was echoing in my mind. So, I asked, *"Are you sure?"* To which they replied, *"Of course we are!"*

As we got to the dump, I reluctantly pulled in, but as soon as we did I was met with a huge pile of lumber, plywood, and nails. There was enough building material, used as it was, to carry on with my treehouse project for quite some time. 2x4's with nails sticking out all over, a couple of doors with hinges, and lots of sheets of plywood that aside from a few nails were like brand new. I instantly got to work on the pile, while David and Heidi ran down to *"the pit"* laughing and giggling like children. The smell that was coming from there was noxious, yet they sounded like kids on Christmas morning. *"David! Look at what I found!" "Heidi! Check this out! Woo Hoooo!"* My curiosity got the better of me, so I walked down to investigate. They had found some long, tall boxes and were in the process of going through them. I asked them what all the excitement was about. David explained that the tourist train, Rocky Mountain Rail Tours, had just dropped off their trash in Boston Bar and it had just been delivered to the dump. I still didn't get it. They were romping around in the dirty diapers and potato peels, not my idea of a good time. He continued to explain, *"The train leaves Vancouver in the morning and serves breakfast and lunch in these sealed trays. Not everyone eats everything and if it's still in its hermetically sealed container or package, it's still perfectly good. In fact, a lot of people don't even open the trays so the whole meal is still perfectly safe."*

Feeling the pit in my stomach and seeing the glee with which they were processing their new-found treasure, I decided that dad was wrong and jumped into the pit and began going through the boxes myself. The rule was simple, if it was unopened it was good to go. Yogurt, bagels with creme cheese, grapes, butter, honey, and jam packages, not to mention about one in five still sealed. It was a bonanza for sure. My pride swallowed, I began to see the true blessing that this was. We loaded as much as we could into the old Olds and went to stash it before heading to town. We had also picked up enough recyclables so that David and Heidi could get some tobacco and toilet paper and I could get gas. We stopped on the way back, and loaded our bounty then headed back to camp. When we got there, I dropped them off and continued a little further up the track to my trail head. I hauled my box of food to my place and sat down on my wood round seat. I opened the box and on the very top, one of the last sealed trays that I found, that was marked *"Crew Only"* and was still warm. I popped it open and almost cried. This was way fancier than the rest. There was smoked salmon, scalloped potatoes, and vegies. I had spent $50.00 for a meal like that only months before. Then it hit me. It was 4pm Friday, exactly 48 hours after I asked the Lord to confirm if I was to be staying there or not. I dropped to my knees and gave Him thanks. I had a car loaded with all kinds of building materials and a big box full of food. My prayers were not only answered but I was so blessed that I wept tears of joy as I gave Him thanks. He truly is awesome.

The Oldsmobile was still alive and doing the job, and I made as many trips as I could to the Valley to find supplies. The 30-gallon food grade barrels Roy knew about, for a buck each, to the bed frames thrown out by a charity mattress fixers place (it was a big building with handicapped and challenged people to rebuild mattresses and box springs for low income folks). They said take as many as you want, so load on the roof racks started with about fifteen box spring frames. Then the load of barrels, and I could get six on at a time, then back to the house to fit whatever I could into them. Like I said, I gave everything else away.

The last trip of the Olds was around the end of September, when the transmission started slipping. I made it into camp, but it was done. I limped it in and out of town, but it was getting bad, so I parked it. But I still had a few things down in Chilliwack and I knew the snow was coming soon. It was my first walk to town, 25kms away, but not my last. The first five km's was an old logging road that David Lillos and Mountain Ed cleared back in the mid-seventies, and it had been kept up because that used to be the way up and across to the Nahatlatch Valley. Anyway, there was absolutely no traffic on it, so it took about an hour to get to the main road. The chances of seeing anyone on that road were slim. I was about 10 km in when a pickup came along, and I jumped in the back.

Now it was strange. When I got to Boston Bar I knew that hitchhiking was part of the plan. I knew that Dennis had an old pickup that belonged to a long-departed tenant and he said if you can start it, drive it away. It was a 65 F-150, straight six and a Hurst shifter. A fresh battery and some gas and it fired right up. Gotta love an old Ford truck. He didn't have any papers for it and all I had was my car tag, which is obvious, and illegal, in BC, and I broke the law. I sure hope the statute of limitations is up on that one. I stuck the plate on and threw mud at it.

Every Christian trucker knows this prayer, *"Oh Lord, please don't let the law see me."* If you need to ask why, you need to try it. I'll ask it this way, would you embrace or run away from someone who wants to take your money? The spirit of the Law gives life, but the letter of the law brings death. It's in there.

So, I made it back to the house in Chilliwack and loaded up the last of my stuff. Now for the big faith push, I had only $10, and a two-hour drive ahead of me. I pulled into the last gas station before the freeway and proceeded to pump gas. As I was standing there, I felt a wave of the Holy Spirit hit me. Suddenly, everything around me was covered in thorns and thistles. I could see the evil in the air, and then I saw it, an old Ford Pinto, scourge of cars, but it was glowing and quite a contrast to the darkness surrounding us. Click! Oh, I forgot about the gas. I looked, let go of the handle, and it stopped at exactly $10.

The old truck was doing fine, and if I didn't over work the old girl, she would get me home. Up and over American Mountain, I was traveling along nicely, almost to Dogwood Valley, when I heard a small pop, and suddenly I had no power to the wheels. I just coasted over the last hillcrest and aimed for The Dogwood Husky Truck Stop, run by my, and every trucker running through there, old friend Ralph. I coasted in to the parking lot, around the back, and way off to the side. I knew it wasn't going anywhere anytime soon. I went and found Ralph and asked him to keep an eye on it for me and that I would be back as soon as I could. Of course, it was no problem.

I went into the restaurant to see if there was anyone I knew in there, hoping for a ride to Boston Bar. I didn't know anyone in there, but this young guy came running up to me and asked me if I want to buy some pot. I told him I wasn't interested and asked him where he was headed. North, like me. Well, two guys hitch-hiking never works well, so I told him since he was there first, he should get out there and put his thumb up. I could wait. He was friendly enough and we were talking when I asked him if he knew Jesus. The poor guy almost jumped out of his skin. He got shaky and said, *"I, uh, gotta go."* As he left, I prayed aloud that he would get a ride right away. He looked over his shoulder as he was running, jumped the no-post, crossed the highway and not more than a minute passed and a car stopped and picked him up. Now it was my turn.

I went back into the truck stop and talked with Ralph. I told him the whole situation and he was amused. I said he could give the truck to his son, since he was looking for a project for him, and about then a driver I knew pulled in for fuel. He drove me to Boston Bar, so I had a little more than half an hour to share the gospel with him.

Once I got to Boston Bar, it was a long, 25km walk to Tranquility Station. It had been raining earlier but had started to turn to snow. I was almost to the 6-k bridge when a pickup stopped and gave me a ride to the turn off. I walked the rest of the way, groceries hanging from a stick across my shoulders, and an hour later was sitting in Richard's cabin, explaining my predicament. He volunteered to drive down there and get my stuff and we were on our way back down to the Dogwood.

When we got there, I found that someone had already rifled through the stuff in the back, no lock, so we grabbed everything that was left, threw it in the back of Richard's truck, and we were gone. It was a cool old truck, and I hope Ralph and his son got some good out of it.

I was *"home"* with no easy way out and winter coming. One of the main economic drivers for the Nahatlatch Valley has been the Pine Mushroom, or Matsutaki in Japanese. These mushrooms can grow to enormous sizes. One mushroom can get to be over a pound. They have been known to lift rocks. They are also considered a rare delicacy in Japan, so they are willing to pay any price for them. Although the market has been flooded every year since China opened its borders, they used to pay as much as $300.00 cash per pound. If you found ten pounds of Matsutaki in an afternoon, you were rich. It wasn't uncommon to find at least that much on an outing, but the prices were usually around $50.00 to $100.00 per pound, still a respectable amount.

With the mushrooms come the mushroom pickers. Some are just locals coming to make a few extra dollars, and some have RV's that they travel to the various picking spots as the mushrooms *"pop"* starting in Alaska in September and going as far south as Oregon by December. The Nahatlatch Valley was world famous among Pine pickers.

David knew the mountain, the Nipple, like the back of his hand. He would stay up all night fellowshipping by the fire then sleep until noon. He would get up, have his coffee and breakfast then saunter out to his private patch and pick mushrooms until dark. He would come back with his pack overflowing with mushrooms and pre-grade them. All #1's were going to the buyer. Some #2's as well. But all the rest would be cut and dried so that they could still be sold when the season was over or added to soups for us all to enjoy. It wasn't all perfect. Some of the characters that showed up were die hard bush whackers. They had all the morals of snakes and would slit your throat as soon as they look at you. I was meeting some rough guys out there in the woods and they were far more dangerous than cougars or bears.

There were lots of things to work with around the place. Tranquility Station had already been there for over twenty years and lots of folks had come and gone, a lot of them leaving their stuff behind. Tarps, sheets of plastic, old nails, etc., it all came in very handy.

One of the coolest little treasures was an old pool cover. It was like an insulated tarp and it made the best roof cover. I found some asphalt sealer at the dump and painted it all flat black. The best roof ever. As time went on, I dug into the bank for a basement. I built a barrel stove and it lived down there. I had all my main beams done and the mattress frames all hanging over a pony wall for flexibility. Insulated with old sleeping bags, foam, styrofoam, etc., then covered in paneling from my old friend Will. It was two floors but needed a roof and loft. I found that cedar branches have about the best tensile strength, so I used a bunch of them to build the roof framework, then covered it with the pool cover.

I'll never forget it. It was October 5th, 1996. Everyone else had gone pine mushroom picking but I just felt in my spirit that I was to keep building. I had just used my last roofing nail and staples on the roof, climbed down my ladders and went outside. You know that smell that happens just before it snows. I was like, *"No way."* I couldn't believe it. Sure enough, not a minute later, little snowflakes came down through the trees. Then it really started coming down. I could just imagine David and everyone out there in the mushroom patches somewhere in the storm. I went down to the summer kitchen and Heidi, or Adelhite as she liked to be called, was preparing dinner when they all started coming in, spinning their tires all the way.

Later that night, I knew I had to make my way to my place through the crashing snow loaded branches and see how it held. I was amazed when I got up there. It was perfect. I went upstairs expecting to find water leaks, but it was totally dry. Big, heavy, snow loads were falling off the branches above, a good 100ft fall, and bouncing off my roof like no problem. My cedar branch idea worked, and I got to test it out right away.

I moved my tent and cot up into the loft and prayed, *"Lord, if I'm supposed to get hit by a load of snow, then so be it. I ask you for a good night's sleep in Jesus name, amen."* I slept like a baby, even with the sounds of breaking branches, falling snow and all the rest.

I installed the barrel stove, patched up as many holes as I could and was ready to hunker down for the duration. I was burning wet birch and alder, but once that wood got going, it made the tarps on the place bulge out from the heat. I can't even begin to describe how much fun it was in a wind storm. The creaking and cracking just added to the rush. Sadly, I don't have a single picture of it. I can see it in my memory quite clearly, maybe I should try to draw a picture and use it for the book cover (hint).

One Third of a Bean Soup

It was Christmas, 1996. We had already had a few good dumps of snow and more was coming. It's interesting how you can smell it before it snows. I had been enjoying the place as much as I could. I found some skis and boots, so I hiked up the logging road as far as I could and skied back down. It was a lot of work for a small reward, but I had fun. But what I wasn't ready for was the sharp pain in my right knee that came that night. I know I worked hard to get up to where I skied from, but this was more than just sore muscles. The pain persisted and got progressively worse. I fashioned a tourniquet from some rags and it helped a little, but it became a constant throbbing pain centered in my knee. I was getting concerned and I knew that I needed to go see a doctor, but I kept putting it off, praying to the Lord to heal me. I experimented with all kinds of different medicinal herbs. Devils club root, willow bark and other plants but none of them had any effect. As Christmas drew closer, I was being drawn into a deep depression. I had no idea if I was going to see my children at Christmas or not. I was praying that I would, but it didn't feel like it was going to happen. The last time I spoke with Sandy, she told me that I had no part in her or the children's lives and that they didn't even want to see me. I knew that wasn't true, but it's strange how your mind can begin to play tricks on you when you are alone in the forest.

It was Christmas day. I was working on my treehouse, trying to keep my mind off not seeing my children, or any of my family for that matter. Darkness came early, and I went down to David and Heidi's to see what she had found for dinner. When I got there and asked her, she said, *"Well, we have a bean."* *"A bean?"* I asked. *"Well we have some lentil leaves too."* Ok, I thought, this is what it is. As much as I didn't want to think about it, I could picture my friends and family all eating and drinking and feeding the dogs the scraps from the table, and I thought about my children, and we had a bean.

Heidi did the best that she could with what she had. She prayed as she prepared the soup. She added some spices and the lentil leaves, and finally the bean. A little while later she served us all our Christmas dinner in wooded salad bowls and I was sad as I held my Christmas dinner. But I trusted God and knew that he had a plan. I asked the Lord to bless our meal with tears in my eyes and began to eat. I sipped the broth and avoided the lentil leaf, saving the 1/3rd of a bean for last. I took my 1/3rd of a bean into my spoon and suddenly we heard voices. *"Where the hell are we!"* *"We're here."* *"Where the hell is here?"* Then the door to David and Heidi's shack flew open and there stood Roy, perpetually late Roy, his beard covered in ice. *"Merry Christmas!"* he proclaimed. There was a guy behind him who was trying to see over Roy's shoulder. *"We brought food!"* I could barely hold back the tears of joy as I helped them get the food into the shack. Roy had quite the pack train going. First, he had on his backpack that had two frozen turkeys, a frozen ham and fifty pounds of potatoes. Then he had two ropes tied around his waist that were tied to a plastic garbage can that had fifty pounds of carrots and fifty pounds of onions in it. Tied to the handles of the garbage can were two more ropes that were tied to a crazy carpet, and on the crazy carpet were two boxes full of all kinds of other treats like stuffing, chocolate bars, flour and most important of all, coffee.

The boxes needed to be stabilized and that is where George came in. It seems that Roy had met him at a restaurant in Chilliwack that afternoon and drafted him into helping him get the food to us. Roy drove as far as he could before he got stuck in the snow, about a mile away from the camp, then they began their trek. George was not a happy camper. He wasn't a Christian and he didn't appreciate hearing how he had been tricked into helping Roy and blessing us. He was cursing and mad, but he did finally calm down and have some coffee with us. It was a very sweet Christmas after all. Although the turkeys and ham were too frozen to cook that night, we did enjoy some potatoes, onions, and carrots as well as the chocolate and other treats. All I can tell you is that it was, by far, the best Christmas I have ever had, before or since.

Pain In The Knee

I had to get to the city to have the pain in my knee checked out. It had become excruciating and I was having trouble walking, not to mention trying to sleep. I was looking at a long walk, 25kms to Boston Bar, if no-one came along to get a ride from, then hitch hiking to Abbotsford where I knew an old couple from when I played at network marketing. God has an amazing way of providing, even when you don't ask. One of the locals, Eddie, bought the old dump CAT and, with a 50-gallon drum of diesel fuel strapped to the back, drove it up to camp, plowing snow all the way. He said it was a gift to us, but it was old and tired, so snow plowing was all it was good for. We were so blessed. The next day I decided it was now or never to head out. A young fellow, Daryl, who was staying with Richard, decided it was time to head to town as well so we set out walking. He was twenty years old, and I was thirty-five with a very sore leg but he was stopping all the time and whimpering that he couldn't keep up with me. I waited a few times until I lost my patience with him and just started walking. I was far ahead of him, on the main road, when a pickup full of natives stopped to give me a ride to town. Daryl was already in the back.

When we got to Boston Bar, we stood out in front of the Husky gas station hitch hiking. Nobody was stopping, and it was getting late in the afternoon. Daryl went and called his mom who paid for a bus ticket for him, but not for me. Oh well, I would just trust the Lord and at least it should be easier to get a ride by myself.

Car after car went by and no one would stop. It was obvious that most of the traffic had full car loads of people moving between Christmas and New Year. Picking up a scruffy, long haired, bearded, and probably smelly guy was low on their to do lists.

As it got dark, the snow started to fall lightly. Still no ride. I was getting cold and my leg was throbbing from being on it all day. I was getting worried as the snow got heavier. The southbound traffic had virtually dried up. The son of some Christians I knew in North Bend, Jerry and Wendy, came to the gas station and I went and asked him if he could call his parents and see if I could spend the night. He called, and I spoke to Wendy. She said that the Lord must have had that in mind because there was an accident up the road and the highway was blocked from avalanches as well, so her daughter and son in law were stuck until the next day, so I could sleep in their bed. It sure was nice to be in a warm house, have a shower and get my laundry done. Since most of my clothes were basically just rags, they gave me some. We had nice fellowship that night as the snow kept falling. We woke up the next morning and it was still coming down. There was about four feet of snow that had fallen over night. Everything was still and very quiet. We found out that there were avalanches up and down the Fraser Canyon and the highway was very closed. It looked like I wasn't going anywhere for a while. I spent New Year's Eve at Jerry and Wendy's home and the next day, Jerry got a call from the manager of the gas station, Orval, asking if he could send someone over to dig out the diesel pumps for when the road was cleared.

The scene was surreal. There were cars and trucks parked all up and down the main drag and snowmobiles buzzing up and down the highway. There was a semi with its driver unloading meat out of the trailer. I was pressed into service along with a few of his sons and neighbors. I was put to work clearing the snow from the diesel pumps. As I was working away, Orval drove up in his pick up and said, *"Get in."*

We went up to the highway department's maintenance yard where we met a helicopter filled with emergency supplies; milk, eggs, and bread. We went back down to the gas station where there was a hungry crowd who quickly cleaned us out. I went back to clearing snow from the diesel pumps when Orval came by again and said they had another helicopter coming in and to get in. We went and got the second load and brought it back. I was riding in the back of the pickup and was surprised to see David and Heidi standing there as we pulled up. I said, *"What are you two doing here? And HOW did you get here?"* David held up his right hand that had a blood-soaked bandage wrapped around it. He explained that he had almost cut his finger off while he was splitting firewood. I was still wondering how they got from camp to Boston Bar. They walked; in six feet of snow for twenty-five kilometers. I was stunned as he explained how they knew that he would need medical attention and had to get to a doctor.

Heidi baked three loaves of bread and they headed out. David held his old Lee Enfield rifle above his head as they literally swam through the snow, David in front and Heidi pushing from behind. They would go for about half an hour at a stretch then stop and rest with some coffee and bread before going again. The one hour walk from camp to the main road took them eight hours. He held the rifle over his head the whole time because, to a predator, all that was seen above the snow was their heads which would look awfully tempting.

Once they got to the main road they found that it had been plowed but still had a couple feet of snow that had fallen since. They trudged through until they reached John Findlay's, whose place was across from the dump. He let them rest there and in the morning, the day I saw them at the gas station, they started walking again. I stood there, speechless. They had spent eighteen hours walking to town. On a normal day it took three hours. There was a helicopter from BCTV News and the reporters were getting their story. I heard them say, *"I guess we're done here."* I thought, no, I don't think so, as I went and pointed David and Heidi out. *"You see that couple right there? They just spent the last eighteen hours walking out of the woods."* They almost knocked me over getting to them. They interviewed them. As David explained their story, Heidi was hiding behind him. Their story was on the BCTV Evening News, then it was picked up by the CTV National News, then the BBC picked it up where it was broadcast all around the world within twenty-four hours. How's that for from obscurity to the world stage?

The Canyon was cleared of the avalanches, 178 of them, by the next day, so I had to leave Jerry and Wendy's. I had found someone who was going to Vancouver and they gave me a ride to Abbotsford.

When I got to the home of the old couple, Dave and Mina, they were thrilled to have me stay with them. I was very grateful as they fed me and prepared a room for me. The next day they took me to their doctor. He was a stern oriental fellow and he was looking at me sideways from the moment he saw me. He asked me what was wrong, and I told him about the pain in my right knee. He had me lay down on the examining table and manipulated my leg while he asked me if I did drugs or smoked. What did that have to do with anything? I told him no but I did smoke the occasional cigar. Which I had just started doing at Christmas because there were some in our care package. He thought I was there to con him into giving me drugs so he told me to get out before he called the police. Dave and Mina were both surprised, but somehow, I wasn't. I wasn't giving up because this thing hurt.

I found another doctor on my own and made an appointment to see him the next day. He was a lot nicer than the first one. He ordered some x-rays and that afternoon I had them done. He called and asked me if I could come to his office first thing the next day. When I got there, he told me that there was some kind of dark spot on my femur. He called it a Nidus and he arranged for me to have an MRI and a CAT Scan. They both showed a tumor growing on my femur and that it was right under my sciatic nerve, which explained why the pain was so intense. He then gave me a prescription and when I went to have it filled, I found out that there was no way that I could afford it. The pharmacist told me to try Ibuprofen. I did, and it worked, even though it made my guts tighten up if I took it without food. I was sent to the Cancer Clinic in Vancouver right away where they did some more tests. It was soon discovered that while it was a tumor and it was painful, it was benign, so it wasn't life threatening. I met the head oncologist and he explained the situation. He then asked me if I was interested in being the first to have noninvasive surgery via radio waves. I asked how long my wait would be until it could be done, and he said about three months until they had the new machine installed and running at VGH. He said the wait for conventional surgery was the same. I figured hey, why not, I would be the first one in Canada to have this procedure done and the wait was the same either way.

Since there was nothing to do but wait, I decided to head back up to camp. Dave and Mina protested and said they were concerned about me. I appreciated their concern but there was no way I was going to let them be my surrogate parents. I hitch hiked back up to Boston Bar where I got a ride to the foot of our road, then I walked the rest of the way. The road was plowed by the old CAT and it was a nice walk back. After that, there was a lot of going back and forth to the Cancer Clinic.

The spring and summer of '97 were filled with lots of work to be done. My treehouse was my focus and the building materials from around Tranquility Station were very valuable indeed. I used anything I could find, from pieces of plastic to bent rusty nails. If I needed it, it was there somewhere. I was flat broke by the world's standards, but I felt like the wealthiest man in the world. God was meeting my needs in small but very tangible ways. From having something to eat every day to the fellowship around the fire every night, it was slightly heavenly. As my project continued, I found myself needing a big spike to hold two logs together. I had no idea where I was going to find one as I had scoured the whole camp and couldn't find one. I prayed and asked the Lord for a nail. I occupied myself with other things until lunch time when David and Heidi would be up and about. While walking down the trail, there it was, a big bent rusty spike. I dropped to my knees and gave glory to God for answering my humble prayer. I was so grateful for a rusty nail. I had walked that trail many times over the course of a day for months and that nail wasn't there, until I needed it. Was it always there? Who knows, but it was right there when I needed it.

H e i d i

The place just wouldn't be complete without a woman's touch. A year before I made the move, I was going up regularly, every second or third weekend to get away and bring David and crew supplies. I remember David sitting in his chair by the fire, stroking his beard and suddenly announcing, *'Her name is Heidi."* We had come to expect these things from him, so it was no surprise, but a few of the guys laughed at him. He got mad and scolded them for their unbelief. Life went on and it was forgotten. One hot August Saturday morning, as I was driving up the trail, I came around the corner and I saw someone in a big fur coat carrying a duffle bag in one arm and a hockey bag in the other, wearing a backpack. It was obviously a woman's figure and she heaved a sigh of relief as she put down her load. I pulled up beside her, rolled down the window and asked if she was going to Tranquility. She smiled meekly and said yes. So, I told her to load her things into the car and I would drive her the last two kilometers. At first, she refused, saying that she was fine and that the Lord had her walk that far and that she could walk the rest of the way. I insisted that she let me drive her the rest of the way.

As she got in the car, I introduced myself and she did as well saying, *"I'm Heidi."* I commented that she had an awful lot of gear and asked her how long she was going to be there. She said, *"As long as the Lord has me there."* We parked at the side trail and made our way to the summer kitchen. As we got closer, I saw David's eyes light up and he had a smile from ear to ear. There was a rather large fellow sitting on a stump at the edge of the summer kitchen. He stood up and asked, *"Well, who have we here?"* *"Heidi,"* she answered. He stood up and saluted and announced, *"Welcome Heidi, Queen of the mountain!"* It turned out that the fellow who made the official announcement was

Chad Allen, the bass player from the rock band The Guess Who. You never knew who you would meet up there.

Heidi got right to the job at hand. She went straight to the sink that was filled with all manner of disgusting things, and probably a few alien life forms, and started cleaning. She set up a pup tent in a small clearing and David and her dated. I guess that they loved each other because they were *'married'* a couple of months later. There was some controversy about their *'marriage'* with some of the local Christians. They were all talking about how David and Heidi were living in sin because they never had a proper wedding. Please describe a proper wedding when you are alone in the woods. They stood before God and committed their lives to each other, you know, the way it's been done since Adam and Eve. Life wasn't easy up there. But Heidi toughed it out, through snow, rain, whatever.

One source of food for the camp was from grain that leaked out of grain cars on the railroad tracks. The trains would sit on a siding, sometimes for hours or days, and the slow leaks often resulted in huge piles of grain. What was destined for foreign markets ended up at Tranquility Station. Heidi would grind it with an old-fashioned hand grinder and make flour. She would then use that flour to make bannock, bread, muffins, cakes, pies, and anything else she could think of. It was always blessed. Her stove consisted of the stacks of brake drums and she managed to produce some of the most amazing meals from them. I noticed how the Lord always provided just enough for however many people were there. Sometimes there would be thirty or more people there and yet there was always enough for everyone. It was awesome to watch how the Lord provided for us.

Heidi was referred to as "the toughest guy up there," not in a disparaging way but because she worked non-stop. She was tough. When their chainsaw didn't work, or they couldn't afford gas for it, she would head out into the forest with a bow saw and fell a tree. I'm talking a wet birch tree that was fourteen inches across at the butt. Once she felled it, she cut it up into man sized pieces and pack them down the trail to their cabin. Then she cut it up into even smaller pieces and feed them into the brake drum stoves. Of course, the whole time she is doing that, she was baking bread, making coffee, and doing a million other chores. Occasionally, we found her sitting quietly somewhere. When asked what she was doing, she would reply, *"I'm being still"* as per the scripture *"Be still and know that I am God."* Her faith in the Lord to provide was huge. She would ask Him for specific items that she needed and then trust Him to deliver. Sometimes He would deliver to the North Bend Mall, aka *"The Dump"* but nevertheless, He would answer her requests, usually adding more than she asked for. Although she did drive, when they didn't have a working car, she rode an old bike. She would load it up until it couldn't take any more, and ride it uphill for the ten kilometers back to camp, towing a small trailer. As soon as she got there, she would get right on to making coffee for David, and meals for everyone else.

I remember one time I was following her as she was carrying a 250lb birch log on her shoulder. I could barely do it and I was in excellent shape and strong. Not only did she have that big log on her shoulder, she would walk like a proper lady doing it. An amazing woman who wouldn't want the attention because she simply lives to serve others.

The Summer Kitchen

I saw many miraculous things at the Summer Kitchen. I was delivered from the darkness of my past there. There were so many different people that came and went that there is no way to remember them all. Some famous, and some infamous, a very diverse group of people found themselves breaking bread in the Summer Kitchen.

David's son, Matthew, lived with his mom and step dad in the Okanogan. He would come up a couple of times every summer to visit David. He got a job driving for Coca-Cola and was collecting all the rejected items. One sunny day he brought a truck load of pop, juices, yogurt, and other goodies; not good for the teeth, but good for the soul. It was cool to have a stranger show up and then offer them a cold pop from the coolers in the creek.

One afternoon Matthew showed up with someone walking behind him. He had a look of bewilderment on his face as he surveyed the place. David was happy to see his son and we were curious as to who it was that he brought up with him. He introduced us to his friend.

As we sat there, we went to the subject of creation versus evolution. He asked me a very technical question, for which I had no answer, but I said I would ask God. He looked at me with a doubting look as I took a stick and drew the answer in the dirt. He was astonished. He asked me, *"How do you know that?"* I told him I didn't have a clue but that was what God showed me and I drew it in the dirt. I can't remember what the question was, or the answer, but it was enough for him to be convicted of his sin and get down on his knees right there and ask for God to forgive him of his sins.

Dave and Mina showed me a cheap supply of generic Ibuprofen. 500 tablets for $10.00 was a good deal. I was taking four or five at a time, every six hours. It was hard on my stomach, but it was much better than suffering the excruciating pain in my leg. I would always wait until I felt the pain start to come on before I took more pills, just in case the Lord healed me. I knew that He could heal me at any time, and I didn't want to miss it because I was medicated.

I was down to my last few pills and didn't have any money for more. I was quietly trusting God for more pills, or healing, whichever came first. Roy came up to camp with a one-ton flat deck and a car trailer with the plan to haul some of the dead cars to the scrap yard. I helped him load the cars until late into the night and then we drove the rest of the night to Surrey, where the scrap yards are. We arrived just as they were opening, and I had taken my last Ibuprofen. It was only a matter of an hour or so before the pain would be back, and I was anxious to get back to Chilliwack where Roy could cash the check from the scrap yard. We were running on fumes and then, just past Abbotsford, we ran out of gas. We coasted to the off ramp, almost to the rest area, and came to a silent stop. I was not a happy camper as I could feel the first twinges of pain coming on. I didn't handle pain well.

We stood beside the truck and Roy suggested that we pray. Better than nothing I thought. As we were praying, we heard air brakes coming on and chains hitting the back of a headache rack. A headache rack is the large piece of steel or aluminum behind the cab of trucks that haul flatbeds trailers. They are supposed to stop anything from coming through the cab in the event of a hard brake application or other sudden stops. I spun around to see a truck sitting in his lane about 100ft from the stop sign. It just sat there with cars starting to back up behind it. I wondered if it was for us, so I ran up to the door and was shocked to find my old friend, Matt, Ted's son, sitting there. I said *"Hey Matt! What are you doing?"* He replied, *"God just told me to stop. So, I stopped."* I could hardly believe it. Not only did he stop as we were praying but it was an old friend.

I quickly explained our predicament and he said, *"Well get in then, let's go get you some gas!"* We hopped up into the cab and within five minutes were at a gas station. He took a windshield washer jug, drained the last bit of it into his washer tank and proceeded to fill it up with gas. The attendant came out and said, **"You can't do that."** To which he replied, *"I already did. You want me to pay for it, or put it back?"* She decided to pay for it was the easiest choice. He also bought me some Advil and, although the pain was starting, the excruciating pain was avoided. God answered my prayers long before I had even prayed them.

Matt said that he had another truck and needed a driver and asked me if I was interested. It was going to be hauling oversized loads all over North America. I was a bit hesitant due to the tumor, and fearful in my ability to handle it. I said I would pray about it. He said that was a good idea, but he already knew that

I would because God had told him. After seeing how he just slammed on the brakes because God told him to, I had to take that seriously. I honestly wasn't too thrilled at the idea of crossing the border either, but I prayed, and wouldn't you know it, I took the job. Before I ventured out on my own in his other truck, he wanted me to come with him on a haul way into the wilderness of Northern BC, to a very remote gold mine. It was an uneventful run up to where we turned off the highway and began a 450KM trip on the back roads. It was slow going and Matt was calling out his miles on the VHF radio, since most of the roads were only one lane wide and there was a lot of truck traffic on them. It was late at night as we rolled into the dark, when Matt looked at me with a tear rolling down his cheek and said, *"You know Jonny, ever since I was a little boy, I've wanted to be a Hells Angel, but they won't let me join because I can't deny Christ."* I sat there in shock at his statement. I mean, if that wasn't dedication to the Lord, then I don't know what is. We stopped occasionally to check the load and finally stopped for the night in the middle of nowhere. The next day we stopped at a little place in the middle of the road, Louisville. We met the owner, Maurice, and his wife Nicole, both very French Canadian and they were very friendly, although Maurice was a little on the rough side. He told us about a driver of a truck who hauled in and out of the mine, but never stopped. He said that made him mad. So, the next time he heard him calling his miles on the VHF radio, he grabbed his shotgun and went and stood in the middle of the road, waiting for him. He said he leveled the shotgun at the driver. He laughed and said to us, *"He stop."* He walked up to the driver and asked him why he never stopped at their truck stop, and that he was visibly shaking. He told us that the driver has never come back on that road, and thought it was the funniest thing ever. Tough folks up there.

Matt had a very nice older truck for me to drive and he leased it with a company that hauled oversized loads. They had me hauling a few things here and there around the continent, but nothing over dimensional. I guess they wanted to see if I could handle the small stuff first. I bounced all over North America and did the job as expected. Then my big break came; take a load of railroad switching spurs to Cheyanne Wyoming and Birmingham Alabama, then pick up a slightly over sized boat in Savannah Georgia to bring back to Vancouver. It was going to pay well, and I was finally going to get an oversize load. I loaded the switching spurs, those big cast steel things in railroad switches, in Richmond BC and headed for Cheyanne. I had loaded late, so I only made it as far as Pocatello Idaho that night. I pulled off the interstate and found a nice quiet side road to get some sleep. The irony was that I had parked right across the street from a huge cancer hospital. If I had the money, they probably could have zapped the tumor right there. But it wasn't meant to be, so I popped a few more Ibuprofen and went to sleep. I could never sleep more than four to five hours because the pills would wear off and I would wake up in pain. I like to describe the pain as this; it was like a small monkey had a ball-peen hammer and it was allowed to strike my leg anytime and anywhere he wanted as hard as he could. It wasn't fun.

The next day I set off for Cheyanne and my first drop. I arrived there around 4:00 in the afternoon and they took off the few that were going there, signed my bills and it was off to the truck stop for some fuel and food. After I fueled, I spotted a parking space right in front. I figured it was a small miracle. I noticed the cattle truck in the next spot but didn't pay much attention to it, until a cow that was in it decided to back up to one of the vent holes and pee all over my sleeper. I got right mad and proceeded to back out of there, only to get my cab, window shut thank God, and my hood covered in cow pee too. I found another parking space, went inside to get something to eat and get some cash from the bank machine. The instant teller spit out two US$100 bills. That has never happened before.

As I was chatting with another driver at the counter, he warned me to avoid Colorado at all costs. He said there was a good two-lane highway that went around Colorado and still got me to where I needed to go. I thanked him for his advice, but there was no truck wash at the truck stop in Cheyanne and I had cow piss all down the driver's side of my truck. I wanted to wash it off as soon as possible so I figured, how bad could it be.

So down I-25 and into Colorado I went. I made it to the first official weigh scale and pulled in. There was a huge stop sign and a small sign under it that said, *"All trucks MUST come to a complete stop before crossing scale."* So, I did. I didn't know the routine, so I played it safe. Then a voice came from an equally huge loud speaker that was three feet from my window that blared, *'PUT YER AXLE ON THE SCALE, BOY!'* Somehow, I just knew I was about to meet this guy. I put my steer axle on and got a red light. I stopped. Then a *"next axle"* light. I put my drive axles on the pad and got another red light and this one stayed red for a long time. Then, as I had predicted, he yelled through another giant loud speaker, *'COME ON INSIDE BOY AND BRING YER PAPERWORK, BOY!'* So, I pulled off to the side and went in.

This guy was a classic troll, from the wart on the end of his nose to his sweat stained shirt with his big fat belly hanging out from under his uniform shirt. He was a caricature in real life. He asked for my logbook, driver's license, and registration, which I produced. I figured that everything was in order, so I didn't think I had anything to worry about. He kind of glared at me for a few seconds then he asked, *"Where's yer Special Southern States permit,"* or something like that. I said, *"I didn't know I needed one, but the company told me that every permit, except for special over-size permits, was in this binder."* It was a huge binder with everything pertaining to the truck, trailer, fuel permits, ton mile tax permits, reciprocity tags, and I'm sure the lost books of the Bible. He said, *"Y'all don't know about the Special Southern States permit?"* With a sound of distain in his voice. I was getting irritated by this fat badge heavy blowhard, so I replied, *"No sir, I'm afraid not. But tell me, do you know Jesus as your Lord and personal Saviour?"* He was a bit shocked, which was the intent, then he shocked me when he replied, *"No, but I do chant in Latin."* I honestly had no come back for that one. He then informed me that the price of the permit was $25.00, and the fine was included in the cost of the permit. It sounded like a scam to me but I said, *"OK, give me a permit."* I put one of the hundred-dollar bills on the counter and he looked at it, then me and said, *"I jest started mah shift. I ain't got change fer that!"* Well isn't that perfect. He said I could drop my trailer and bobtail down to the truck stop that was about thirty miles away and get change there. I had about an hour left on my logbook and there was no way I would be able to legally do that. I knew that he knew that, and that fat old troll was trying to entrap me. I stood there for a second, then I remembered standing on a scale platform trying to bum a ride when I was a kid. I asked him if he would mind if I asked drivers who were crossing his scale if they had change. He was a bit taken aback but he said, *"Sure, why not, just don't get hit."*

There I was, at a scale in Northern Colorado, standing beside the scale platform at around 8pm, asking every trucker that came by if they had change for the hundred-dollar bill that I was holding up. Most said they wished they did. Then a Safeway truck pulled up and the driver pulled out a wad of bills and made change. I thanked him and went back into the chicken coop and handed the troll his $25.00. He almost seemed relieved that I was leaving. So, off I went to Denver where I would get some sleep and get the truck washed in the morning.

The next morning, I awoke at the Sapp Brothers truck stop on I-70 just east of Denver. I called Matt and he said that the truck needed an oil change anyway, so I was to get that done. All clean with fresh oil and grease dripping from the zerk fittings. I headed east on I-70. A little way down the road, there was another weigh station. I pulled in, feeling confident that I was nice and legal, when a voice came across the big speaker, *"Pull it around back and come inside, BOY!"* Here we go again. So, in I went, Special Southern States permit in hand, and stood in line behind all the other poor wretches that were getting their pockets picked. When my turn finally came, I handed them the SSSP first. The woman trooper looked at it and was satisfied, then she asked for the license, registration, and logbook. She studied my logbook for a while and unable to find a reason to lighten my pockets snarled, *"You're good to go. NEXT!"* Note to self, when trucking, avoid Colorado.

When I got back out to the truck, I checked the truckers Atlas and sure enough there was another scale that I had to cross before I was out of Colorado. I studied it and saw a nice country highway that led me out of Colorado and into Kansas, without a scale in sight. So off I went, with my detour route planned. I found myself on the backroad and was having a nice time, cruising along at 65 MPH, listening to Dust in the Wind by the rock band Kansas, figuring that since I am going to be there in a little while, I might as well get into the spirit.

It was November 22nd, 1997, as I was cruising along, I saw two cattle trucks heading the other way. I overheard them on the CB as they blew past, *"Where's Billy Bob?" "I don't know, he's back there somewhere, let's go!"* I was rocking to the stereo, listening to Kansas playing the song, Point of No Return, when I saw him, a cattle truck, and I was assuming it was Billy Bob. As he got closer, I saw that it was one of those brand new Western Stars with the Canadian Government paid for redesigned cab. It was ugly, I thought. He was almost where I was when he drifted across the center line. All I had time to say was *"WHAT THE....!"* His mirror hit mine at a combined speed of at least 150MPH. Aside from the loud bang, glass blew into the cab and my door was almost ripped off its hinges. My first reaction was to stand on the brakes but that's when I looked in the passenger side mirror and saw my chains and straps dangling and blowing in the wind. He had scraped along the side of my trailer, breaking my chains, and shearing of my straps so nothing was holding my load down. So, I feathered the brakes and brought it to a nice gentle slow stop.

I came to rest right in front of a farmer's driveway. There was the farmer, standing in his driveway, holding a pitch fork with his jaw almost on the ground. I cussed and tried to get out of the driver's side, but the door was too mangled. I brushed some broken glass from me and climbed over my stuff that was now all over the formerly clean cab and out the passenger side door. The farmer asked me, *"Are you all right?"* I angrily replied, *"I'm still here. I thought I was going to be with the Lord a second ago."* He looked puzzled. All I wanted to do was to kill Billy Bob.

I went around to survey the damage. It was one of those God type, angels all around, head on collisions. He had hit my mirror but missed the front fender and air cleaner. He managed to crease the sheet metal on the sleeper, just enough to make it impossible to open the jockey box so I couldn't get my cinch bar out to beat Billy Bob with. It was weird, I was trying to share the Gospel with the farmer, but I wanted to kill Billy Bob. His cattle truck was still upright, but he ripped his fuel tank open and there was diesel fuel dumped on the road. I saw that he managed to peel all three of the outside tires off the rims on my trailer as I stormed towards his truck.

Cows were mooing in distress as I got closer. I was almost to the front of his truck when I saw him. He was freaking huge. Suddenly hitting him wasn't feasible. He was holding his left arm and crying. I looked at him and said, *"Billy Bob, I want you to know that you just messed up my day, maybe my life, it's too early to tell, but because God forgave me, I forgive you."* He looked at me shocked that I knew his name, and the floodgates of tears poured forth. He said, *"I'm so sorry! I fell asleep! I'm sooooo sorry!"* I said, *"You're going to tell the cops that when they get here, right?"* He said he would.

We went back to the farmers place and they had already called the Sherriff. It wasn't long before the authorities arrived and began to assess the situation. Billy Bob confessed, and I was cleared of any fault. Then the tow truck arrived, hooked on to Billy Bob's tractor and another tractor hooked on to the cattle trailer, with much concern for the cattle. Billy Bob was loaded into an ambulance, in hand cuffs. It turned out he did not have a logbook, and he didn't have a driver's license. It got better. That Western Star tractor was a brand new one that the good old boys had taken from a dealer's lot for a test drive, so there was no insurance on anything. Just before they closed the ambulance doors on Billy Bob, I told him again that I forgave him, and that Jesus had died for his sins and that he might just want to talk to God about that. The ambulance drove away and there I was, standing there with the farmer, and a mangled truck. No tow truck came for me. Now I was mad. The farmer took me into his house to use his phone, so I could call someone who cared. I called Matt. The farmer and his wife were super nice people and they even offered to let me use their car. I was very grateful for their kindness. I asked them if they believed the Gospel to which they basically replied, *"We were raised Mormons. We've never heard the Gospel before."* I'm still amazed to this day how, only half an hour after having my truck hit head on, I was sharing the story of Jesus' death, burial, and resurrection. They had an appointment they had to get to, but not before I led them both to salvation in Jesus Christ.

The truck was finally towed to Amarillo Texas where it sat for a week before an insurance adjuster came to assess the damage. The company that we were leased to, Motrux, assured me that all expenses were covered so not to worry about that. I got a hotel room and spent my 36th birthday in the lounge of the Amarillo Radisson Airport Hotel. I am an evangelist. Wherever God puts me, so I started sharing the gospel with the hotel staff. Why not? Brandy, the girl who worked the front desk during the day, the Mexican woman who worked in the lounge, and Joel, the hotel shuttle bus driver. Did they get saved? I don't know, but I did some serious seed planting.

My schedule was completely shot. My boat from Savanah was given to someone else. They finally got me a rental tractor so that I could at least get my load to Birmingham. I had to go back to Lamar Colorado to get my trailer and of course, nothing had been done to it. I had to buy all new chains and straps, as well as three new tires and rims. Once again, being assured that it was all going to be covered by the insurance settlement. Liars, but I'm getting ahead of myself.

I headed for Birmingham. The weather was starting to get cold and icy, so I headed south. I went through the Dallas/Ft. Worth mix-master and headed east on I-20. It was late Saturday night when I realized that I didn't need to be in a huge hurry since I was only three hours away from Birmingham. I prayed and asked the Lord, *"Well, Lord, I would like to go to a black church somewhere here tomorrow."*

As I came around the bend in the freeway, there it was, a HUGE cross on the top of a radio tower. Turn signal on, this is where I stop for the night and hopefully go to church in the morning. I pulled around the back of a BP gas station and parked, in West Monroe, Louisiana. I went inside and there was a sweet looking little old lady with blue hair behind the counter. *"Is that your big truck that just came in here young man?" "Yes ma'am,"* I replied. *"Well, how can I help you?"* she asked. I explained that I wanted to go to church somewhere the next morning. She said, *"Well, you are in luck. My husband is a deacon at our church and they are having a big pancake breakfast there in the morning. There is a big parking lot there and they would love to have you there tomorrow."* I said, *"Well thank you ma'am, but I was kind of wanting to go to a black church."* She narrowed her gaze at me and replied, *"What do y'all want to go to a nigger church for?"* I stood there stunned. I had just met the antebellum deep south face to face. She was so sweet and as ugly as it gets at the same time. I said, *"Well ma'am, I'm from Canada and we don't judge people by the color of their skin but by the content of their character." "Suit yourself,"* she said, *"there's a phonebook on the back wall by the payphone."* I became invisible to her.

I went back to the phone booth and found the phone book. When I opened it, I couldn't believe how many churches there were. It was overwhelming. It was like looking up OIL in the Edmonton Yellow Pages, probably 50 pages of nothing but churches. So, since it wasn't tethered to the wall, I took it to the front counter. I waited for a break between customers and asked grandma if she could help me. She wasn't impressed, but she did answer my questions. As I flipped through the pages I would point to different churches. *"My sister and brother-in-law go to that church. It's very nice." "Sorry, no, not what I'm looking for."* And then, there it was. The smallest possible print for a Yellow Page's ad, **"The Faith Filled Fire Baptized Church of the Holiness of the God of the Americas!"** I pointed to it and she said with a voice dripping with distain, *"That's in the nigger part of town."* I said, thank you and went to the pay phone on the wall in the back. I dialed the number and a voice answered. I didn't understand a single word that she said. I said, *"I'm sorry, we must have a bad line, could you repeat that please?"* I was at a complete loss. I thought she said the service started at 9:30 so I said thank you and hung up.

There was no way I was leaving my trailer at that gas station the next morning, so after finding White St. on the local map, I headed to my black church service. Man, those roads were narrow. With huge ditches on both sides. Once I was on White St. there was no way I was turning the thing. Even if I left the trailer behind, there was no way I could have turned the tractor on to a side road. I watched as the numbers got smaller, until I came to a dead end and realized that I had passed it. So, I backed up.

There it was. A double wide mobile home that was sinking into the ground on one side. Hmmm, not quite what I had imagined but I was there. I put on the four-way flashers, shut off the truck and walked towards the place. A bunch of children came outside curious about the big white truck and the white guy with the long hair and big beard. Then a woman came out and asked me, *"Are y'all the fella that called last night?"* I said I was. She said, and I could sort of understand her when I could see her lips move, *"I tried to tell you last night, the pastors gone to a conference today and we ain't havin church t'day."* I felt like an idiot. Then she said, *"Well, iffn y'all want, we can try to make the best of it. Ain't no one here but me, my brother, and the children. Come on inside and we'll do the best we can."*

It was humble in there, let me tell you. She asked if I knew a few of the songs that she showed me. I didn't. Her brother looked like he wasn't all there. The children were fascinated by me. So, we tried singing as her brother tried to cut his violin in half. It was sad. She got behind the pulpit and read some scriptures. That was okay. I got up and told them that I had come from Canada and was blessed to be there. She asked, *"What's Canada?"* *"It's where the snow comes from,"* I replied. She asked, *"What's* snow?" I couldn't believe the culture gap. I had zero in common with these folks, other than the Lord, but I wanted so much to connect with them. I asked if I could read from the Bible and she agreed. I don't remember what I read. Then she said, *"I hope y'all don't mind but the children have to practice for their choir recital next week."* I said, *"Hey, no problem."* It was clear that the gap was just too big to jump. I felt like a total idiot for going there. Then the children came out. They were all dressed to the nines. There were probably ten of them, from a little boy about five to a beautiful young girl around fifteen. Then they started to sing. I was so blessed. Their singing was straight from heaven. As they sang, I swear that there were angels sitting on either side of me in the front pew. I cried with joy as they sang. I have never, before, or since, felt so blessed.

I hugged them all and thanked them, and the Lord, profusely as I left. I backed all the way down White Street, West Monroe Louisiana, and headed to Birmingham on that Sunday afternoon. It was one of the most blessed days of my life, that is, until I arrived at my destination in Birmingham. It was Sunday afternoon, so everything was closed. I decided to drop my trailer and go find something to eat. As I swung the rig around, BANG! I had driven over a big chunk of steel that punctured one of my tires. Be careful when you are in the *"blessed mode."* That's usually when the devil takes a swipe at you. Again, more money out of my pocket, about $200, to fix a tire on a rental truck that I would never see again.

Aside from getting a big chunk of steel in one of the rental truck tires, Birmingham was uneventful. I had no back haul. Dispatch was telling me they were looking but there just wasn't anything available. I deadheaded back to Amarillo. Matt's truck still wasn't fixed, so I sat there for another week where I continued to share the gospel with the folks at the hotel.

Finally, the truck was fixed. It looked better than before too. So, I called dispatch and asked what they had. Nothing. What's happening with the insurance claim? *"Not your concern, we are* dealing with it. Just wait and we will get you something." So, I waited.

Finally. A load. I went to Missouri. I had a Sand blasting unit that weighed 200 lbs. going to Prince George BC, then some Chinese CAT parts going to Edmonton. Well, at least it was going to Canada, and I was going home. I loaded it all up, scaled it to make sure I was legal, and headed north. I had crossed a few scales on my way, and they all gave me the green light, but when I crossed the Sioux City South Dakota scale, I got the red light. I went inside to see what the problem was, and they told me I was 200lbs over on my drives. *"Impossible!"* I said, *"I've crossed three other scales today and haven't had a problem!" "Well son, you have a problem here."* They said they would give me a small fine, only $200.00 and let me go if I could get it legal. That meant sliding the fifth wheel, which normally wasn't a problem, but I had no way to dump the air in the suspension which meant that it was nearly impossible to slide. I made sure the jaws were unlocked and the landing legs were down to take weight off, then tried to slide forward. Nope. Tried to slide backward. Nope. Tried forward. Nothing. Tried backwards. I blew a U-joint. Now I was screwed. It was a Friday night.

As they closed the scale, I used the payphone and called Matt. He was surprisingly calm. Did I mention that he was a biker and that he hung around with the Hells Angels? Anyway, there I was, in another hotel room. Not what I had planned. The next day, Saturday, I found a machine shop that was open. I don't think I need to tell you what a miracle that was. The machinist took one look at the U-joint and called his buddy over. *"Dang Bubba, look at the size of that thing. We shore ain't got nuthin like that around here."* That's not what I wanted to hear. Seems they don't have use for super big U-joints in the USA since they only pull little girl weights. So, there I sat all weekend. Waiting to have one shipped down from Winnipeg. Monday Afternoon and I was finally rolling north. The whole experience was unreal.

Everything that could go wrong, did. I had worked my butt off and wasn't sure if I was even going to get paid. As I was heading north in the dark, there it was. Just before a rest area in South Dakota, there was a small sign that read, *"Truck Inspection Ahead. All Trucks Report."* After all I had been through, there was no way I was going through that. I turned off all my lights and drove right on by. Crazy, for sure. I was scanning my mirrors for the police. I was expecting to get popped at any time. Every headlight in my mirrors looked like a cop car. What was I thinking? I put the hammer down and was going as fast as that old Freightliner would go, about 85mph, checking my Atlas for an alternative route to the border. And there it was, in Minnesota there was a two-lane road that runs parallel to the interstate and no scales. But I was low on fuel. So, I took a chance and headed over to the Flying J in Grand Forks North Dakota.

As I was standing there fueling up, this good old boy, American driver at the pump next to me asks, *"Y'all er from Canada... eh?"* I said, *"Yep,"* since it said so on the door of the truck anyway. He just started laughing and said, *"Well I know you ain't got a gun!"* I can tell you, I felt mighty vulnerable right then and there. I wondered, how many other people knew that.

I headed back to the two-lane in Minnesota and went north, praying every inch of the way that no one had seen me sneak past the inspection and that they weren't lying in wait for me up the road. I was almost to the border when I saw the sign. *"BRIDGE LOAD LIMIT, 60,000LBS"* No way! After all this and so close to home. I figured, What the heck. I am so deep in it now, what difference will it make. I stuffed my foot on the throttle and hit that old bridge at about 70mph. I made it ten minutes later I was at the border. The agents on the US side checked my paper work and it was good. Then they asked how long I had been down in the US. I said six weeks. They asked why. I said, *"Buddy, you have no idea. I just want to go home."* They saw the look in my eyes or something and said, *"Okay, have a nice trip."* I went across the line and to Canada Customs. I almost wanted to kiss the ground when I got out of the truck on the Canadian side, but I thought having my lips would get stuck to the ice, so I didn't do it. Canadian Customs were great and now all I had to do was get to Edmonton, unload the Chinese CAT parts, then to Prince

George to deliver the sand blaster then back to the Fraser Valley and, home. It was an uneventful trip to Edmonton where I unloaded the CAT parts, then off to Prince George to unload the sand blaster. I spent the night at my sister and brother-in-law's place, then loaded lumber south of town the next morning. It was a quick trip back down to the coast from there.

So, there I was, back in Abbotsford. I didn't know where else to go except Larry Black's. I parked in his driveway and woke up to a huge American flag draped across the hood.

Larry Black

A few months earlier, while I was waiting for my surgery, I was renting a room at Dave and Mina's. They were a nice enough old couple, but she had a nasty habit of going through my stuff, ostensibly to wash clothes, but with the side effect of finding my phone book and calling people in it. Anyway, I was smoking then and used to go up to their carport to have a smoke. I noticed this long-haired character who had a house across the street. He had quite the car collection and even had an old car hoist in the middle of his driveway. Now that was cool. I didn't feel like I was supposed to go and introduce myself, so I would simply have my smokes in the carport then head back inside.

One morning, as I was leaning on the car and having my morning smoke, he walked out of his house, looked over at me and waved. I took that as my cue and went over to say hello. I liked the guy right away and as we chatted, he told me that he was a bit pissed off because he had been diagnosed with leukemia and was going through chemo and was feeling sick. I was very sympathetic since I was dealing with the tumor in my leg, although it wasn't malignant. I could relate to the very real pain though. I asked him if I could pray for him. He just looked at me like I had threatened to shoot him or something. Then he said, *"You don't believe in that hocus pocus fairy tale about God, do you?"* Well, it was do or die time. Funny how that happens. I said, *"Not only do I believe, I have a personal relationship with Him through Christ."*

He lost it, *"But how? You seemed like such a smart guy. There's just no way."* All I could tell him was that God made Himself very real to me in more ways than I could count and that it was looking obvious to me that He had me there to share His love, and gift of salvation, before Larry went to meet Him. Unbelief goes very deep in some people and Larry was one of them. He told me he was raised catholic and he and his twin brother were sexually abused at their catholic school and his brother was now a raving homosexual. *"Where was God then?"* he asked. I told him that I too was abused but I chose truth and love over anger, resentment, and bitterness. God was always there, despite the horrible things that happened. I wished I could have explained it better, but I was still trying to figure lots of stuff out myself. Larry said he had an appointment and had to go but that he wanted to meet again sometime to discuss it further.

As the weeks rolled by, I found myself going back and forth between camp and Dave and Mina's and the cancer clinic. I saw Larry regularly and he always brought up God and if He did exist, he hated Him for what He did to him and his brother. All I could do was be there as God's witness and do my best to share His love with this dying man. But, frankly, I was getting tired of his hatred of God and wasn't too enthused about hanging out with him anymore. There is only so much a guy can take, even with the Holy Spirit, and I had reached my limit.

One evening, Larry came outside as I was having a smoke and waved for me to come over, so I did. When I got there, he offered me a beer. I didn't drink so I politely refused but he said he was having one. He told me that the doctors had forbidden him from drinking alcohol because of the adverse reactions it would have due to the strong medication he was on. I started to get a bit concerned when he ran out into his front yard and yanked up the for-sale sign and threw it at a passing bus. Then his wife came out and said that dinner was ready, come on inside. As soon as we got in the kitchen, he grabbed a knife, bent me backwards over the stove and held it to my throat, saying, *"You're scared now aren't you? I bet you're filling your pants right now!"* I was surprisingly calm and replied, *"Larry, I had no idea you were going to be the one who was sending me home. Just a little off the top please."* He was shaking with rage and I really did think I was going to die right there, but I was totally at peace because of the thought that I was finally going Home. He yelled at me some more but when he saw that I wasn't afraid to die, he grabbed his family Bible that his wife had brought out, threw it on the floor, dropped to his knees and began stabbing it, crying, and screaming. His wife came up alongside me and said, *"I think you should probably go now."* To which I said, *"I think you're right."* I walked out the door, never to see Larry again.

Soulish Prayers

I had enough of Mina snooping in my stuff. I told her that it was beyond unacceptable and I was not staying another minute. As terrible as this sounds, I was convinced she had pretty much driven Dave crazy. He had horrible migraine headaches that I am sure could be attributed to her. Anyway, I walked out of their place one Sunday morning and she asked me, *"Where are you going to go?"* I said, *"Camp."* They both freaked out and started yelling, *"That place is evil. David's the devil. Oh Jon, nooooo..."* I couldn't believe it. I knew they had some issues but that was over the top.

I limped the mile or so to the freeway on-ramp and stuck out my thumb. It was unreal. I usually would get a ride within a few minutes, but I had been standing there for an hour and no one would even look at me. If they did, they would quickly look away. Since it was around noon Sunday, the church crowd was going by, and I even recognized a few of them, but they looked the other way and kept on going. I was getting mad. I asked the Lord, *"What is going on here today?"* I heard the Holy Spirit answer, *"Someone is praying soulish prayers for you right now."* I had never even heard of such a thing and asked Him, *"What do I do about that?"* *"Rebuke them in the Name of Jesus."* So, I did. I said, *"Soulish prayers, I rebuke you in the Name of Jesus."* As soon as I said that, a car literally stopped right in the travel lane, right where I was standing. It was an older native guy and he said,

"Well, get in!" He told me that he had no idea why he had stopped and he never picked up hitch hikers. I knew why but didn't think it was wise to tell him. He didn't take me far, but it was far enough to know that not all prayers to God are Spirit filled. I don't hate Dave and Mina. They didn't know any other way and they are believers. I was sad that they had missed so much of the freedom in Christ that was available, but I knew that they had to answer to God, not to me. I have prayed for them a lot and only God can heal their hurts.

It was Christmas of '97. I had just finished the trip from hell. The Freightliner was parked in Larry Black's driveway and I woke up to find an American flag draped over my hood. I wasn't too overly fond of the USA at that moment, considering everything I had just been put through. I called Matt and he came up to meet me at Larry's. It turned out that they knew each other since Larry was a full patched Hell's Angel. A fact that I didn't learn until right at that moment. Matt took me to lunch and told me the news.

Due to the accident, and all the lost revenue, and, since Motrux was living up to their reputation as the scum of the earth by not paying him and preventing him from collecting the insurance settlement, he was losing everything, including the truck. He said that he felt bad for me and gave me $200.00 as he apologized for the way things had worked out. That was it. After everything I had just been through, $200.00.

Well, God has a plan I guess, so I called a few of my brothers and sisters to share the news and it was then that the idea of putting a *'care package'* together for Dave and Heidi came up. Since I had been on the receiving end of the miraculous care package the Christmas before, I thought it was the least I could do to take one up to them. My friend Phil sold me a Ford Escort Diesel car and it was super cheap to run. I found Roy and we loaded up with supplies and food and headed up to Tranquility Station.

We encountered snow about half way between Boston Bar and camp, so I put my tire chains on and we continued up the trail.

When we were about 2kms from camp, the snow was just too deep for the little car, so we turned it around and left it pointing downhill. We loaded up the backpacks and trekked through the snow the rest of the way. I still had that tumor in my leg. The snow wasn't too deep, maybe a foot and a half but no one had cut a trail through it, so it was hard going. We climbed the last hill up to David and Heidi's shack, saw the smoke coming from their stove pipe and yelled, *"HELLO THIS HOUSE!"*

When we got inside, David and Heidi were sitting on their respective chairs and David said to me, *"Ah yes, Jon, you're right on time!"* I said, *"You bet, we figured you guys could use some food and tobacco."* He said, *"That's great but it's not what I'm referring to. But we're grateful for the food too."* Okay, I thought, what is he talking about? He said, *"We have a package that needs to be mailed by tomorrow and were trusting the Lord to send you here, so you could mail it for us."* I was like, *"Whoa, I just got here, and after everything I've just been through I have no intentions of going anywhere until after New Year's, at the earliest."* *"Well, God told us you were coming and that you're going to mail the package for us."* I asked, *"What is it?"* David replied, *"We can't tell you. But let's just call it a trinket."*

"What was that? Let me get this straight. You expect me to go to town and mail a package without knowing what it is? Not going to happen."

"But God assured us that you were coming here to mail it and here you are."

"I haven't even begun to tell you about the nightmare trip I just had, getting hit head on by a cattle truck and then Matt losing the truck and all he gave me was $200.00, $150.00 of that spent on getting here, and this food. All I have left is $50.00!"

"That should be more than enough Jon." I was stunned. *"Are you kidding me? Ok, where is it going?"*

"Sorry, we can't tell you that either."

"Okay, let me get this straight. You want me to not only mail this mystery package and pay for it too, but I can't even know where it's going? I'm sorry but that's just nuts." I just flatly refused to do it. I thought they had been in the bush for too long and it had finally cracked them. I asked, *"Can I at least see it? If I'm going to mail it, I'll see it anyway."* David and Heidi whispered to each other then she went to get the package. She handed it to me. It was a small box wrapped in brown paper, like a package would be wrapped, with the proper twine wrapped around it as well. It was rather heavy for such a small box and when I shook it, it rattled a bit. I asked again, what is it? And they replied again, *"We can't tell you. All we can say is that it is incredibly important, and that God wants it mailed before the last business day of the year, which is tomorrow."*

"Why didn't He tell me anything about this?" I asked incredulously.

I sat there holding the little package. David and Heidi just smiled at me. Roy was there in the background somewhere, but it was like I had just entered the Twilight Zone. I said, *"Okay, let me pray about this. If I am going to do it, then God will have to make it obvious."* *"That's fine,"* David said, *"We already know the answer."* To say it was annoying and frustrating is an understatement.

I went outside to pee, and while I was out there making yellow snow, I asked God what I was supposed to do. It seemed insane to the rational mind, but God has been known to override that. Then it started to snow lightly. I knew what that meant. If I stayed, there was a good chance that my car wasn't going anywhere until spring. I decided to do it on my way back down to the city. I reasoned I needed to be down there in case there was a breakthrough with the insurance settlement anyway. I went back in and told them what they already knew, that I was going to mail it. They were pleased, and we sat up until the early morning hours fellowshipping in that cramped little survival shack.

The next day I was up before anyone else and was anxious to get going. The days are very short at that time of the year and the day was half over already. I woke everyone up, whether they liked it or not, and tried to motivate them to get a move on. It was unreal. Now they were all dragging their feet. There was another few inches of fresh snow and I wanted to get out of there as soon as possible, just to go mail the stupid trinket. Roy decided that he was going to go check on his junk pile. I said, *"I am not letting you out of my sight."*

So here I was, the guy who was dead set against this only a few hours before, now being the motivator to get everyone going. Richard was up there at the time and had agreed to drive us all to where my car was. We helped him chain up his 4x4 and got in the back for the ride. He drove like my grandmother. I yelled for him to put his foot in it or we are going to get stuck. He refused to. We got stuck. The clock was ticking and the post office in Boston Bar closed at 5:30pm. I said to heck with it and jumped out and walked while they dug his pickup out of the snow. Roy came with me.

When we got to where we were sure we left the car, it wasn't there. There were a couple of empty beer cans in the snow, but no car. Did someone steal it? Then we saw the tire tracks. We could see that there was a vehicle that had come up the road, turned around and left. Then we spotted my car. They, whoever they were, had pushed my car over the bank and down into a ravine. The snow had acted like a cushion and had stopped it from going too far but it was till 15ft down the bank, stopped inches from a big stump. I was mad, perplexed, confused and then suddenly I was convicted that the enemy did this to prevent *"the package"* from getting to wherever it was going. We stood there for what seemed like an eternity until Richard, David and Heidi arrived. I pointed out where my car was and asked Richard if he had a chain to pull it out with. Of course, he didn't. But he did have some small nylon rope. We doubled it up, but I thought there was no way that it was going to get the car out. He tied it to his front bumper and me to my trailer hitch. He backed up and it was like God sent angels to push, because it popped up out of there like it didn't weigh anything.

The car was out of the ditch and it was 5:05, twenty-five minutes until the post office closed and it was a twenty-five-minute drive on a nice summer day. I said, *"I'm going for it. I'll try to get there in time and hopefully she will wait for you to get there!"* Roy and I flew down that mountain not stopping to take the chains off when we got to bare road and got to the post office at 5:35pm. Too late. But the lights were all still on in the post office. I ran up the sidewalk, opened both doors and was inside. Lauren, the post mistress was talking to David's niece, Theresa. Women, they like to talk. She said, *"I'm sorry but we're closed. I just haven't got to locking the door yet."* It was do or die time. I said hello to Theresa and informed them both that her crazy uncle David was coming right behind me with a very important package that needed to be mailed. She said she was closed but she would wait until they got there. About ten minutes later, they rolled up. David came striding up the walk, package under his arm. He entered the post office and greeted his niece and Lauren. She said, *"I understand you have an important package that needs to be mailed today?"* *"Yes ma'am,"* he replied. She said it was out of the ordinary but why not, she would do it. I was shocked. She asked him where it was going, and he replied, *"To Windsor Castle, England."* as calmly as if he was saying, just down the street. No wonder he wouldn't tell me where it was going, there is no way I would have done it, if he had told me that. She asked if he had the address. He did. He didn't have the postal code though, so they had to look that up. Then he asked for a pen and some paper so that he could include a note with the package. He went out into the foyer and wrote something down and came back in. He had written two letters. One to Queen Elizabeth II, and the other to our then Prime Minister, Jean Chretien. I was floored but I had agreed to do it. She weighed everything and, since it was all going double registered, the total was $42.00 and change. There went my last $50.00 and it was in the mail.

We all kind of stood there looking at each other for a minute. We had just mailed a mystery package to the Queen of England and the Commonwealth. I asked David one more time what it was, and he said that God would reveal it to me when it was the right time. Just trust Him and have faith. It's all good.

Roy and I jumped back into the car and started to head back to the city, normally an hour and a half drive to Chilliwack. As soon as we got to the outskirts of Boston Bar, the car just died, and we coasted to the side of the road. Perfect. I popped the hood and couldn't see anything obvious, but it was a diesel and it had a small primer pump. So, I pumped it up and had Roy turn it over. It started. I got back in and away we went, for about a mile before it died again. Obviously, it was a fuel problem, but I couldn't see anything wrong, so I pumped it up again and away we went, for about two miles, then it died again. We repeated this process all the way to Aggasiz, about a 60-mile drive, to where the battery was finally dead from over use. It was dead, in the middle of the Aggasiz Bridge, a narrow two-lane bridge that is a major truck route. The lights didn't work, so they couldn't see us. It was a dangerous place to be. So, we pushed the car over the hump and coasted to the other side, just in time to miss being smeared by a truck.

It was 4:30am and I was done. I told Roy that I was reclining the seat and going to sleep, we can deal with it in the daylight. He decided to go for help. At about 9am, he was there with his pickup and some rope. He towed me the rest of the way into Chilliwack on the back roads, about another 15kms. I called Phil and explained the situation. He said he would come and look at it during his lunch break, which he did. The fuel filter had a pin hole in it, and it was sucking air, which is why it would only run if we pumped it up.

It was now January 1998, and now, we wait. I headed back to Abbotsford to Peng Cheng Chua's missionary outreach and asked him if he knew of a place that I could stay. He told me that he had just bought a house for training future missionaries and I was welcome to sleep on the couch.

I waited for news about the insurance settlement, and about *"the package."* Motrux, as I already mentioned, screwed Matt out of the insurance settlement. Since David's brother, Mike, was about half way between the cancer clinic and Abbotsford, I would have the volunteer drivers drop me off there sometimes. He was a great guy and always had a bed for me to sleep in.

One morning, in late March, I called Mike from Abbotsford to see what he was up to. He said, *"Jon, you are going to jail. My idiot brother mailed the Queen a gun."* I was like, "What did you just say?" He repeated, "You told me you paid for my moron brother to mail a package to the Queen. It was a freaking GUN. You're all going to prison. What a bunch of idiots!" I couldn't believe what I just heard. I said, *"Don't go anywhere, I'll be there as soon as I can!"*

I jumped in my car and flew. I got there in record time, ran up the stairs and into his house, out of breath. He said it again, *"I don't know why you came here, I already told you what happened, you idiots are going to jail. I was woken up by the phone at two in the morning by some guy from Scotland Yard. They asked if I knew a David Lillos and I said that's my brother, why? Then he told me what he did. You boneheads mailed the Queen a gun. You are all going to jail."* I said, *"A gun? Are you sure?"*

"That's what he told me, and he had two questions. Who the hell is David Lillos and where the hell is Tranquility Station?" He said that since he was the only Lillos in the phone book they thought he might be related. *"Man, now you idiots have me involved."* I was in shock, perplexed, and steaming mad. I said, *"There's no way I'm going to jail. There has got to be a good explanation for this. I'm going up there right now to find out."*

I jumped back into my car and flew up to camp, normally a three-hour drive from Mike's. I did it in just over two. I was angry and wanted answers. I got up there and woke them up. I was yelling at them to get out of bed, NOW. They got up and were a bit upset that I disturbed their sleep. I was way more disturbed that I had been used to mail the Queen a gun.

"She got it then?" asked David. "How the heck should I know. All I know is that Scotland Yard, CSIS, and who knows who else have been on the phone asking Mike all kinds of questions since two in the morning and he is convinced that we are all going to jail." David was calm as a cucumber and he said, "Don't worry Jon, we're not going to jail. We will probably even get a reward."

"A what? Did you just say a reward?"

"Yes, Jon, I told you God would let you know when it was time, now come inside and let us explain. Heidi, can you put some coffee on for us?"

I said, "This better be good because I paid the freight for that thing!" He said it was and began to explain.

"It was near the end of November when Heidi announced that we were out of food. She said she thought that there might be some boxes in the wood shed that she remembered seeing and went to check. Folks would bring food up during the summer and sometimes it would get placed off to the side. She found a box in the wood shed that had some food in it, but a lot of it was spoiled because it was only in cardboard boxes and there was a drip above it that had ruined most of it. There were some cans of food though, and the hermetically sealed packages from some Kraft Dinners."

"Okay, get to the good part." I implored.

He said to be calm because it was all important. Fine, but tell me what this has to do with mailing the Queen a gun. He said, "Heidi found a paper bag at the bottom of the box. She picked it up and the bag disintegrated. What she found was the gun. She took it back to the shack and showed it to me."

Now, he had to back up a bit himself. One morning, months earlier, David went to Boston Bar. As he was sitting in the Charles Hotel café, reading the paper, and having a coffee, he read the story of how Jimmy Pattison's house had been broken into. Jimmy Pattison, one of the wealthiest men in Canada, had indeed had his house broken into about a year earlier. The article mentioned that precious antiques had been stolen and among the things stolen was a gun. But this wasn't just any old gun. It was the personal side arm of Sir Winston Churchill. The man credited for his decisive role in winning World War II. I asked him how he knew. He told me how the Lord had lead him to town around the time that Pattison's house was broken into and he saw the article in the newspaper at the cafe. There was a small picture of it with the description of it. It was a Webley five shot revolver that had a pool cue butt for a pistol grip. It was unique, and David said that he knew whose it was as soon as he saw it. It even had the bullets in it.

My next question, how did it end up at Tranquility Station. He said he had no idea, but he did think he might have known who brought it up, but there was no way to verify it. Apparently, there was one character that would come up, when he wasn't in jail for breaking and entering, and he was the only one he could think of. I had no idea who that was, but since there were probably close to a hundred people that came and went from Tranquility Station over the course of a summer, it was impossible to even speculate.

I had paid the freight to send the Queen Sir Winston Churchill's personal handgun. Suddenly, I'm expecting a reward instead of jail. What a wild tale. Only God could arrange that. David figured that the reward could be monetary or the title deed to the land, or both. I liked the sound of that. If I had known that I was squatting on Crown Land when I first got there I doubt very much that I would have stayed.

So now we wait, again, only this time we are not in fear but in anticipation of a great reward. Then I saw it. Literally right in the very middle of the Bible. Psalm 118 verse 9. *"It is better to put trust in the Lord than confidence in princes."* Yes, it is, but what about the reward?

A month or so went by with no word about it. Then one morning I thought I heard a vehicle down below, so I went to investigate. David was up early, which was unusual. He had a big smile on his face and told me that they just had a visitor. He said it was the same RCMP Constable that I met the day I stopped the woman from jumping off the bridge, Constable O'Kell. He was sent up on official Queen's Business and had a few questions for David on behalf of Her Majesty, Queen Elizabeth II. I was excited as I asked him what the questions were. He said, *"She had three questions. 1, Do you expect a reward? To which I replied no. 2, Do you have anything further that you wish to say? To which I replied, no. 3, Do you have anything else that you wish to send? To which I replied, no."* I stood there, speechless. *"No? You said NO? Are you out of your mind? What were you thinking?"* He said not to worry, that it was all just formalities. That *"no"* doesn't really mean *"no."* I kind of figured otherwise. Bye-bye reward, child support debt will keep piling up. I am having an incredible adventure of a life but it's not looking very promising at that moment. I couldn't believe it, he said, no.

An Old Friend Gets Saved

When I was born again, the few friends I had all told me to get lost. I was no longer welcome because I was *"a downer."* It really hurt me to lose my only friends, especially when I had something that they didn't understand, but desperately needed, Jesus. One of my friends was Mark. We called him Mark Tank because if he spotted you across the room at a party, he would just lean forward and start moving his legs, knocking over anyone who was in his path. He was a master gunsmith, but, this being Canada, his talents weren't in high demand. He suffered from depression and consequently he drank heavily. He was always there to help everyone, but he didn't know how to help himself. It had been over ten years since I saw my old friends, and although I prayed for them, I had no idea how they were doing. One day, as I was getting my ride from the cancer clinic, I had a crazy idea and asked the woman who was giving me my ride if she would mind if she took me on a little detour. She was a sister in the Lord and was more than happy to. So, just out of curiosity, I wanted to see if my old friend Bill still lived in the same house he lived in when we parted ways. As we drove down his street, I saw his '72 GMC pickup parked in front of his house and asked her to stop. She waited while I went and knocked on the door. Wouldn't you know it, Bill answered the door.

Normally, when you see an old friend you would be excited and happy to see them, but not Bill. He said, *"Hey, what are you doing here?"* I told him I was getting a ride from the cancer clinic, and if it wasn't cool I could just leave. He said, *"No, you can come in."* So, I waved to my driver and she left.

When I went inside, nothing had changed. He had Star Trek on the TV, he had a beer in his hand and a joint in the ashtray. All his crystal dragon collection was there, as well as his model cars. Nothing had changed in over ten years. The only place to sit was on his couch so I sat down, and we made small talk. I was really wondering what I was doing there when he asked me, *"Hey, did you hear about Mark?"* Of course, I hadn't. He said, *"He has become one of you"* with much anguish in his voice. Wait, what? What do you mean, *"one of you?"* He rolled his eyes and said, *"You know, a Christian."* I was in shock. *"You heard me, he's one of you now. It sucks because he used to be such a good guy."* Suddenly, I knew why I was there. I asked him where he was, and he told me, *"He'll be here in about five minutes."* Now I was getting excited, Mark Tank, a Christian? And he's on his way here. Only God could put this together.

Sure enough, about five minutes later, Mark was at the door. I asked Bill if I could answer it and he said, *"Knock yourself out."* When I opened the door, Mark's eyes got big and said *"JON!"* I replied, *"Brother?"* And he said, *"BROTHER!"* We hugged and went inside. Like I said, the only place to sit was on Bill's couch, so we sat on either side of Bill, who was trying to watch Star Trek. As we were fellowshipping, and he was telling me how he was saved, Bill's head was turning back and forth, looking at each of us as we were talking. We must have hit a nerve because all the sudden Bill held his head in his hands and exclaimed, *"Oh my god, I've got it in stereo!"* Well that cracked Mark and I up and poor

Bill was even more depressed than usual. I can't remember where I went from there, probably hitchhiked back to Tranquility Station, but I got Mark's phone number so we could stay in touch.

My Crazy Life Went On

One afternoon, Richard came up to my place and said he needed to discuss something with me. He said that, *"It says in the Bible, "If a man doesn't work, neither shall he eat.""* I knew the scripture that says, *"Do the work of an evangelist,"* but I don't think that is all that the Lord had in mind there. He said he felt a real burden to get a job, and thought that I might be in agreement. He was right.

Sitting there, waiting for someone to just randomly come up the trail with tobacco and food was proving to be hit and miss at best. I knew that he was right, and he asked me what I liked to do. I knew that he was big time into the *"prosperity Gospel"* thing. Frankly, I didn't think it was ALL bad, I just have no respect for those guys who pry money from the poor to buy Lear Jets in the name of Jesus. Anyway, he said to be as specific as you can and ask God for it. So, I said I didn't want to drive trucks anymore due to being gimped from them already, but I couldn't think of anything else to do, at least that I was qualified for. I thought about it and said, *"This is what I want. I never want to leave BC. I only want to work part time. I want to be loaded one way, but never have to load the trailer myself. I want to get paid to bobtail somewhere and hook on to preloaded trailers so all I have to do is bring them to a yard and drop them and then go home. I want to be paid cash!"* He asked, *"Are there jobs like that?"* I replied, *"I don't think so, but if there are, that is what I want."* He asked for something specific as well, and then we prayed and held our requests before God and waited.

I had been helping Ralph out at Dokkside Transport, just as a friend and brother. Since we didn't have any phones or any other form of communications up there, Ralph would just show up and away we go, with me as his co-driver.

One day, Brian, the owner of the trucking company Ralph worked for, Dokkside, came and asked me if I would be interested in working part time. It was on weekends only. He would have the trucks that went out on Thursday nights and take two empty sets of trailers to the lumber mills, load them both and leave one of the loaded sets at the mill while bringing the other back to the coast. All I had to do would be to wait around the yard on Friday until the first available tractor was ready. Then, I would bobtail to one of the mills where there was loaded set of trailers, hook on to them and bring them back to the yard. I even had until 5:00am Monday morning to do it. It was exactly what I had prayed for only a month earlier. He said he would pay me in cash. My prayer was answered. It was like having the pickup for the weekend. I could bobtail to friends or relatives' places on Friday, hang out all day Saturday, hook on to the wagons on Sunday morning and be back by 5am Monday. and get paid to do it.

Getting Into The Word

One of the first things that I found out about living in the woods was that since there were no phones or other distractions, I could spend focused time reading the Bible and praying. Since my church life began at a Pentecostal Church, I found myself quite confused about many things. One person told me that I had to have the *'gift of tongues'* or I wasn't truly saved, while another said I didn't have to at all. One said I had probably committed the unpardonable sin and that all I could do was beg God for mercy while another said there was no way I could have committed it because it was for the early church. And on and on it went. I came to Christ and had great inner peace, then I came to the church and ended up mad and confused. I know they don't intend to do that, but that was the result. Up on that mountain, I had lots of time to explore the Bible; God's love letter. It was amazing to me how it always seemed to come with a test shortly after reading certain passages. We have no idea just how deep the selfish, evil wicked nature is in us, until we allow God to expose it. Then we can cry out, *"Amazing Grace! How sweet the sound that saved a WRETCH like ME!"* I soon discovered the most important aspect of our walk with the Lord is His free, unmerited favor and grace, not because we are all that and a bag of fries, but because He loves us and gives us His unmerited favor, despite ourselves. He blesses us so much and we don't deserve a single bit of it. If we all got what we really deserved, we would be smoking piles of ash in the parking lot, getting hit by lightning about every three seconds. This is not meant to sound morbid or morose. It is a fact that we, in our own strength, can do nothing to please God. He has become our Salvation. He is our redeemer and deliverer. He is our faith. He is such a wonderful loving Father that no one can come to him except that He draws them.

Unfinished Business

It was about a month or so later, and I had the volunteer driver drop me off at my mom's place in Langley. The evening news was just starting when I walked in and her and Jack were both sitting there watching, unaware that I was standing there behind them. Then the news anchor, Tony Parsons, dropped the bomb, *"We have a very unusual development tonight. Prince Charles and his sons, Harry and William, are making a surprise visit to BC this weekend. Normally these trips are planned months, if not years, in advance, but this one has come as a total surprise. The reason given is to go skiing at Whistler/Blackcomb and then sightseeing by helicopter on Sunday. We go live to Canada Place where they are having a brief impromptu press conference before heading up to Whistler Mountain."*

There they were, Prince Charles and his sons William and Harry, on TV, sporting ROOTS Wear sweatshirts and posing for the photographers. I knew why they were there. Then it dawned on me, I must be one of only a very few who knew *why* they were there. If I hadn't been dropped by at that precise time, the chances of me knowing what was going on were slim to none. God had me see that just in time.

Mom and Jack realized I was there and asked what I was up to. I had hoped to sleep in the camper there that night, but my plans had just been changed. I said I just stopped in to say hi.

I walked the couple of miles to the freeway where I hitchhiked home. I got some groceries and arrived there late that night after walking almost all the 25kms from Boston Bar. I shared with David and Heidi that Prince Charles, and sons, were in BC and that I knew that they were coming to Tranquility Station. They didn't seem overly impressed and I was a bit confused. I thought they would be excited, or at least happy, but they were both like, *"Yeah, that's nice Jon."* Well not me. I thought *"This is it. They are coming to make it official."*

The next day, Saturday, I went up to a logging landing not far from camp, the only place that a helicopter could possibly land, and did some brush clearing. With a bit of work, I had it all cleared and ready for the big meeting the next day. I could hardly sleep that night. Now I remembered the scripture about not putting my trust in Princes, Psalm 118:9, but it was not every day you meet one, and his sons. It snowed lightly that night, about two inches, and I was up early in the morning getting a small fire going at the landing site as I cleared the small brush away from the edges. I stomped out a big H in the snow, just for reference. Then I sat there and waited. And waited. And waited. Then about 11:00am, I heard it, a helicopter. It was heading our way. David and Heidi and everyone else were still sleeping, but I was wide awake and ready to do my duty as the official greeting committee. Then I saw it, a Canadian Armed Forces Chinook Helicopter. It came to the edge of the camp and hovered there for a minute or so. I could see the people in the helicopter pointing at the place. It was then that realized that there was no way they could land that huge thing in my little landing spot. They did a slow circle around the camp and then they spotted me. They waved to me. I waved back. They did another circle around the place, tilted the helicopter back west, towards

Whistler, and left. That was it. I guess I could have slept in like everyone else. When I told everyone what had happened, they still didn't seem overly impressed. Do not put your trust in princes.

So, there we are, after the big trinket incident and a visit by Prince Charles and sons, all is quiet around the camp. I was coming and going to and from the cancer clinic in Vancouver as needed, but I had to hitchhike to and from Hope, which was as far as the volunteers could drive. It was back to the usual routine. One late Spring afternoon, Richard brought a strange fellow to stay at his place. They met at a rock and gem show, which Richard was into because of all the soapstone that was around the place. The fellow's name was Nigel. He was from New Zealand and just happened to bump into Richard at the show. He told Richard that he was an avid soapstone carver and he would be delighted to spend some time up there, carving.

I had a feeling right from the start that all was not as it seemed with this guy. For one thing, he needed to go to town every single day to get a bottle of wine and mail a post card to his daughter. Every single day. I saw the printing on one of his post cards and it was miniscule. I mean tiny, 1/16th of an inch high at best. No one writes that small, except maybe someone who is getting paid to do a report on the weirdos who send the Queen guns. I poked at him for information but came to believe that he himself had no idea what he was there for. He spent time with each one of us, asking lots of questions that you only ask if you are digging for information. David and Heidi figured out who he really was as well, but Richard, Lloyd, and Darryl had no clue. It was almost comical really.

I had been doing my part time trucking for Dokkside, and I took Nigel on a trip to the Chilcotin area of BC, where I was picking up the trailers that were pre-loaded with lumber. I remember telling him, before we left, that I owned the road, to which he replied, *"That's preposterous mate."* Well after being in the truck with me for a couple of days and seeing how 140000lbs of truck and load move down the highway, he exclaimed, *"You really do own the road!"* I peppered him with questions myself, trying to figure out if he knew why he was gathering information about us. He didn't. I proclaimed, "God Bless the Queen," hoping that would stir him a bit, but he just said, *"Whatever mate, I don't like the old bat."*

He was there for about two months and he had done what he was sent to do. He had also carved one of the most hideous soapstone carvings that I had ever seen. Then one day, Richard drove him to the airport and our *'spy'* was gone.

The Prayer of Jabez

It was easy to lose track of time at Tranquility Station. We had no electricity, so there weren't a lot of clocks around. My watch battery had died long ago and it just didn't matter much. I was reading the Bible from cover to cover, forwards, backwards and sideways. One day I felt like I had skipped past 1st and 2nd Chronicles for long enough. It was some dry reading in there. So and so begat what's his name, who begat so and so, and so on. But I soldiered on, reading about Anub, and Helleliponi and their relatives.

And then I saw it, *"And Jabez was more honorable than his brethren: and his mother called him Jabez, saying, Because I bare him in sorrow. And Jabez called on the God of Israel, saying, Oh that thou would bless me indeed, and enlarge my coast, and that thine hand might be with me, and that thou wouldst keep me from evil, that it may not grieve me. And God granted him that which he requested."* (1st Chronicles 4: 9,10). And then right back into all the begats. Wait a minute. What's that doing in there? I read it repeatedly. Then I prayed the same prayer as Jabez did some 3000 years before, because, why not? I began to see God doing increasingly amazing things on my behalf. I started thinking grandiose thoughts about how I could get cleaned up and hit the church circuit with this amazing revelation from the Word of God. I studied it and prayed and agonized over it. Then I thought, now is the time to take this amazing little passage of scripture to the masses of Christians who needed to hear this powerful message from eons past.

I made it to the city with the idea that I would go to a couple of my friends who were in ministry and ask them to help me spread this powerful message of Jabez. I went to church on a Wednesday evening and there were Prayer of Jabez memorabilia EVERYWHERE. Prayer of Jabez coffee cups, Prayer of Jabez placemats, Prayer of Jabez casserole dishes. It appeared that while I was completely cut off from the outside world, learning all about Jabez out there in the middle of nowhere, so was the rest of the church. There were books, CD's, TV interviews with famous authors. It had already been done. I was so disheartened. All I could ask was, *"Why God?"* I thought this was a great thing to share with everyone and I was late for the party, it had been commercialized already. Then God let me in on a little secret. He reminded me that I had tuned in to the exact same thing that the rest of the Body of Christ was, at the exact same time, with no outside, physical connection. I was in tune with my brothers and sisters, even though I had no idea what they were in to. Of course, like most of the church *"fads,"* Jabez faded back into the obscurity of 1st Chronicles, and life goes on. Once again, all was quiet at Tranquility Station. But not for long. It was the spring of 1998 and, after spending a few weeks in the woods by myself, I found that I was needing some basic supplies, like bread and stuff, so I headed into town. We had talked about putting a cross at the entrance of the camp, at the Branch 30/Tranquility Road intersection. I had made a cross out of cedar poles and it needed to get taken the couple of kilometers to the corner. I put it on my shoulder and started walking. It felt surreal to be walking down the mountain carrying a cross. As I walked along the road by the beaver pond, I saw a logging crew up on the hillside on a logging landing working away. I could hear as one of them yelled, *"Hey! Look at that!"* I just kept walking with that cross and even though it was made from light weight cedar, it was starting to dig into my shoulder, feeling heavier and uncomfortable. I carried it, with the bottom of it dragging behind me, up to the corner of Tranquility Rd. and Branch 30.

When I got there, I just picked it up and drove it into the ground. It stayed put right where I stuck it. There was a logging truck idling in the middle of the road and the driver was buckling up his pants after doing what bears, and loggers, do in the woods. I said Hello, as I walked up behind him, and he almost jumped out of his skin. He spun around and stared wide-eyed at me walking towards him, then he noticed the cross that was standing there that wasn't there before. He went into the woods, then looked back at me. I asked him if I could get a ride into town and he said, *"Sure, why not."* I tried to share the Gospel with him, but sometimes it's best to just let God do the work.

He dropped me off in Boston Bar and I picked up a few things at the store. As I was standing in line to pay for my stuff, there was a fat old logger, complete with his obligatory Husqvarna Suspenders, standing in front of me at the counter. He turned around and glared at me and asked, *"Hey, aren't you one of those Jesus freaks that lives out by the Nahatlatch?"* I said, *"Yes."* He then said, *"Well, it's too bad about you poor buggers, we are going to start logging that entire area this fall, for the next twenty years. And, we're putting our base camp right where you are. Looks like you're going to have to find somewhere else to live."* He was laughing. I was ticked off at the guy's attitude, but I just prayed to the Lord that His will would be done in the matter. I then started heading back to camp.

The same driver I caught the ride into town with was going back for his last load of logs of the day and he picked me up and gave me a ride right back to the corner where he picked me up that morning. The cross was still standing. As I was walking back into camp, I stopped at Pill Bill's spot. He was a straggler that came from the very nasty bunch of squatters that had a cabin down by the river. He wasn't a Christian, but he had been kicked out for not being evil enough, or so he said. He was carving out a little camping spot and had it looking nice. I stopped in to say hi. He said he was ready for winter and I asked him how so. He said, *"I have 72 Star Trek novels. That's enough reading for the entire winter."* *"Star Trek novels?"* I asked. *"Why not read the Bible and get something good out of it?"* He replied, *"The Bible? Ha! Why* would I read that bunch of fiction?" That disturbed me, and I headed up the trail towards camp.

I stopped at Richard's cabin. He had a generator and a satellite dish, and we had spent many nights watching Pastor Arnold Murray on it, but there he was, sitting there watching the Brady Bunch. *"The Brady Bunch Richard?"* I asked. He replied defensively, *"I happen to really like this show."* I thought, *"Okay bro, whatever turns your crank."* My spirit was grieved as I continued up the trail.

I got to James' place. He came storming out of his shack angrily demanding to know what I was going to do with my old Oldsmobile. I told him, *"Well, James, the transmission is shot, and I don't have any money to fix it. Besides that, it's been here longer than you have/ I'll tell you what, why don't we pray about it?"* He said that wasn't good enough. *"Well that's too bad,"* I said, *"it's all I have to work with right now."* So, I prayed, *"Dear Lord, here's James, and he's upset about my old car being in his way. If You want me to put it back on the road then thank You for a new transmission, and if not, I thank You for making that obvious too. In Jesus name. There you go James, I've set it before the throne of God. I expect we'll have our answer soon."* He grumbled and went back into his shack. I went up to my treehouse, grieved in my heart about everything that happened that day. On the one hand, I was blessed and had some more bread and tobacco, on the other hand, this so called *'Christian Camp'* seemed to be anything but. I dropped to my knees as I prayed, *"Lord, this place is a mess. Please do something. If you can't change the hardened hearts, then get them out of here."* I found plenty of scriptures to call upon the Lord with, mainly in the Psalms, and I prayed them as if they were my own words.

The Nipple Is On Fire

It was August 5th, 1998, and one of the hottest days on record at 105 F in the shade. I abandoned my project of building a road through the forest to my place, mainly because of a massive cottonwood tree in the way that was just too big for me to deal with and at 105 degrees, it was not a pleasant task. I took a lawn chair and my Bible and went to sit in the creek with my feet propped up on a board because, as hot as it was there, that creek was just too cold to leave your feet in. I was stripped down to my underwear, reading my Bible when I came across the scripture, *"My ministers are a flame of fire"* (Psalm 104: 4). I remembered seeing it before but hadn't really given it much thought. As I contemplated that, it was mid-day when I dozed off. I'm not sure how long I slept, but I started to wake up to the smell of smoke. Before I opened my eyes, I remember thinking to myself, who would have a campfire in this heat? Then I opened one eye and saw it. The smoke was thick in the trees. Then it dawned on me, IT WAS A FOREST FIRE! What do I do?

I ran to my treehouse and went upstairs. I was trying to be calm, but it was obvious that we were all going to be evacuated, soon. I prayed *'Lord, what do I take?'* and then His still, small voice said, *"A couple changes of clothes will be fine Jon,"* as clearly as if he was standing next to me. A couple of changes of clothes. That made sense to me. I grabbed my small back pack and tossed in two pairs of pants, two shirts, two pairs of socks and two pairs of underwear. I didn't think to take my leather jacket with my wallet and driver's license in it. I even left my Bible right where it lived on the table and booked it out of there.

I had no idea where the fire was, which direction it was travelling or how we were going to get out of there. As I was running down the trail, I met another one of the many Richards that were there heading up the trail. I thought maybe he was running from the fire and I was going the wrong way, so I asked him. He said he had no idea where the fire was either, but he had *"laid a fleece before the Lord"* in the form of a ring left on a tree branch and he needed to go back to see it. He had just arrived there the night before with his girlfriend, Tammy, which is a whole other story. I said, *"You're nuts. We can't go that way. What if the fire is coming up over the ridge? You'll get burned to a crisp."* He was determined, so I decided to go with him, just in case anything happened, and to try to get him to turn around.

The smoke was getting thicker and he finally decided to turn around. We ran back to the Summer Kitchen, where everyone who was at the camp had assembled. It was quite a mix. Ten of us all together. We were an unlikely mix but there we were, all gathered in the Summer Kitchen. A red helicopter flew over us and announced through a loud speaker that we were being evacuated. I suggested that we pray. We all held hands, believers, and unbelievers alike, and I lead the prayer. *"Dear Lord, we know that this fire comes as no surprise to you. But we sure weren't expecting it. You know how hard we have all worked here to build this place of refuge for weary travelers. We ask you now, that if this place is supposed to be here when this fire has passed through then it will, and if it's not, it won't. Have mercy on us Lord for we are just a poor and wretched bunch and without you we are less than nothing. In Jesus name we pray, Amen."* There was a hearty amen from everyone, believers, and unbelievers alike.

I had a Bible tract that I found in a phone booth in a truck stop in Omaha Nebraska called, *Why No Revival?* It laid out, plainly, why God had been holding back the revival for His children in America, Canada too. It wasn't intended for unbelievers and it had many strong rebukes for the soft, demanding, wimpy Laodicean church. The last page had in big, bold words, *"JUDGEMENT BEGINS IN THE HOUSE OF GOD."* David attached it, open to that page, on a clipboard in the Summer Kitchen.

Moments later, the RCMP and Search and Rescue were there, telling us all we were being evacuated. We were all present, accounted for and more than ready to go. We all got into the various trucks they had there, and were hauled off the mountain, uncertain about our future there. Richard tried to turn around because he forgot something and one of the cops told him that if he did, he would be arrested on the spot. He didn't go back. It turned out that everyone for miles around was also evacuated, including everyone in the Nahatlatch Valley and up and down the west side of the Fraser Canyon.

We were taken to the Green Canyon Motel, about ten miles south of the mountain, on the East side of the Fraser Canyon. It is situated on a bluff above a big bend in the river. We had front row seats because there were a bunch of beach chairs set up, overlooking a bluff, that faced directly towards our place, as if God had placed them there just for us. It was surreal to watch the entire mountain burning.

As the night set in, the scene became even more unreal. There was the wildest light show imaginable, and the fire created its own weather system. The winds it was generating were fierce. There was lightning shooting out of the smoke and flames too and we had the best seats in the house. While we were sitting there. I started to get drowsy. It was probably around two in the morning, when the doubts started to flood my mind. In my mind, I saw the rafters of my house burning and falling in on themselves. I said, *"Oh Lord, no."* But then I heard His still small voice say, *"That wasn't from Me."* I snapped out of it and said, *"I rebuke you satan, you liar!"* From that moment on, I had complete peace about my treehouse and everything else up there.

We were put under the care of the Provincial Emergency Program, who David's brother, Danny, just happened to oversee for that area. God had set things up perfectly. Here was this crazy guy from the woods, David, whose brother oversaw the PEP, who was only second in command to the fire chief. Only God could come up with that one.

After the first few days there, we were sent across the highway to stay at the Canyon Alpine Hotel and given $39.10 per person per day towards our food. In fact, our very first meal was at the Canyon Alpine Restaurant at the big truckers table. The people that owned the restaurant were part of the good old boys' network and they decided that they didn't like us for various reasons, not the least being that we were Jesus freaks. Well, as the ten of us were sitting at the big table, it became a literal fulfilment of Psalm 23, *"They prepared a table for us in the presence of our enemies."* Now, don't misunderstand me here. As far as I'm concerned, those who don't like us, simply didn't know the whole story. *"Our enemies"* are folks who are ignorant to who

God and Jesus truly are, and what He did for them. They are not people we hate, but people we are trying to love, despite their hostility towards us because of their lack of full understanding. It was an intense time. There we were, the scourge of the Fraser Canyon in the eyes of the locals, being fed and housed while The Nipple burned. There were rumors flying around that we were the ones who had started the fire.

After a few days, Richard left, heading back to Alberta saying, it's all over. Sadly, his lack of faith was obvious. But as for the rest of us, we were eating steak until we couldn't stand it. It was such a contrast. Before the fire, we had lots of hard work to do but not much food. At the motel, we had tons of food but nothing to do, except wait. The fire fighters were staying at the same motel and they were dead tired at the end of their shifts. Wouldn't you know it but Rick, Veronica and James, the unsaved party animals, were in the rooms right underneath them, partying. There was a lot of conflict between them unfortunately, but it had a positive outcome in that the locals could see who the trouble makers were and who weren't.

Heidi was quick to volunteer to help around the motel and restaurant. The other Richard and Tammy both got jobs at the restaurant. I met my old trucker friend, Ralph, who stopped in for lunch one day. We all knew Ralph and it was a blessing to see him there. Since I was bored stiff anyway, he hired me to help keep him awake when he got tired. During that time, the fire raged. We would ask the fire fighters if they had any news about our places every day, but they said it was just too hot to get in there and find out. One of them told me that it was so hot in the area near the camp that when the water bombers would drop water on the fire, it would turn to steam before it even hit the trees. It was getting harder and harder to keep the faith that my place was still there.

It was day 21. David, Heidi, and I were sitting in a booth at the Alpine Restaurant. We were getting frustrated at the lack of news, wondering when, or if, we were going home. At the same time, the Husqvarna Suspender guy, the same one who taunted me in the store a month or so before, came in and sat down at the counter. He ordered a beer and a steak. As he was sitting there, he said in a voice that was intended to be loud enough for us to hear, *"Yeah, too bad about those Jesus freaks. Looks like they're going to have to find somewhere else to live."* We sat there, looking at each other and gritting our teeth, unable to do anything but silently praying for God to do something.

Husqvarna guy's steak arrived, and he cut off a bite and was lifting it to his mouth, when just then, Danny, David's brother, Number Two man in charge of the fire, came running in to the restaurant looking for us. *"Dave! Jon! Heidi! It's still there!"* Just like in the movies, Mr. Husqvarna spit out his bite of steak and it flew across the counter and hit the back wall. It was priceless. As Danny was telling us how they had finally made it to the camp and that everything was still there and better than we left it. Husqvarna dude pulled out a $20, slid it on the counter and quietly slinked out. Danny was telling us how the chickens had had chicks and they were running all around the place, how the garden was exploding with corn stalks that were fifteen feet tall due to the massive amounts of nitrogen the helicopter water bombers were dumping on the place. We were thrilled. I asked him about my place. He said he didn't know where my place was, so he couldn't tell me. So, everyone but me knew that their places were okay. But I had faith.

The head of the entire firefighting operation, Steve Grimaldi, was a Believer himself and he had taken quite a liking to us. Once he could drive in and out of Tranquility Station, he took it upon himself to pick up chicken feed at the local feed store and feed the chickens. Apparently, it had become such a common occurrence that the fire crews even laughed about it. *"Where's Steve?"* they would ask over the radio. *"Where else? He's feeding the chickens!"* would be the reply.

So, with the knowledge that everyone else's places were safe, we had peace about our circumstances. I was still helping brother Ralph but staying at the Alpine when he went on into Vancouver. It wasn't much, but he did give me some spending money and it was good to get away from the boredom of that motel. Then, on day thirty-seven, we were told that we could go home and take stock of the place. Since James Barret's old pickup was the only working vehicle there, we all piled in and went up. We were allowed past the check point and we drove up the trail. The smell of smoke was still very thick, but you could see that the fire was mostly out. James parked his old truck at the bottom of the camp and we walked in. I was reminded of the scripture written when the children of Israel returned to Jerusalem after their 70 years in Babylon, *"Our mouths were filled with laughter."*

As we went up the trail, Rick and Ronnie's bus was still there. A little further up and there was Pill Bill's camp. As we surveyed the area, I noticed a fire path about 2ft wide that had travelled down the small slope and had burned his tent, the one with the 72 Star Trek novels in it. Amazingly enough, his other tent, only a few feet away was completely untouched by the fire. Then, as we made our way up the trail a little further, there was David and Heidi's garden. It was incredible. The watermelons must have been 2ft long and 18 inches in diameter, the corn stalks were 15ft high, and chicks and young chickens were everywhere. They obviously were blessed amid adversity.

Then we walked through the Summer Kitchen, where our bible tract was still attached to the clipboard, and up to Richard's. His cabin was still there, but there was his satellite dish, just a blob of melted plastic. Like Pill Bill's tent, there was a narrow strip of burnt ground that wound its way down the ridge to the stump that the dish was on. His generator was only a few feet away and was completely unburnt.

Then Up to James Barret's. We didn't need to wonder about my car anymore because it had been burned to a crisp. There was nothing left of it, except the burned out, rusting hulk. The other vehicles on either side of it were untouched by the fire. Then I saw the fire break. They had simply followed my road that I was building, and that big old cottonwood was not only gone, but the road they left behind was almost a highway.

Then I started up the trail that lead to my treehouse, not knowing what I would find. There were no obvious signs of fire in that part of the forest, but it was on the wrong side of the fire break. As I walked up the trail and over the ridge, there it was, just as I had left it thirty-seven days before. I stood there with tears of gratitude in my eyes as I thanked God.

As I got closer, I saw that there wasn't even a singe mark on it. God had answered all my prayers and protected it. I went inside and upstairs to where my Bible was open to the 23rd Psalm. I didn't remember leaving it open to that, but there it was. Maybe one of the firefighters opened it. I will never know on this side of glory. I went up to the loft where my bed was, and it was exactly as I left it. My roof was made out of an old pool cover, about as flammable a material that there is, and yet it didn't have a single hole in it. I was in absolute awe of God. I dropped to my knees right there with tears of joy and gave Him thanks and praise. I was speechless. His ministers were literally flames of fire.

> *The Lord is my shepherd; I shall not want. He maketh me to lie down in green pastures: He leadeth me beside the still waters. He restoreth my soul: He leadeth me in the paths of righteousness for His name's sake. Yea, though I walk through the valley of death, I will fear no evil: for thou art with me; thy rod and thy staff they comfort me. Thou preparest a table before me in the presence of mine enemies: thou anointest my head with oil; my cup runneth over. Surely goodness and mercy shall follow me all the days of my life: and I will dwell in the house of the Lord forever. (Psalm 23).*

Going Home

After we were all allowed to return home forty-four days after the fire started, it was obvious that things would never be the same again. The lush garden that was seen by us all on our inspection seven days earlier was trampled by the cattle from the Washtock Ranch, who had a free cattle ranging permit for the area. It seemed like a cruel blow after the incredible miracle of Tranquility Station being preserved through a massive forest fire. Did someone deliberately run the cows up there? Or did they just find their way there? One of those questions we will never know the answer to down here.

The entire forest smelled like a giant fire pit. There were still a few spot fires burning and lots of smoldering going on, but the worst of the fire was over. Whenever the wind blew, there were trees crashing down all over the place. It was kind of eerie.

Since our little patch of forest, about ten acres, was the only one left for miles around, all the birds that had been displaced took up residence there. The sound of them every morning was almost deafening. There were thousands upon thousands of birds.

There was a definite change in the spiritual tone too. Pill Bill felt that he wasn't welcome. None of us told him that, but after seeing how his 72 Star Trek novels had been burnt, but his sleeping gear hadn't, he said, *"It seems pretty obvious that God doesn't want me here."* I tried to tell him that it didn't mean that God didn't want him, but he wasn't the type to want to be comforted with that kind of knowledge.

James was set back quite a bit too. His *"garden"* was toasted, so he had no source of income from that. He was always a strange dude. He talked about God, but his actions didn't. He was no Christian. Veronica had left Rick while they were at the Alpine because he was a very mean drunk. So, when he got back without her, he was even meaner. He had two months of welfare checks to buy beer with and he was getting drunk every day. He also had some guns, and as he got drunk he would fire them randomly towards us through the forest from his bus, which was about 1/2 a km away. Richard and Tammy had continued to work at the Alpine restaurant, until they split up and both went their separate ways.

Roy, the least punctual person I have ever known, went up to Tranquility Station during the fire in the middle of the night, completely unaware that the fire was raging, and no one was allowed up there except for fire crews. He made it to the checkpoint but there was no one there, so he moved the barricade, drove through, and closed it behind him. He drove up to camp and dropped off a load of his junk, then went for a walk around camp to check on things. He got up to my place and noticed a small lick of fire that was working its way closer and closer to my treehouse. The firefighters had left a small fire pump and some hose there, so he started the pump and soaked down my place and put out the fire lick. Once again, he was right on time despite himself. He might have even saved my place from the fire.

Richard and Tammy

The day before the fire, Richard and Tammy arrived at camp. What a story they had. They had been together, on and off for a few years, but they had split up that spring. Tammy went back to Saskatoon Saskatchewan and Richard went to Vancouver. I guess there was a guy that was in love with her back there and he must have had some money, because they were having a huge wedding. I remember when Richard stopped by camp and was agonizing over it. He wanted her but didn't, if that makes sense. We all prayed for him and one day he was gone.

It seems he went back to Saskatoon, to the wedding, where he stood up and objected to the marriage at the time when the minister asks if anyone objects. Tammy, unaware that Richard was even there until he spoke up, abandoned the poor guy at the altar and the two of them ran to the highway, where they started hitchhiking. Imagine, if you will, a scruffy Metis guy and a lily-white girl in a wedding dress, hitchhiking.

They made it to Jasper Park, Alberta, where they were dropped off. I assume they managed to find a change of clothes for Tammy by then. Anyway, there they are hitchhiking at the intersection of Hwy's 16 and 94, at Jasper, westbound. Tammy says to him, *"Richard, I'm hungry."* He replied, *"Tammy, we're in the middle of nowhere, what do you want me to do about it?" "I don't care, I'm just hungry."* He lifted his arms to God and yelled, *"Do you hear that God? The woman is hungry."* He said that he felt like God was asking him to ask her what she wanted, so he did. *"What do you want?"* She thought about it for a second and answered, *"I want chicken."* He held his arms up and yelled, *"Did you hear that God? She wants chicken."* The next car to come along was a big old Lincoln Continental. He pulled over in front of them and rolled the window down. When they got up to him he said, *"Sorry, I can't give you a ride, but I thought you two might be hungry."* He handed them a bucket of KFC chicken, not more than a minute after Richards prayer. They arrived at Tranquility Station the night before the fire.

Richard M

There was another character that popped in and out of camp, another Richard. He had picked me up when I was hitchhiking once and was fascinated enough with my stories about Tranquility, that he made a point of finding the place. Like everyone else up there, he had a story. He was a smart cookie, very high IQ, an honor student in school, and he was on track to be a doctor with acceptance to med school. He was also a bit strange, and one day he was feeling happy and free after church, so he went for a walk. He got to the Mission Bridge, took off his shoes and socks, and proceeded to walk, tight rope like, on the guard rail. It was a long way down to the Fraser River if he slipped.

He said he was in complete control and wasn't even slightly worried, when the police arrived and ordered him to get down. He said he wasn't hurting anyone and was completely at ease so what was the big deal. They forced him down and took him for a psychological examination. These are not usually fun. He was kept in a glass cell, completely naked, and forced to perform like a lab rat to prove that he was sane, for months. They found him to be *"unfit"* and committed him to Riverview Hospital for the Insane. All because he was having a really great day, according to him anyway. So, fast forward to when he found Tranquility Station. He was quite a character. He had his Bible with him and knew it very well. Since he told me his story, I was watching him extra closely and he seemed to be a bit strange, but clearly wasn't dangerous or insane. He kept coming up to visit and always brought food and tobacco for us. He added to the fun around the campfire. Sometimes he would arrive in the middle of the night, in a snow storm, with bread bags under his socks to keep his feet dry. He hang out for a bit, then just as mysteriously as he arrived, he would vanish.

James B

It was the end of October, 1998, when James received a letter telling him that his father had cancer and didn't have long to live. There was a pilot's strike in Canada that had just ended, so he was able to get return tickets to and from Nova Scotia for almost nothing. Richard Miller was there and had agreed to drive James to the Vancouver Airport. It was a typical day in camp for the fall; cold in the morning but the sun was out, so we knew it would warm up. I wanted to come along for the ride, just to get away from the place for the day.

As we were waiting for James to get his stuff together, I was getting a bit impatient and thought I should probably get another layer of clothing, just in case it was late when we got back. I walked up to my treehouse, went up to the loft and got a sweater, then stopped at the Bible that was open on my desk. It was 2nd Corinthians chapter 5. I felt compelled to stop and read it.

> *"It is actually reported that there is immorality among you, and immorality of such a kind as does not exist even among the Gentiles, that someone has his father's wife. You have become arrogant and have not mourned instead, so that the one who had done this deed would be removed from*

your midst. For I, on my part, though absent in body but present in spirit, have already judged him who has so committed this, as though I were present. In the name of our Lord Jesus, when you are assembled, and I with you in spirit, with the power of our Lord Jesus, I have decided to deliver such a one to Satan for the destruction of his flesh, so that his spirit may be saved in the day of the Lord Jesus. Your boasting is not good. Do you not know that a little leaven leavens the whole lump of dough? Clean out the old leaven so that you may be a new lump, just as you are in fact unleavened. For Christ, our Passover also has been sacrificed. Therefore, let us celebrate the feast, not with old leaven, nor with the leaven of malice and wickedness, but with the unleavened bread of sincerity and truth. I wrote you in my letter not to associate with immoral people; I did not at all mean with the immoral people of this world, or with the covetous and swindlers, or with idolaters, for then you would have to go out of the world. But actually, I wrote to you not to associate with any so called brother if he is an immoral person, or covetous, or an idolater, or a reviler, or a drunkard, or a swindler—not even to eat with such a one. For what have I to do with judging outsiders? Do you not judge those who are within the church? But those who are outside, God judges. **Remove the wicked man from among yourselves."**

I thought about all the overt sinfulness in the camp, especially after the fire, and knew that it was house cleaning time. I honestly was looking forward to James being gone. He had some questionable tendencies, like making moonshine and growing pot in the woods, and was not a real Believer in the deep calls unto deep category. So, having just read that, I was praying that the Lord would do the removing because who was I to take on the task? I have never been the toughest guy on the block, but I could hold my own, but some of these characters clearly had nothing to lose. The scripture in Proverbs that tells us not to argue or fight with unbelievers is very good advice.

When I got back to James' cabin, he was still packing. But we had a new guest, Rick, and his Rottweiler. He took one look at me and I guess the spiritual restraint had been removed because he said, *"I hate your guts!"* as he took a swing at me and broke my nose. I was wearing my *"going to town clothes"* and didn't want to get blood on them, so I cupped my hands and caught the big blood clot that came out of my nose. Fighting with this guy would have been foolish enough, but he also had that snarling Rottweiler beside him, so I just sat down, holding the blood clot in my cupped hands. He was yelling and cursing at me as I sat there.

He picked up an empty five-gallon water bottle and began hitting me with it. I thought it was funny and started to laugh. I think he realized the absurdity of the situation and he kind of laughed too but he was still enraged so he turned to leave. I stood up and threw the blood clot at him as I said, *"The blood of a righteous man is upon you, God have mercy on your soul."* He and his dog stormed down the trail, the hideous collection of demons driving him on.

Now that he was gone, Richard and James came out of hiding and we headed towards the airport, three hours away. I now had a broken nose and a black eye, but hey, at least we were putting the wicked out of the camp. I had enough though and made Richard stop at the Boston Bar RCMP detachment to file assault charges against Rick. He was plainly getting dangerous and call me a wimp if you must, but I was concerned that he was going to kill someone, most likely me. I gave a full report and told them I was pressing charges.

We drove to the airport and that was the last time we saw James. We heard through the grape vine that he was there when his dad passed away. Then we heard that he had gone out with his brother, on his brothers fishing boat in the Atlantic Ocean, where his brother fell overboard and drowned. The curses follow them that curse God.

I can't remember what time it was when we got back that night, but there was a noticeable calm around camp the next day. I heard the rest of the story from David and Heidi that afternoon. It seemed Rick was out of beer and didn't have a way to get to town to get more. So, he improvised. There was Pill Bill's old Toyota sitting there, but it didn't have a battery. There was Roy's truck that had a battery. He stole Roy's battery, put it in Pill Bill's car, hotwired it and headed for Boston Bar. He made it about a kilometer down Chaumox Rd. when the police, who were coming up to camp to arrest him, saw him blast by going the other way. They spun around and pulled him over.

Heidi was riding her bike back from the dump when she saw Rick spread eagled on the hood of the cop car as they cuffed him. He yelled obscenities at her as she rode by. He had stolen a car with a stolen battery. He obviously didn't have a driver's license and the car was uninsured. He was drunk. And, he had just assaulted the guy who was working hard to bring food to the camp, food that he had eaten the night before. He was being put out of the camp. He was immediately given a peace bond prohibiting him from coming within 5kms of Tranquility Station and to avoid all contact with me.

As much as I hated having *'the system'* fight my battles, I was happy that he wasn't going to be around. I remember thinking, *"Boy, I hope he gets what's coming to him."* But the Lord quickly put the brakes on that attitude. That night I picked up my Bible and, as was my habit, turned to a random page and started to read, *"Rejoice not when thine enemy falleth, and let not thine heart be glad when he stumbleth: Lest the Lord see it and it displease Him, and He turn His wrath away from him"* (Proverbs 24: 17,18). That smartened me up and I forgave him and prayed for him.

Rick received a fine and was forbidden from coming anywhere near camp, and me specifically, for nine months. Not much of a punishment but at least I didn't have to worry about the guy, if he played by the rules. He played by the rules.

Nine Months Later, To the Day

I had gone to the city and had bought a chub of ground beef that was on sale. I had no way to refrigerate it, so I had to cook it all right away. I was grilling burgers on my little outdoor cook stove when Rick, and his personal sycophant Pill Bill, came walking across my log bridge. He was announcing as he came, *"Yesterday was the last day of the peace bond, what are you going to do now?"* I sat there, calmly cooking burgers. He got closer. *"Didn't you hear me? I don't have to stay away from you anymore."* He was laughing. I just kept cooking meat. They were finally standing right in front of me when I asked, *"You guys hungry? I got more than I know what to do with here."* Pill Bill said, *"Yeah, that looks and smells really good."* Rick snarled at him and said, *"We don't want your stupid meat."* It was obvious that Bill was disappointed but since he didn't want to be on Ricks bad side he meekly agreed. I asked them again, *"Come on guys, you must be hungry, grab some bread and make yourself a couple of burgers."* Bill was visibly drooling but Rick wasn't going to bite. Rick said, *"I can come and go as I want now, so watch out.'* I said, *"Yep, you can. Jesus still loves you and you can have a burger if you want it."* He growled and stormed off. Pill Bill was eyeing those burgers, but his fear of Rick was stronger as he followed him back down the trail. I didn't have any trouble from Rick from that day on. Bless your enemies and do good to those who despitefully use you, for in doing so you heap coals of fire upon their heads.

During this whole time, I was always holding my children up to the Father, believing that someday we would be reunited. I had no idea where they were and couldn't have done anything about it even if I did.

My memories about that winter after the fire are slim, but I did spend most it on the mountain. One thing I remember very clearly was the sound of trees crashing down all around us from the weight of the snow on the dead trees. Some nights it sounded like a war was going on, with tree after tree coming down. Some of them simply exploded from the combination of snow load, being weakened by the fire and then the extremely cold temperatures at night. It was a thrill to climb into bed at night, with all the noise from crashing branches and falling trees, then say a quiet prayer, *"Lord, I'm yours. If I'm not supposed to be hurt out here, then I won't. I love you Lord."* I would fall into a blissful sleep, waking the next morning feeling quite loved by God.

I was still trucking for Dokkside on the weekends, throughout the winter and somehow managed to drive in and out of there in my old van no matter how deep the snow was. I guess it never got that bad because I don't remember ever getting stuck. One trick I learned from trucking is to have lots of weight over your drive axle. I found a bunch of railroad track cleats at the dump and laid them on the floor of the van. With all that weight adding to the traction, I could go pretty much anywhere with a good set of tire chains on that thing. Trucking in the winter has its own challenges but at least I had the sleeper to crawl into at the end of a long day.

Ricky

The next spring, I came off the road and found a whole new crowd of people up there. There was another kind of mushroom that grows after a forest fire, the Fire Morrel. It seemed like the fire had made the conditions perfect to produce a bumper crop, and these guys were there to cash in. There weren't any Christians in that crowd though, so I took it as an opportunity to share the gospel.

Of all the characters that were up there that spring, one stuck out. His name was Ricky, and he was an avowed satanist. He made no bones about it, going as far as to say he believed in the same God as us, he just chose to fight him, rather than serve him. I was trying to find a way to witness to him about the awesome salvation available through Christ, but his heart was as hard as a rock. I shared some of my experiences with him, telling him about the time Dennis Hammer and I prayed one Halloween night. He made me stop right there and he asked me what year that was. I scratched my head and tried to remember. *"1995,"* I said. He asked me where we were when we prayed. I wondered why it mattered and he grew angry and yelled, *"Because it matters!"* So, I told him we were in Greendale. He went pale, then he began to explain.

It turned out that he was preparing to do two human sacrifices that Halloween night, not even a mile from Dennis' house. He then told me about how everything started to go wrong. How he lost his resolve to do it, and how he even went as far as to rescue the two young girls he was supposed to kill and flee into the night with them on foot. He said the people he was *"working for"* were driving up and down the streets, searching for them with flashlights, and he knew that if they caught them, he and the girls would all be killed.

As he was telling me this, I kept getting chills. It was an incredible confirmation to me that the Lord had indeed used me in the simple act of prayer that night with Dennis and had saved the lives of two young girls in the process. As much as I was edified, he was ticked off. He was talking to the guy who, through our simple prayer, had derailed his career as a warlock and had caused him to have lots of the wrong kind of people as enemies. I shared the gospel with him yet again and this time he said he honestly believed that Jesus was who He said He was, the living Son of God. There was a bit of a transformation in him but frankly he was still very much the old Ricky. He would say what he thought we wanted to hear to our faces but was someone very different to others. He thought he was fooling me until I had an unintentional confrontation with him one day.

He was sitting at Richard's one morning when I came down the trail. He was in obvious pain and was holding his head in both hands. I asked him if he was okay and he said he had a horrible earache. So, without a second thought, I walked up to him and asked if I could pray for him. He wasn't able to refuse so he said, *"Sure, why not."* I reached out and as soon as my hand touched the side of his head, he screamed in pain. I jumped back, not sure myself what had just happened. I knew he was still in serious satanic bondage and was expecting him to lunge at me or something. Instead, he said, *"It's gone! The earache is gone."* I hadn't even started to pray yet.

God had healed him of that earache without me uttering a single word. I was giving glory to God for doing such a wonderful thing, but Ricky didn't quite see it that way, he was mad at me. The power he had so earnestly sought through satanism was a free gift from God. It seemed to drive an even bigger wedge between us and he was always hostile towards me after that.

Love your enemies, do good to those who despitefully use you, bless them that curse you. It goes completely against the grain of our natural inclinations of the worlds expectations and of our desire for revenge, but trust me, it is God's way and it works

Rick's Salvation

I was walking down the trail to David and Heidi's one afternoon, when I heard someone weeping. I stopped. I listened as he said, *"Oh God, I didn't know. I just didn't know. I'm so sorry."* It was Rick. I walked a little closer and saw him sitting on a log with a Bible in his hands. *"God, I have been such a wicked man. I am so sorry. I just didn't know."* He didn't see me standing there. He kept repenting and crying out to God, then he turned and saw me standing there. *"Jon. Oh, my God, I am so sorry. I had no idea. Can you ever forgive me?"* I was in shock, but it was a good kind of shock. I said, *"Of course I do!"* I sat next to him on the log and asked him what he was reading. It was the 27th Psalm. We read it together as tears flowed down both our cheeks. He looked at me and said, *"You must have hated me so much."* I looked him right in the eyes and said, *"No Rick, I've always loved you with the love of God. Because honestly that was the only way I could."* We both laughed and cried at the same time about that.

> *The Lord is my light and my salvation; whom shall I fear? The Lord is the defense of my life; whom shall I dread? When evildoers came upon me to devour my flesh, my adversaries and my enemies, they stumbled and fell.*

Though an host encamp against me, my heart will not fear; Though war arise against me, in spite of this I shall be confident. One thing I have asked from the Lord, that I shall seek: that I may dwell in the house of the Lord all the days of my life, to behold the beauty of the Lord and to meditate in His temple, for in the day of trouble He will conceal me in His tabernacle; in the secret place of His tent He will hide me; He will lift me up on a rock. And now my head will be lifted up above my enemies around me, and I will offer in His tent sacrifices with shouts of joy; I will sing, yes, I will sing praises to the Lord. Hear, O Lord, when I cry with my voice, and be gracious to me and answer me. When You said, "Seek My face," my heart said to You, "Your face, O Lord, I shall seek." Do not hide Your face from me, do not turn Your servant away in anger; You have been my help; do not abandon me nor forsake me, O God of my salvation! For my father and my mother have forsaken me, but the Lord will take me up. Teach me Your way, O Lord, and lead me in a level path because of my foes. Do not deliver me over to the desire of my adversaries, for false witnesses have risen against me, and such as breathe out violence. I would have despaired unless I had believed that I would see the goodness of the Lord In the land of the living. Wait for the Lord; Be strong and let your heart take courage; Yes, wait for the Lord. (Psalm 27).

It was the most amazing thing. I was privileged to witness a man, who had previously declared to everyone that he was my mortal enemy, falling on his knees in repentance to God. He was forgiven, justified, and redeemed right there. God had given me the ring side seat. I didn't deserve to be a part of that, but our awesome God made it happen.

What happened after that was even more amazing. We became friends. Rick had never had a real friend in his entire life. He was always a cast off, even his own family had rejected him when he was a small boy. No wonder he was as bitter and angry as he was. He had tons of hurt in him, and as tough as I thought my life was, he had it much worse. At least my parents didn't just kick me out when I was little and force me to survive on the streets. His childhood made mine look positively idyllic.

Pine mushroom season was fast approaching, and it had been a wet summer and fall, perfect conditions for them to *"pop."* Rick had set up a camp about 3kms from Tranquility and I would stop in every morning and pick him up, so we could get to the mushroom patches before anyone else. We did pretty good there for a while. No huge strikes, but we each made a few hundred bucks a day. It was positively cool to be friends with my former enemy. With God, all things ARE possible.

God Moves Mountains, and Bureaucrats

One day, Ralph tracked me down. He wanted me to do a run for him, but he also told me that the government had put a hold on my driver's license because of my unpaid child support debt. This was serious. I prayed about it and I knew I had to get down to the city and deal with it. Without that, as a trucker, I was completely screwed. It was the first week in November when I left.

Another five years had passed since the last time I had fought to keep my driver's license from being seized because of the child support nightmare, and I had to go back to the city once again to deal with it. It was extremely difficult to leave Rick there, but I had no other choice. I headed back to my mom's house in Langley and was once again allowed to sleep in the camper in the back. It wasn't luxury, but with a small heater I did have a warm, dry place to sleep.

My sister Patti and her husband Roger were renting a couple of rooms in my mom's house, so I was *"allowed"* to stay in the old camper out back. I got in touch with the DMV and told them my situation. They said their hands were tied, and I had to get the hold removed from my license by the Family Maintenance Enforcement Program, or FMEP. I wasn't looking forward to dealing with them, but I didn't have much choice. Once I found the woman who oversaw my file I explained to her that I had been living in a bush camp, that I had no access to my children and didn't even know where they were anymore, and that if they didn't allow the renewal of my license, a Class 1 commercial driver's license, then they could forget about ever getting another penny from me since they would have taken away my ability to earn a living. She said she was sympathetic to my problem and would consider it for me. I didn't hold out much hope, but it was my only option. Of course, I was praying for the Lord to intervene. She wasn't the friendliest person I have ever dealt with.

The next week I called and asked to speak with my case worker but was told that she was on sick leave and her replacement would be handling my file. It was an interesting conversation. As believers, we often know when we are talking to another believer simply because *"deep calls unto deep"* as the scripture says. So, after about fifteen minutes on the phone with her I asked her, *"Are you a Christian?"* She answered, *"Yes."* So here I was, on the phone with this woman who was filling in for the one who would usually be assigned to my case, but who had to be off work because of an illness. I told her my entire story, how Sandy left when I got serious about God, how she had completely disappeared with my children and how I didn't even know if they were alive or dead. She said she sympathized with me and would investigate it deeper for me. That was the hand of the Lord working. I talked to her a few days later and she told me that even the FMEP didn't know where she and my children were, so even if I did send them the $400 every month, they didn't have anywhere to send it.

My birthday came and went with no reply from FMEP. My driver's license, and my ability to work, were gone. I wasn't a happy camper. Then three days later, I received a letter from the feminazis at the FMEP telling me they had removed the hold from my driver's license and I could go and renew it.

My children were out there, somewhere, and I took comfort in knowing that God knew exactly where they were. They are His children before they are mine anyway and I knew He would do a far better job of looking after them than I ever could.

I was soon back trucking, this time running team with Ralph. We covered all Western Canada with a set of Super-B trains, hauling steel, lumber, machinery, and even live trees. We had a load of used railroad ties from Swan River Manitoba. We loaded it right to the absolute limit, since we were paid by the number of ties. At 63.500kgs, or 140,000lbs, it was as heavy as it could legally get, once we got back to Alberta and BC., since Manitoba and Saskatchewan's max gross was 62,500kgs. It was early morning and I took the first shift. While Ralph was sleeping, I started the climb up a pretty good grade. It was slow going. With my speed around 30kmh, as fast as it would go with all that weight, I caught a glimpse of something to my left. It was a bull moose, and he was running up the road beside me. I couldn't believe it. Then, he put it in a higher gear and started to pull away from me.

He crossed in front of the truck, ran down into the woods, and disappeared. All I can say is they are big, fast, and built like tanks. One night, Ralph and I were heading to Winnipeg. We left Calgary at a reasonable time with Ralphie behind the wheel, and I fully expected to be a lot farther down the road than we were when I woke up. Man, I was mad. *"What were you doing Ralph? We should have been much closer to The Peg than this. We had to be there by 9:00am and now I won't have time to stop for ANYTHING."* I don't remember what his excuse was, but I wasn't happy about it. I was working for nearly nothing to help him out and here I was expected to break all the rules to get us there on time. Well, only one thing to do. I grabbed my Bible off the dashboard and opened to a random spot. The scripture for the night was, *"He came even unto them, and cometh not again: and the driving is like the driving of Jehu the son of Nimshi; for he driveth furiously."* (2nd Kings 9: 20). It wasn't in context but who cares, it was perfectly timed for my situation and hilarious.

Speaking of Ralph, once when we were on our way to Winnipeg from Calgary, we loaded to the maximum legal weight, for BC and Alberta, 140,000 lbs. or 63,500kgs. Only one problem, back then Saskatchewan and Manitoba had gross weights of 62,500kgs. So, we were about 1000kgs overweight. We were well on our way when we realized our mistake but what could we do, the load was coiled steel and there was nothing we could do to get legal. All that *"legal weight"* was numbers on paper. The *'legal'* weights are harmonized across Canada now anyway. It was my turn to drive as we were heading East.

The snow was blowing sideways across the highway and it was -15C at 8:00am. We were both nervous as I was approaching the Eastbound Scale by Swift Current. Ralph was literally on his knees in the sleeper, praying for us to make it through without being fined, shut down or both. I was about half a kilometer behind a Trimac tanker and saw the sign change from OPEN to CLOSED, right as he pulled in. We rolled right past the scale and made it all the way to Winnipeg without further incident.

Another time God intervened in our trucking adventures was when we were both driving for Dokkside Transport. The owner of the company was known to be as cheap as they get. He made his drivers pay for their own windshield washer fluid. Drivers barely made anything working for him, so they would just put water in them, which would freeze solid at the first cold snap, thus making them useless. One of the other drawbacks of working for such a company was the quality of drivers he attracted. Bottom of the barrel is a good description. From alcoholics who openly drank while driving to heroin addicts, he had quite the crew. The only reason I was there was because God put me there. Dokkside was given many disparaging names by the other drivers on the road due to their high accident rate. Sad to say there were people killed by these idiots he had driving for him, all because he was too cheap to pay to have quality drivers. One of the downsides of working for Doorslide was that the DOT were always looking for them. It didn't matter if you were a good driver or not, if it said Dokkside on the door, they were going to look for anything they could find and give you the tickets. Funny how they punished the drivers, but the owner is not affected, until there is enough tickets that his safety rating is up for review. So there we were, one sunny summer morning, cruising down the road. We had loaded out of Prince George that morning and were scheduled to unload in North Vancouver by 4:30pm that afternoon. In perfect conditions, which we had, it was a nine-hour drive. We had loaded by 7:15am, in two separate trucks, and were drilling it down the highway, without time to stop for anything if we wanted to make it.

I had a VHF scanner in my truck, so I knew what *"The Boys"* (aka, the police and DOT inspectors) were up to. As we were rolling through Clinton, I overheard the DOT on the radio as they were getting ready to set up for truck inspections in Cache Creek, about half an hour away. We knew that two Dokkside trucks would be a prime target, and we didn't have time to stop for their little get together. I got on the CB and told Ralph and his reply was, *"We don't have any choice but to keep moving. Let's pray."* So, we did, right over the radio, *"Dear Lord, You know what's up ahead and how we don't have the time to stop, or the desire to have our pockets looted. If there's any way You can help us get through the inspection, preferably without even having to stop, then let Your will be done. In Jesus Name. Amen."*

We kept rolling towards Cache Creek on that beautiful sunny morning. But then we saw something that was truly amazing. A big, dark cloud was forming over Cache Creek as we were getting closer. Then, about a mile from there, it started to rain, and when we got to Cache Creek it was raining so hard that the two DOT officers were running for their cars using their clipboards as umbrellas. It was awesome! As we rolled by them, they were running for their cars, and they didn't even see us. Then, just as suddenly as it had started, the rain stopped and once we climbed the little hill out of town it was clear blue skies and sunny all the way. Coincidence? I don't believe that for a second. It was a full-blown miracle and powerfully answered prayer.

Clean Up Time

There was a huge cleanup, or salvage logging operation, the next spring. The plan to log our side of the mountain for twenty years was cancelled, since 10,000 hectares, or basically all the lumber mill's timber license for the area was toasted. It was quite a gong show there for a while. There were three heli-logging operations, at least fifteen spar towers, and a few small players with grapple yarders and other small equipment, all working from dawn until dusk every day of the week for months. At one point, I was told that there were around 700 logging truck loads, a day, leaving there. The noise was unbelievable. Helicopters constantly flying. Engine brakes echoing down the hills all around. The horns from the yarding towers. It was unreal. I had to put in ear plugs if I wanted to sleep.

As they were slowly clearing the forest, I was a bit saddened to see it go. I was assured that there was no point in letting the trees stand because they were all dead anyway. Many of them were green and standing and they looked fine, but the fire had burnt around their trunks, so they would all slowly die anyway. After six months of nonstop logging, it was starting to slow down a little. The little patch of forest, about thirty-five hectares around our place was pretty much untouched by the fire, so we were confident that since God had preserved us, the loggers would too. We were wrong. I went for a walk in the forest near my place one morning and saw "FALL BACK LINE" ribbons tied to the trees right next to my house and deep into the unburnt forest around our place. That was it. In righteous indignation, I went around the entire fall back line and pulled the ribbons off every tree. My pockets were bulging with them as I stepped on to Branch 30 Road. I emptied one pocket full and put them in a pile on the ground, then put a big rock on top of them. I was steaming mad. How dare they try to log what God had protected. I figured that someone would be coming to find out what happened, and that what I had done might have been illegal, so I prayed and asked the Lord what I should do. As I searched the Word, I came across an obscure little scripture in Ecclesiastes:

> *There was a small city with few men in it and a great king came to it, surrounded it and constructed large siege works against it. But there was found in that city a poor*

wise man and he delivered the city by his wisdom. Yet no one remembered that poor man. (Ecclesiastes, 9:14,15)

As I prayed, I felt that I should go and act preemptively, so I got in my car and drove to the Ministry of Forests office in Rosedale, about two hours away. I walked into the office and asked if I could look at their maps in the map room. This was before everything was computerized. They had a huge table and large 5' by 10' maps in a large chest. The secretary let me in and a couple of other Forestry employees came in with me, asking which map I needed to see. I told them the Nahatlatch Valley, specifically where the fire of '98 was. They pulled the map out and I took the wad of fall back line ribbons out of my pocket and threw them on the table. *"I'll bet someone is looking for these, right about now,"* I said angrily, *"As I'm sure you all know, the only part of that mountain that wasn't burnt was Tranquility Station and a few acres around it. If God protected that place from a fire, so that even the fire fighters admitted it was a miracle, then there is no way I'm going to just stand here and let the loggers have it. Not going to happen. Call the cops if you want, but there is no way it's happening if I can help it."* Just then, Jim Reid, our local forestry cop, came in. I said, *"Hello Jim, just the man I wanted to see. Can you come over here please?"* I had him come around to the side of the giant map that we were looking at. I pointed to the map and asked him, *"What is the name of that road?"* He hesitated. I asked him again, *"Come on Jim, I know you know it. What is the name of that road?" "Tranquility Road,"* he mumbled. I asked him to say it louder so that everyone could hear him clearly. *"Tranquility Road,"* he said a bit more clearly. I asked him, and everyone else who had gathered in the room, *"So if it's called Tranquility Road, on your own map, why would that be?"* They all kind of shuffled and shrugged, knowing where I was going with this, but not wanting to admit it. I said, *"It's called Tranquility Road because Tranquility Station, unpopular as it might be, was there long before any logging activity was even considered for up there. And you all thought you could just come in there and cut the only trees down that the fire didn't touch."* I was mad by then. They said they would have a meeting about their plan for the area and get back to me. They also told me that they had promised that area to the Native Indian bands in the area and they probably weren't going to be happy. I said I would worry about that later, and if necessary would go to court to settle it. I thanked them for their time and the use of their map room and left.

About a week later, I was awakened by a knock at my door. I got up, looking like the long-haired freak I had become by then, and answered the door. It was Jim Reid and the local Native Indian Chiefs from the local reserves they had mentioned in our meeting in their office. I recognized one of them right away, Sonny. I had met him through James and he seemed like a down to earth guy. I didn't know the others, but Sonny seemed to be able to speak for them. He said, *"Hello Jon. I thought it might be you who we would be talking to. Sorry to get you up so early."* "No problem Sonny, good to see you my friend," I replied as we shook hands. Jim started to tell us how they wanted to settle this in a fair way and I agreed. He said they had been given twenty-five hectares of the salvage permit and that meant our place. It was a touchy situation. I didn't want to get on the natives' bad side, but there was no way they were logging our little patch of forest. Then Jim suggested a compromise. He would make sure that all the big firs and cedars that were 50cm and bigger across the butt and bigger would be left and they would only log what was smaller. Realizing that most of the trees there were that big anyway, I agreed. Sonny was happy and so were the rest of the chiefs. Jim Reid was relieved, and I felt that a fair compromise was reached. *"And yet no one remembered that poor man."* I never stopped praying for my children.

I Need A Bath

After years of sponge baths and cold creek dips, I decided that I needed a bathtub. David and Heidi had a tub with a fire box underneath it and a fire heated tank for the water. It was lovely, but it was theirs, and it was just an awful lot of trouble to use. I needed my own. I prayed and asked the Lord for a tub. It didn't have to be fancy, it just had to be a bathtub. I can't remember who it was that asked me to take them to town one day, but off to Boston Bar we went. As I was getting a run at Horseshoe Turn hill, we zipped past the dump, and there it was, right at the entrance, a bathtub. I said it had better be there when we got back. It was. We loaded it into the truck and hauled it home. It was heavy, and since there was no real road to my place then, we had to carry it up the hill. I set it off to the side and began the task of building a small shack to put it in.

I had been hauling over dimensional green lumber and the dunnage for those loads was 10ft long. Perfect. I collected the nicer dunnage from every load until I had about twenty lengths. I roughed out the frame for the floor, levelled it on some rocks, and got to work. I had lots of 8ft dunnage as well, so I decided to make it 8x8x8ft., with a 10ft overhang for the roof. I was getting right into it when I came to a small impasse. I didn't want any trusses for my roof because I wanted to have a usable loft above it. That meant having a ridge beam. I wasn't much of a carpenter, so the angle thing was a bit of a challenge to me.

I managed to cut a few 2x4's on the right angle to the ridge board. I had a ridge board. I built some scaffolding out of some barrels and some planks. I had it all up there, ready to be nailed together, except for one small problem: I needed four hands to hold the boards and to nail them together. I tried a couple of different ways, but it was hopeless. It was getting late anyways, so I called it a night.

The next morning, I had my time in the Word and some prayer time. I knew what was waiting for me at the bathhouse project and the last thing I said to the Lord was, *"You know what I need, I'm not going to tell you how to do it."* I walked up to the bathhouse, strapped on my tool belt, climbed up the scaffold, held the pieces of lumber up to where they were supposed to go, wondering how I was going to do this, and then I heard a voice saying, *"Hey buddy, you need a hand with that?"* Keep in mind that this place is in the middle of nowhere. The few others around slept until noon and were still counting sheep. This stranger just came up the hill, climbed up the scaffolding, grabbed the pieces of wood and said, *"Okay, I got this end, nail her up."* I stood there for a second, my jaw hanging, before I declared to him, *"Buddy, you are an answer to prayer."* He was like, *"I don't think so pal. But whatever, glad I was here to help."* Ladies and gentlemen, meet Eddie Albright.

As we were standing on the scaffolding nailing the ridge board and rafters together, I couldn't stop grinning and praising God for sending Eddie at the exact, perfect time. I kept telling him what an answer to prayer he was, but he didn't want to have anything to do with it. I just said to him, *"Too bad buddy, you just are."*

It turned out that he was a pine mushroom picker and that he had heard from someone that it was good picking up around our area. He had driven as far as the beaver pond late the night before and stopped to sleep. When he woke up the next day, his battery was dead. So, seeing the obvious signs of vehicle traffic, he walked on up the road, where he saw my van parked and he simply followed the trail to where I was. He was on his way, while I was praying for help. Truly, God answers our prayers while we are praying.

He asked if I could give him a jump start and normally I would have, but I was using the battery from my van for some 12-volt lights in my treehouse and it was a big job to haul it back to the van, put it in, then go jump start his car, drive back up and haul the battery back to my treehouse. I told him, *"If you want, you can just borrow the battery to start your car, then bring it back when you are done."* I didn't know this guy, so I told him that God was watching him, so he better come back with my battery. I unhooked my house from the battery and he took it down to his car by the beaver pond. About an hour later, he was back, his car running and my battery back in its place in the house. He then helped me with my bath house project. As we worked, I kept telling him that God had brought him there for a purpose, that it wasn't an accident that his car died where it did, and that he needed Jesus. He was not into hearing that message at all. He was adamant that there was no God and he had no intention of ever believing in one.

Still, he was a likeable little fellow. He had a sense of humor and was full of funny stories. It was about 10:00am when he announced that he was going to his car to get a beer and asked me if I wanted one. I hadn't touched alcohol of any kind for eight years and didn't have any desire for it then, especially at 10 in the morning. So, he came back up to the bath house, sat down and proceeded to drink beer. I had dealt with lots of characters up there, so I wasn't going to judge the guy. But some guy standing there getting drunk while I was trying to get my project finished was a bit trying. He started to tell me all about his hemorrhoid problems. Wonderful. He couldn't sit down. He had problems *"going."* He hated his doctor. He needed another operation to fix the problems from the last one. Basically, everything you could imagine from having problems with hemorrhoids. Not my idea of good conversation. As he got more into his beer, he started to tell me his story.

Almost Started A War With The USA

It would have been in the late eighties when this incident happened. It was near the Portland canal, the fiord that separates BC and Alaska. The 200-mile limit applies from there out into the Pacific Ocean, mainly to delineate the border for keeping American and Canadian fishing boats on their respective sides of the border.

The Coast Guard from each country regularly patrols that area to keep everyone honest, and on their respective sides. Eddie Albright was the First Mate on one of those Canadian Coast Guard vessels. It was the early morning watch, about 2:00am, when he noticed some American fishing boats drifting into Canadian waters. He got on the radio and reported it to the American Coast Guard ship near him. Their reply, *"So what are you going to do about it."* Trying to remain professional, he simply repeated his original statement about their ships drifting into Canadian territory. Once again, they replied, *"So what? Tough luck,"* and other less than nice things. He then threatened them, *"If you don't get your boats back on your side of the line I will be forced to take action."*

"What are you going to do you dumb Canuck?"

"If you force my hand, I will fire a shot across your bow."

"You wouldn't dare," came the reply from the Americans. Eddie went below deck to where the Captain was sleeping and woke him up, telling him what was happening. Instead of getting up and taking charge, he just mumbled, *"Do whatever you think is right soldier,"* and rolled over and went back to sleep. Eddie went back up on deck and saw that even more American fishing boats had drifted into Canadian waters. He again requested that the USCG get their ships back on their rightful side of the line. They made farting noises over the radio in response. He then told them if they didn't honor his request, he would be forced to fire a shot across their bow. They laughed at him.

He ordered the 50mm gun on the deck to be loaded with a single tracer round. He then advised them that his gun was now loaded, and he made one more attempt to get them to call their boats back to their side. He figured they must have been drunk because they all took turns calling him names, taunting him, and making rude noises over the radio. He declared, *"You have left me no alternative. Prepare to be fired upon."* There was silence on the radio, until once again they started to taunt him saying, *"You wouldn't dare."* He said, *"I have been as patient and as reasonable as a man can be under these circumstances. You are going to be fired upon in one minute, unless you act towards calling your ships back."* By then even the people on the American fishing boats were on the radio saying that he was just bluffing, and they were generally being rude.

He then announced, *"You have been given more than enough opportunities to do the right thing. You are being fired upon, NOW."*

He gave the order to fire the 50mm tracer across the bow of the American Coast Guard ship. At that moment, Eddie Albright had become the first Canadian to fire at an American since the war of 1812. As you can imagine, this sparked an international incident, with the ambassadors from both countries issuing statements to the press. I can remember hearing about this on the news when I was in my early twenties.

It seemed the Canadian Government did not have Eddie's back in the matter and he was promptly drummed out of the Coast Guard and put ashore in Prince Rupert BC. At least they didn't hang him or put him in the brig. He found himself unemployed and without the ability to collect Unemployment Insurance benefits because of how he was let go. Someone told him about how they were making great money picking pine mushrooms up in the Nass Valley north of there, so he gave it a try. He did very well at it. He had become quite the expert Pine Mushroom harvester, until he fell off a cliff and hurt his back. He was laid up in the hospital for a while and it was there that he developed a taste for prescription drugs. His back was messed up, so he was taking the drugs and drinking a few beers to cope with the pain. Unfortunately, the beer made him a bit psychotic.

I had stopped working on the bath house and was sitting there with my jaw on the floor. What a story! I had the only Canadian who had ever fired on an American in an undeclared act of war sitting in my bath house having a beer at 10:30 in the morning. I remember thinking how strange that was, but then I felt like God had brought him there for him to hear the Gospel, and I was the guy who had the job.

He went down to his car to get more beer but came back in a panic about an hour later telling me he lost his keys. He went for a walk around the camp and had met Heidi and some of the others, then, when he went to get in his car to leave, he couldn't find his keys. He was clearly panicking, mainly because his beer was in the trunk and he couldn't get to it. He said, *"I don't care if I have to take a crow bar to the trunk. I'm getting at my beer."*

Never mind driving anywhere, he just wanted the beer. I had an old key ring from my dad that had just about every kind of key you could think of on it, so I lent it to him to see if there was one on there from the GM keys that would open his doors and or start his car. Wouldn't you know it, there was a key on there that let him open his doors and trunk, but not one to start his car. So, he was stuck until we could figure something out, find his keys or something. But hey, at least he could get to his beer.

There he was, stuck sitting at the fire pit in the Summer Kitchen, listening to a bunch of Jesus freaks. He was clearly uncomfortable, but he couldn't go anywhere. God had him there for a reason. He interrupted our conversation a few times to tell us how sore his butt was and how he needed a new hemorrhoid operation because the last one didn't work. It was getting old, fast. I saw how the poor guy had gone as far as he could in his flesh and his own strength. It was obvious the Lord had brought him to us.

The next day, he was right back up at my place, drinking beer and talking about hemorrhoids. He was constantly offering me a beer, but I kept refusing. I was starting to get a little tired of the story. I went to take a leak and as I was standing there I prayed, *"Lord, I know you brought this guy here to hear the gospel, but he just doesn't seem to be getting it. I pray for his salvation and that You would open the door to his heart so that he would hear and understand and be saved."* I went back to working on the bath house while he talked about hemorrhoids. I avoided the Summer Kitchen that night because I didn't think I could take another minute of hearing about his hemorrhoids.

The next morning, as I was sitting there doing my morning devotionals, I felt the Holy Spirit telling me to go and have a beer with Eddie. I was sure it was a bad connection. I prayed, *"There must be some mistake Lord. I don't drink anymore."* I just couldn't shake the feeling that I was supposed to go have a beer with him. I tried to work on the bath house, but nothing was coming together, so I finally gave up and went down to the Summer Kitchen. I found Eddie with a beer in hand, sitting by himself, since David and Heidi were still in bed. I said, *"Hey Eddie. I decided to take you up on your offer."*

"My what?" he replied.

"A beer. I would like a beer please." He looked at me kind of sideways and then said, *"Okay, but I only have a few left."*

"No problem buddy. I only want one." He opened a beer and handed it to me. My first beer in eight years, at 10:00 in the morning. It wasn't long before he started to tell me his hemorrhoid story.

That beer hit me hard and my head was spinning as the hemorrhoid story was told once again. I finished the beer and was wondering what it was all about when he offered me another one. I hesitated but thought, why not, I still haven't shared the gospel with him yet. So, there I am, on my second beer and it was not even eleven in the morning yet.

As Eddie was going on about his hemorrhoids, I waved my hands in his face and stopped him. I said, *"Eddie! Stop! I have something that I have to tell your heart. Your head probably won't get it, but your heart will."* He sat there, kind of stunned. *"Eddie, Jesus was born of a virgin. He lived a perfect sinless life. He was crucified for our sins. He rose from the dead, and He's coming back again. Now, what were you saying about hemorrhoids?"* He looked at me and said, *"Hey! You can't do that."*

"Do what?" I asked.

"What you just did. You can't do that."

I said, *"I was talking to your heart Eddie. That is what needed to hear that."* He was still just kind of staring at me, shaking his head, then he started talking about his butt problems again. I had no idea if what I said had done any good, but I thought what the heck, why not have another beer.

I asked him for another beer and he started to get all defensive saying he only had about forty left and didn't want me to make a habit out it. I assured him that I wasn't ever going to ask him for another beer. I finished that third beer and staggered back up the trail. As soon as I got home, I passed out for most of the afternoon.

Later that day, as I was working away on the bath house, someone came up to my place and told me that Ralph was there and he needed me to co-drive for him. So, I packed up my stuff, got my travel bag together and went down to the Summer Kitchen. When I got there, Ralph, who was a big old boy and who liked to wear his ball cap low over his eyes like a drill sergeant, was grilling Eddie, asking him if he was a Christian. Eddie shot back, *"I'm a Tranquility Christian."* I was shocked. Ralph asked, *"What the heck is a Tranquility Christian?"* He said, *"That's right, you big oaf, a Tranquility Christian, because WE LOVE EACH OTHER."* Eddie looked right at me and said, *"My heart heard every word you said this morning."* I assured Ralph that it was good and we could just go. I hugged Eddie and said, *"God bless you Brother,"* then we were off.

When I got home a few weeks later, Eddie was long gone. A few of the folks there were talking about how big a change the Lord had made in him before he left. He found a key that worked in his ignition and he had to hit the road. He said he would be back soon. Years went by, but there never was another sign of Eddie. I was seriously doubting that what I had witnessed was in fact true. Then I stopped at the mailbox one day and there was a letter from Eddie Albright, Oyster Bay, BC. I didn't open it, until I got back to David and Heidi's place. It read, to the best of my recollection,

> *Dear Jon, David, Heidi and crew,*
>
> *I just wanted to let you all know that I'm blessed and doing Okay.*

Two years ago, if someone would have told me I would be reading a concordance and studying Hebrew, Greek, and Chaldea, I probably would have hit them. But here I am, studying the Word and praising God for Jesus Christ.

I was just diagnosed with a very aggressive form of cancer and probably won't be around for much longer, but I wanted to let you all know that I love you, pray for you and think about you all always. In Christ, Eddie Albright.

Ask and You Will Receive

The bath house was such a blessing. It was awesome to be able to soak in that hot water after a day of sweating and getting dirty from building. There was only one problem, it didn't have any windows. I had made the cardinal mistake of *'reaction'* building; I had framed for windows that I didn't have.

One evening as I was laying in the tub looking at the incredible view but having just about every bug in the woods landing in the tub and flopping around until they drowned, I prayed. I said, *"Lord, thank you for this incredible bathtub. I am so grateful for it and want You to know how much I appreciate it. But there's this little problem. It needs windows badly. I'm sorry to bother You about this but could I please have some?"* I got descriptive of exactly what I wanted. *"Forgive me for trying to tell You what they should be, and I'm not getting out of the tub to measure the exact size I need, because I know You already know that, but if they could be tempered, tinted and double glazed that would be awesome. Anyways, thank You Lord that you know exactly the size I need."* I drifted off to sleep.

Since they had dumped tons of nitrogen all over the place during the forest fire, the miner's lettuce was exploding all over the place too. Miners lettuce is a wild, delicious plant that grows there. Roy had a connection with a guy who bought all kinds of wild and exotic plants and mushrooms and he was buying as much miner's lettuce and stinging nettle as we could supply him with. The only problem was Roy and his inability to be on time for anything.

We had picked a huge load and had to be in Richmond, about 3 1/2 hours away, by 11am Tuesday mornings. Because of his procrastination, we were late one Tuesday. The buyer was mad because he had orders that couldn't be filled because the plane had to leave without the product on it. He was mad at me and I was livid with Roy, who just didn't seem to get it. He said it was God's will that we were late. I wanted to smite him in his hinder parts. We went back to camp, still loaded with miner's lettuce.

Truckers were having a protest at the Canada/US truck crossing and the truckers had shut the border down, so we couldn't get to Zero Ave, which was our short cut. Forced to take the long way, we found ourselves fighting the useless road system that is Greater Vancouver. We took a side road to get away from the traffic and as we were going along, I caught a glimpse of some windows leaning up against a telephone pole. I did a U-turn and went back to get a closer look. As we were approaching them, I told Roy that these were the windows I had been praying for the other night. As soon as I saw them, I knew that they were perfect; tinted, double glazed and tempered. They were about the right size, so we loaded them into the van, without an inch to spare, and away we went.

When I got home, I took a piece of twine and took a rough measurement, then walked up to the bath house and sure enough, they were the exact same size as the opening. God had answered my prayer. I installed them right away and had baths without bugs. God is so good to us, even when we don't deserve it.

A few days later, I was laying in the tub, thanking God for how good He was to me, "Thank You Lord for how wonderful You are to me. I love you so much. This bath house is such a blessing to me. But You know, I sure could use a few bucks. I'll leave that up to You too, since I know You know what I need better than I do. In Jesus name, amen."

The next morning, I decided to clean up my mess from the construction of the bath house. I was picking up little pieces of 2x4 and stuff when I heard a loud *"CRACK."* I spun around to see what made the noise and there they were, three huge male deer standing about fifteen feet from me. I cried out, *"Lord! What is this?"* I heard His still small voice reply, *"You did ask me for a few bucks last night."* I couldn't believe it and I cracked up right there. God has a sense of humor, and He can be incredibly corny too. I laughed at how He had answered my prayer.

Bye-Bye Treehouse

As I was getting into the routine of doing the weekend run to pick up loaded trailers, another Friday was upon me and I headed out at about 9am. It was an uneventful drive down to the Valley. I went to the Dokkside office and got my check, then headed up to their bank to cash it. I bought some road food, then headed back to the yard to wait for a tractor to be available. It was then that the dispatcher told me that, for various reasons, none of the trailers had been loaded that day, so there was no trip that weekend. I wasn't planning on that.

I decided to head into the city and see David's brother Mike. He was always fun to hang around and I hadn't seen him in a while. I got there in the midafternoon and he invited me to stay for dinner. His father-in-law was there too, so there was lots of food. His father-in-law was one freaky dude. He was a Hell's Angel who owned his own limousine service and a store that sold grow op equipment. It was like sitting at the table with satan, only he had some manners.

After dinner, I decided to head back up the mountain. I stopped at the grocery store and picked up the usual, one of everything for me, one for David and Heidi. Again, it was an uneventful drive home, until I got to the beaver pond. I could smell burnt plastic. There was one rule we all kept up there and that was to never burn plastic, so I was a bit upset at whoever had.

My first stop was, as usual, at David and Heidi's to drop off the groceries that I picked up for them. I wanted to know who had been burning plastic and when I walked into their cabin, that was the first question I asked. Everyone was sitting there looking very morose, like someone had just died. So, I asked, *"Did someone die? Why are you all looking so sad?"* No one said a word. I asked again, *"What's wrong with everyone?"* Finally, Richard Barton spoke up and said, *"Your house burned to the ground today Jon."*

"Oh, is that all?" I asked before the news penetrated my brain.

"Wait a minute, did you just say that my house burnt down today?"

Someone said, *"Actually, it was a treehouse, so it burnt up."* I guess I was in shock as I stood there letting this news sink in. David was sitting in his bed. Roy was sitting there with his head hung down. Heidi was, as always, making coffee and cooking something. Richard Barton had just come up for the weekend and was standing there looking sad too. *"So, how much of it burned?"* I asked. *"Everything,"* answered Roy. Someone mentioned that it would have been much worse if it hadn't been raining so hard that day. Then, there was silence for a bit until David spoke up and said, *"It was the sound of exploding propane tanks that woke me up."* I had three freshly filled twenty pounders in there and lots of ammo and a can of black powder.

There were a few things that would have made for some big bangs. *"Everything,"* I repeated as I sat down once the full impact had settled on me. I didn't have much to say. The others started talking, but I couldn't even hear them. I prayed silently to God, *"Why Lord? How? There wasn't anything there to start the fire. I guess I'm finished here then? Where do I go from here? I didn't have much, but it was all I had. Why Lord?"* I curled up on David and Heidi's couch and fell asleep.

I woke up at around 7am and went outside to take care of business. The smell of the burnt plastic still hung in the air. I didn't have anything to go and get, and I had no interest in seeing what was left. I got in my van and drove away from there, not intending to ever come back.

Once I got to Boston Bar, I sat at the crossroads and prayed. I thought I might as well go to the Okanogan and see Greg. He was living in a house full of students and had always had a spot for me to sleep. I got there around 3pm and they were all glad to see me. I told them what happened, and they were all genuinely saddened and concerned. As I was explaining it, things began to come clear in my mind. There were no combustibles. There was no electricity. The fire was out, since I didn't start it again before I left in the morning. Then it hit me, someone torched it. That was not a comforting thought. The only conclusion was that someone hated me enough to burn me out. As my mind was wandering and grasping to make sense of it, I heard the old Hymn, *"It is well with my soul."* The brother who wrote that glorious old hymn had just found out that his wife and three daughters had been killed in a shipwreck. I had just lost a treehouse. I tried to keep that perspective so that I didn't get swallowed up in self-pity.

Greg announced that they were all going to the Tragically Hip concert that night, but they didn't have enough tickets for me to go. I wasn't a big secular music fan anyway, so I didn't mind. After they left, I simply read my Bible and prayed, having that peace that passes all understanding. About half an hour later Malcom, Greg's roommate, came in and asked me if I wanted to go to the concert. Why not, I thought. It turned out that Malcom discovered that asking two girls to the same show wasn't a good idea, so one dumped him and that left him with an extra ticket. His pain, my gain.

When we arrived at the show, it was obvious that lots of folks were gladly smoking pot. Just standing there on the upper balcony was enough to get me stoned. I wasn't into it, but at least it was better than sitting back at their house feeling sorry for myself. I didn't know any of the songs, I didn't even know anything about the band aside from hearing their name in passing. When the first song ended, and everyone was on their feet cheering, I thought just sitting there feeling glum wasn't going to be fruitful, so I got on my feet and started to praise God at the top of my lungs. Everyone was making so much noise that no one could discern what I was saying, in the natural. There was one chick who was a few rows down who spun around and glared at me. I smiled and waved knowing that the demons could hear me, and I didn't care. Less than 24 hours after finding out that my treehouse had been burnt to the ground, I was at a rock concert where I was praising God as loudly as I could. It was surreal to say the least.

I stayed at their house for a few more days until I figured I had better get back to the Valley for my Friday departure to pick up loaded trailers somewhere. That was still happening and who knew where that could lead. I was thinking that since I was now completely homeless, at least I could live in a truck and make some money at the same time.

As I drove over the Coquihalla Hwy, I had the distinct feeling that something was wrong with the van. I stopped on the side of the road and checked things over but couldn't see anything wrong. I got back in and headed down the big hill called The Smasher. As I was rolling along at a clip fast enough to keep pace with the trucks, I had that feeling that something wasn't right. I had gone probably another 30kms when I decided to pull over once more. As I put my turn signal on and started to pull on to the shoulder, the driver's side of the van dropped to the ground as my tire kept on going. It bounced across the exit and over the bank, just narrowly missing a tow truck that was sitting there.

I got out of the van to take stock of the situation, fully aware that only a minute before I could have had that happen at 110KMH. The tow truck driver went to look for my tire and rim and found it. He came back up with it and said that he could tow me into Hope where I could get it fixed. I said thanks for finding the tire, but I don't have any money, so I couldn't afford to have him do anything. He wasn't too pleased since he had just gone and rescued my tire. Once again, I had to think on my feet and improvise. What had happened was the wheel nuts had backed off and the wheel was loose on the studs. The holes in the wheel had finally been worn out enough to fit right over them and, when I touched the brakes, the wheel came off. I had a spare tire and rim. The nuts, as screwed up as the threads were, were still there on the studs. I had my star wrench and I proceeded to remove each nut, painfully and slowly because they were almost welded to the studs and because I had to keep the brake drum on the ground, so I could turn them. It took a while, but I eventually got them all off. I jacked up the van and put the spare tire on. It took a while to screw the nuts back on because of how badly chewed up the threads were, but I got it on tight. I got in the van and drove away, waving to the tow truck driver as I pulled back on to the freeway.

Since I didn't have anywhere to go and was again homeless, I remembered that Roy told me he was renting a room at a house in Chilliwack. I tracked him down and the fellow that owned the place was glad to let me sleep on the couch. I should be perfectly honest, this being homeless stuff does get old after a while. Jesus said that the Son of Man had nowhere to lay His head, so maybe I shouldn't complain too loudly.

Staying at that house was challenging for many reasons. Not the least being that the owners two teenage kids were out of control. His daughter was 17 going on 37 and was not a believer. His son was around 15 and was a little hoodlum. He and his friends made it a game to steal from my bags while I slept. I didn't have much, but they managed to take what little I had.

We never know who is going to land on our door step. One sunny summer afternoon as I was puttering about the place, one of the worst choices in friends of my life showed up with a couple of guests.

When I was doing the weekend, trailer pick up thing, I picked up the occasional hitchhiker. I always used it as an opportunity to share the Gospel. One Sunday afternoon as I was headed through Quesnel BC, I spotted a young man thumbing so I pulled over and picked him up. He kind of resembled the son of my friend Matt, the fellow I drove for when the cattle truck hit me. Anyway, he climbed in to the cab and it was obvious right away that he wasn't who I thought he was. Now, most of these Hell's Angels kids have a certain look. They are hunched over a bit, walk with a swagger and are generally rude. This kid was no exception. He wasn't very talkative, so I figured, why not, let's give him the Gospel. I preached at this poor young man for hours, not letting the demons in him have a word. He slunk down in his seat and listened, albeit not willingly. I figured that since I had to stop and take a break anyway that I would put feet to my faith and buy him lunch and there was no way I was leaving a stranger in the cab of my truck without me being there. He seemed grateful for the meal and began to open up a bit. His name was Chris, and he confirmed my suspicions when he told me that he was raised by Hell's Angels and he was on the run because they had threatened to kill him. For what he wouldn't say. Great, I have a fugitive from the HA riding around in my truck. I thought about ending his ride right there, but I felt like the Holy Spirit wanted me to help him.

We got back in the truck and he wasn't a bad kid. I kind of liked him. As he opened up about his life, it was obvious why the Lord had me pick him up. He had never heard the Good News of Jesus before, not even a little bit. As I explained his need for a Saviour, a light went on. He seemed to get it. It was amazing as he was asking all the right questions and saying that it must have been God who arranged this ride.

I had to get the rig down to Abbotsford, so we went straight through, arriving there around 6pm. I asked him where he was going from there and he said he didn't know. I thought, I can't just share the Gospel with this kid and dump him, he needed to be around real Christians. I offered to bring him up to Tranquility Station and he readily accepted. We arrived there around midnight. I threw a foamy on the floor for him and we crashed.

The next morning, I gave him the tour of the place, so he could meet everyone. He was a very polite and well-mannered young man, which surprised me considering his background. He seemed to fit right in up there and it was amazing to see him wanting to learn as much as he could about God. He had me and everyone else completely fooled.

It turned out that the little bugger was quite the psychopath. He was charming, funny, clever and would rob you blind when he had the chance. Little things went missing, but I put it down to my absent mindedness. Then others started to mention that they were having a hard time finding things. There were some other questionable characters coming and going from there around that time, so no-one could pin anything on anyone. Besides, the scriptures tell us not to think evil of others. Not only that, but I was of the mindset that everything I had belonged to God anyway, so if something was stolen, they stole it from God, not me. Chris started to come and go quite freely. He brought some very questionable people up there and I was regretting ever picking him up in the first place. Which brings me to where I started this story.

That afternoon as I was puttering around my place, Chris showed up with two strangers. It was a hot day and I needed a break anyway, and there was no way I was going to trust this guy to go into my house without me being able to keep an eye on him. He told me that he was hitchhiking out of the Fraser Valley when he was picked up by the cowboy, who was one of my new guests. As they were going along they stopped and picked up another hitchhiker, who was my other new guest. They both seemed like okay guys and they introduced themselves. The cowboy was heading back to his parents' home in the interior after being disillusioned by the outright nastiness of Vancouver. He had been robbed and beaten and just wanted to go home. The other fellow had a thick Irish accent and introduced himself as Jerry.

Jerry asked me if I had a cassette player. I pointed to the one I had from the dump and he asked if he could play a tape in it. I thought sure, why not. *"What is it?"* I asked. He proceeded to tell me about songs he was strictly forbidden to listen to in his home land of Ireland. He said he could go to prison for just having that tape. I asked him what it was about that tape that was so bad. He explained, *"This has been the strangest journey in my life. The house that I was staying in Ireland just three days ago was just blown up by the British Army. All my friends that I left there were either killed or arrested."* I stood there stunned. "For what?" I asked. He said, *"Have you ever heard of the Irish Republican Army? Well, I'm part of the leadership. The other day, as I was sitting there having tea, I heard a voice telling me to leave Ireland, and specifically that house, right away. The voice was so real that I was surprised that no one was there. I had no idea where to go but I had a friend and his wife who lives in Toronto, so I got on a plane. I landed there and took a cab to their house but there was no one home. I asked their neighbor and he said that they were away on vacation. So, I got a cab back to the airport and got on a plane for Vancouver, just because I've never been there before. I got a hotel room last night and when I woke up this morning, I decided to hitch hike around and lay low. That's when your friends picked me up and here I am. Is it okay if I play my tape now?"* We stood there, and if no one else was, I was shocked. What a story, there was no way it was true. I heard so many BSer's that I was getting jaded from the stories by then. Then he played the tape. It was true Irish rebel music. I can't remember the lyrics, but they did strike me as rather violent. My new friend, Jerry, was standing in my treehouse with his hand over his heart, crying as he listened to his tape. The rest of us just looked at each other, not knowing what to make of it. I let him listen to both sides of his tape and he said he was eternally thankful. Eternity, I thought. I wondered if these men had ever heard the Gospel. Being bold in my faith, and sensing that God had arranged this little meeting, I began to share Jesus.

The Gospel does a few things to people. The demons that are riding around on their hosts usually don't like it. I asked Jerry and the cowboy if they knew that Jesus had died for their sins. The cowboy said his parents go to church all the time and that he had heard it. It didn't take long to realize he was doing the prodigal thing and that his parents had probably been praying like crazy for their lost son. Jerry said he believed in God but didn't know anything about Him. He said that the Pope was supposed to be God's Vicar, but he had his doubts about that. Now honestly, I had little to no idea who or what the IRA was. I didn't know then that they were a militant group of Catholics. I started to share the gospel with these fellows and they both seemed eager to hear it, but Chris wasn't. It was as if he was possessed and he couldn't get out of my house fast enough. I continued to share the Gospel as I followed them to the cowboy's pickup. My audience wasn't in a hurry to leave, but Chris was making such a fuss that they decided to leave.

Did the cowboy, Chris and Jerry ever get saved? I have no idea. But the Lord thought it would be a cool way to open the door.

The Sons of Belial

It always surprises me how few of the brethren, elders included, have never heard of these people spoken of in the Old Testament. They are mentioned in four places; Judges 19: 22, 1st Samuel 2: 12, 2nd Samuel 23: 6 and 1st Kings 21. In every instance, they are worthless fellows. They are sodomites, idolaters, liars, takers of bribes and false witnesses. Not the kind of folks you want to have as neighbors. Well, guess who moved in down the hill.

I had met Jimmy briefly, a few years earlier, but had no idea who he was or what his connection was to Tranquility Station or David, in particular. As it turned out, he was a very troubled child who was raised in North Bend, the son of a logger who was the town drunk and a bully. Jimmy's apple fell directly under that tree and he was the same as his father.

David had befriended him way back in the early days when he was still a teenager and had invited him up to help him. David's philosophy was that if you weren't against the Lord, you were for Him, so little Jimmy was included in the founding of Tranquility Station.

He was hated and despised by the folks in North Bend, so he was more than happy to have David as a friend. David tried to share the love of God and the plan of Salvation with him, but he just went along, not ever taking any of it seriously. He was as nasty as ever, as some of the residents of North Bend confided in me years later. Like most people like him, he was eventually forced to leave because of his own doings.

I don't know how or when he arrived in Hope, but while he was there, he met Sue. Sue was a Jewish girl and she was head over heels in love with Jimmy. She overlooked all his faults and they began living together. They had three children, Tyler, Rhonda, and Jordan. I met Jimmy and Tyler when he came up to get an engine out of an old car. That was during my first fall up there in '96 and they were only there for the day. I knew something was wrong when Jimmy passed a joint to Tyler, who was eight at the time. He said he would rather have his kids smoking weed with him than with strangers. I have heard that before, and even though I don't agree with the use of drugs, I guess it is better to get stoned with your dad than some stranger. Little Tyler was also smoking cigarettes then as well. Nice family.

The next time I met Jimmy was in the summer of 2002. He had decided to move his entire family up to Tranquility. I had no idea what we were in for. Right away he started to push himself around and I was instantly at odds with him. Neither he or his entire family had even a rudimentary clue about the Lord and what Tranquility Station was about, nor did they care. He began to bully the weaker folks who were there, threatening them and generally picking on them until they became uncomfortable and left.

Beware of the wolves who will come in unawares and destroy the flock. One by one they left, but the Lord had given me a very simple set of instructions early on in my time there. "Stand. And having done all, STAND." Let me tell you, it is always easier to move when things get uncomfortable, but the Lord's instructions to me were very clear. No matter how tough it gets, you are not the one who is leaving Jon.

Pretty soon, he had a derelict vehicle in every driveway as part of his plan to take over the camp. It was obvious that he had no intention of playing nice. I saw how David and Heidi's addiction to tobacco prevented them from standing up to him, because they were dependent on him for cigarettes and other supplies. I saw the seeds of destruction being sown in the camp but was helpless to stop it from running its course. I tried to explain what I saw was happening to the place to David and Heidi, but it all fell on deaf ears.

I read something that made all the nasty, ungodly and just plain demonic people there make sense. It was supposed to be a true story and I will do my best to recall it. In the mid 1800's, there was a huge push to build railroads that spanned the continent of North America. One such railroad had planned to terminate in San Francisco. The owner of the railroad sent his son to oversee the project as they built from West to East, planning to meet somewhere in the middle. He was a typical New Yorker snob. He went to a restaurant and ordered salmon for dinner. Upon receiving it, he disdainfully sniffed at it and declared, *"This isn't Atlantic salmon"* and refused to eat it. He then ordered his staff to get him some Atlantic salmon. Now this was the mid 1800's and the logistical challenge was nearly impossible. He declared that, *"Money was no object. Just get me my Atlantic salmon."*

They all tried to think of how to accomplish this seemingly impossible task when someone said, *"Hey, why don't we commission a ship from New York, fill it with salmon in special holds filled with ice and sail it there?"* It sounded good, so that is what they did. There was no Panama Canal back then, so the only way was around the tip of South America and all the way back up the West coast, a trip that took six weeks if conditions were favorable.

When the ship sailed into San Francisco harbor six weeks later, the harbor master immediately ordered the ship to be taken out to sea and sunk. It seems that the ice had all melted by the time they were off the coast of Brazil and they intended to continue, hoping to get paid. I have no idea if they ever did.

Little lord Fauntleroy was mad. He had just spent a fortune for nothing and was the butt of jokes about stinking fish. He ordered his men to try again. They thought about it for a while and decided that their mistake was to ship dead fish. They thought that if the fish were alive during the trip they would arrive in much better shape. So, once again, they commissioned a ship from New York to be built with water tight holds designed to hold live Atlantic salmon. They caught the fish live, loaded them into the holds and set sail, once again, for San Francisco. Six or so weeks later it arrived. This time it didn't smell too bad and they unloaded the fish into live tanks. They didn't look to healthy, so they found the best ones and cooked them up for his nibs. He was eagerly anticipating his long awaited for Atlantic salmon, but when he took a bite, he was soon disappointed. *"This fish is mushy,"* he bellowed. *"Can't you idiots do anything right?"*

Back to the drawing board. They were at a complete loss as to how to get him his fresh fish when someone said, *"The catfish is the natural enemy of Atlantic salmon, so why don't we get another ship with live holding tanks and put some catfish in with them?"* I guess they all thought it was a stroke of genius, so they did just that.

Six weeks later the ship sailed into the port of San Francisco and a few hours after that the rich New Yorker had a plate of fresh Atlantic salmon. It was firm and tender, just like he wanted it. The moral of this story? The devil and his minions are like those catfish in our tanks. The Lord allows them in our tank to keep us moving and to stop us from getting mushy, or worse yet, to stink. Suddenly, it all made sense. God allowed these characters to be there to keep me from getting soft. It was a nonstop challenge to rebuke, exhort and pray. I saw so many demons manifesting that it looked like they were winning, but the Lord had promised me that He was in control and that the gates of Hell wouldn't prevail against His church.

I found a job. I scoured the classifieds for work, since going back to the mountain wasn't looking like it was going to happen. It was the beginning of winter and I didn't have anything prepared for the winter. Snow can make surviving up there a wee bit of a challenge. I replied to one ad for a truck driver that seemed promising. The guy was a two-truck owner/operator who needed a driver for his second truck. I went and met him, Rudy, took a short test drive and was asked if I could start right away. He had the truck on with Butterworth Transport, hauling refer containers from the docks to Alberta where they would be loaded with McCain French fries, pork, beef, and the worst load I had ever hauled in my life; horse meat going to Japan. It was good to be working full time again, but deep inside I knew that I had a place on that mountain. I had some interesting trips through the Rockies, and learned to hate driving the Trans Canada Hwy. It was a narrow, winding, two lane road that is subject to closures regularly due to accidents, and or avalanches. What should be a ten-hour trip to Calgary has been known to take up to four days, most of it sitting in the lineup of traffic. There was no public washrooms or any other facilities for that matter, so imagine sitting in your cab for sixteen hours waiting for the road to open.

It was getting old fast and I wanted to have a change, so after talking to Rudy about it, he put the truck on with another outfit and I hauled beer to the Okanogan and back four nights a week. It was the perfect job for the truck and me. Overnight runs so the traffic was light and back to the starting point by six the next morning, when I would go to bed and start all over the next night. I had been driving for Rudy for almost a year and had only been to Tranquility a few times during that time. Jimmy had moved in to Tranquility and was being the bully. He scared the weaker Christians away and an old race horse he found had decided all on its own that my house was his barn. I had built quite the frame work for the new house but had to abandon it when I went to the city. It was quite sad to see the tarps all torn and flapping in the wind when I arrived there one summer evening. I didn't know if I was ever going back.

It's funny how I was making lots of money in the city but never seemed to have enough to do anything there, but when I lived on the mountain I didn't have much money but always seemed to have enough time.

Fun with the Law

While driving for Dokkside, I had a few interesting interactions with the Authorities. Only a trucker knows the apprehension that comes from a sign saying, *"SCALE OPEN."* You can be nice and legal and get a green light and carry on with your wallet intact. Or, you can get the dreaded red *"PARK-BRING PAPERS"* light. You pull over and get ready to go in and meet your new friends. They want your driver's license, registration for tractor and trailer and your logbook. You can only pray that they are in a good mood and you don't dare show them that you are upset in any way or they will make a special effort to make you even more upset. You smile, say hi, give them your papers and let them do their job. Unfortunately, their job is to find things wrong and give you fines, or worse, shut you down on the spot. If they decide to do an inspection of your rig, you get to find out if you missed anything the last time you checked it all over in your pre-trip inspection.

Most of the DOT's are friendly enough, if you keep your cool, but occasionally, you meet one who is having a bad day and you are the next victim. It is times like these that every truck driver should be wearing body cameras. I will share a couple of instances of my interactions with the dreaded DOT, or Care Bears, or Creeper Cops, as truckers call them.

One afternoon, after loading north of Prince George BC, I was heading towards the yard in Abbotsford. The scale on the south side of town was open so I pulled in and crossed the scale. All my weights were good, new truck and trailers, and no outstanding debts or warrants, so I was quite confident. Until PARK BRING PAPERS. Upon entering the scale shack, I was *"greeted"* by a snarling guy in a DOT uniform. I said, *"Good evening sir."* He said, *"Give me your papers."* I smiled and tried to keep it light, but this guy was a jerk. He couldn't find anything wrong with my DL or registration, so he dug deep into the history of my logbook. They were permitted to go back two weeks to find violations. He found one. So, out comes the ticket book and he is going to take $215.00 from me for a clerical error. I tried to reason with him, but there was no way. He was determined to give me the ticket. I was not happy, but didn't dare let it show, in case he decided to do an inspection on the truck. They can always find *"something wrong"* if they look hard enough.

I took my ticket and swore I would fight it. It is always in a court far from home, but if you don't fight, you have lost already. I filed my intent to dispute and waited to hear back. A few months later I was given a court date at the Prince George courthouse. It was inconvenient. I was also becoming friends with one of the pre-eminent pro-life advocates, and legal scholars, Gordon W. He took an interest in my situation and suggested that I file a Constitutional Question, citing that my right to privacy was being violated by having to keep a logbook, among a few other reasons. It was very heady stuff for a guy who lived in the woods in a treehouse. I was notified of the courts acceptance of the new proceeding, and given a new court date, once again, months down the road.

As the court date was approaching, I had no money and wasn't driving for Dokkside anymore due to the physical pain returning, so getting there for court was looking impossible. It was the dead of winter, so the idea of hitchhiking wasn't too appealing. I approached the owner of a Boston Bar trucking company and asked if I could get a ride there in one of their trucks. He said he couldn't guarantee he would be able to get me there on time, but he did offer to buy me a bus ticket, which I gladly accepted.

I arrived at the courthouse half an hour before my appointed time. I went to look on the posting board and couldn't find my name anywhere on it. I went to the court clerk's office and asked them what the deal was. The woman looked my name up, and then told me that my court date was the day before and, since I was a no show, I was convicted in absentia. I showed her my copy of the court document, which plainly showed that my court date was indeed that day. She took it back into the office and a while later came back with one of her colleagues. They didn't know what to do. It was obvious to me that someone was playing games and that I would not accept the guilty by absentia verdict. They disappeared back into the office while I waited. About ten minutes later, they came back and apologized for the mistake, told me the conviction would be removed and that they would send me a new court date. If you think they play by the rules, you are sadly mistaken my friends.

So, back to the woods I went, only to wait another eight months for a new court date. Meanwhile, I had gone back to work for Dokkside, stipulating that there would be no tarping done by me. As I was driving through the Okanogan one afternoon, I was pulled into the Vernon BC scale.

As a searcher for truth, I found myself involved with lots of interesting facts and people. One such group at the time was called The Three Whys Men, or De-Tax Canada. They proved, beyond any doubt, that there is still no law requiring individuals to file or pay the Income Tax in Canada. There is coercion, there are threats, there are the police and courts with jail cells, but there is no law. It is a policy, it is voluntary, and it was made to apply to corporations, not individuals. One of the cute things the De-Taxers produced was a *"Public Servant Questionnaire."* It is a simple document, much like the type that government types give us to fill out prior to interacting with the public, the only difference is that we, the public, are requesting the government employees fill out the form before we interact with them. It can be great fun if you aren't squeamish. There is another little piece of paper that goes with it, just so they know it is legit. It states:

> *"Criminal Code, Section 337. Public servant refusing to deliver property – Everyone who, being or having been employed in the service of Her Majesty in right of Canada or in right of a province, or in the service of a municipality, and entrusted by virtue of that employment with the receipt, custody, management or control of anything, refuses or fails to deliver it to a person who is authorized*

> *to demand it and does demand it, is guilty of an indictable offence and liable to imprisonment for a term not exceeding fourteen years."*

Being the faith filled disturber of all things bureaucratic, I presented the scale men with my PSQ, and asked them to please fill it out before we proceeded any further. They refused. I showed them the law, but they ignored it, and then proceeded to write me two tickets. One for failing to produce my driver's license and one for failing to provide my registration. Both of which were in plain view on the counter, right beside my Bible. Not wanting to leave without sharing the love of God, I opened my Bible to Isaiah 10:1-2, *"Woe unto them that decree unrighteous decrees, and that write grievousness which they have prescribed; To turn aside the needy from judgment, and to take away the right from the poor of my people, that widows may be their prey, and that they may rob the fatherless."*

Well that shook them up a bit. The one DOT officer asked me, *"Are you saying I'm evil?"* He was getting ready to escalate the situation. I replied, *"Of course not sir. I love you and God loves you. I'm simply sharing the Word of God that I think applies to this situation."* That seemed to satisfy him, but they refused to tear up the tickets, even though I never refused to give them my documents. So, we fought this one too. This time Gordon wanted to challenge the validity of the entire system when it came to using the PSQ. I had to count the cost and told him that the Prince George case was enough for now. I was simply going to go to court in Vernon and tell my story and ask for a reduction in the fines.

The time of the PG case had come, and I was driving truck again and had myself dispatched to Prince George for the appointed court date. I was armed with reams of documents and ready to have the entire logbook law thrown out, clear across Canada.

When I arrived, there were a few supporters from the De-Tax group there, and we went in as a group. It is always best to have witnesses in those places. We waited as they went down the list and when they got to my name, the prosecutor announced that he was saving my case for last, so we sat there as the rest of the cases were heard. It wasn't until after lunch that my case began. The prosecutor was a short, well-dressed man, and he came out of the gate swinging. He was doing his job and he was good at it. I was representing myself, so having no knowledge of court procedures, I made a couple of mistakes. The judge allowed for my inexperience, and even helped me a few times, but it was obvious that there was no way he was going to let me win. He called a recess and we all gathered back in the courtroom for his verdict. He said, and this is from memory, *"Mr. Los, I appreciate you bringing this Constitutional Question in to my courtroom. You have certainly done your homework and have given us all a chance to do something we don't normally get to do. Having said that, I want to ask you a question. When you applied for and received your Class One Commercial Driver's License, did you sign for it, and thereby agree to all the provisions it entailed, including the keeping of a daily logbook?"* Of course, I had to answer yes. *"Then, as far as this court is concerned, you are bringing the wrong argument to this court. You, as a professional driver, are required by law to keep and maintain a logbook. End of story."* He then rambled on for almost forty-five minutes, talking about nothing, but making the cost of a transcript very expensive. At the end, I asked the judge, *"So, what you are saying is, as a truck driver, I have given up my right to privacy and protection from unjust searches and seizures?"* He replied, *"That is exactly what I am saying. Now, as for the fines, I am willing to offer you a reduction in the amount, but the conviction will go on your record. This is very out of the ordinary, but so was this case, so I ask you Mr. Los, what do you recommend the fine be?"* I stood there in shock, trying to process everything I had just heard, and I said, *"How does $75.00 sound?"* Judge said, *"$75.00 it is and have a nice day."* Talk about a civics lesson.

When my Vernon court date came, I loaded a bunch of the residents of Tranquility Station into my van and we headed to court. There were about six of us. Once we arrived at the courthouse, I felt the need to drive around it seven times, then for all of us to shout at the top of our lungs, which we did. We parked and went inside.

I found my name on the list and we went to the courtroom. We waited, but since it was a small crowd in there, my case came up quickly. Once I was in front of the judge, he read my charges of failure to produce, and then asked me how I pled. I told him, *"Guilty your honor, but with an explanation."* He said, *"I can't wait to hear it."* I told him how I never once refused to show them my papers and driver's license, I simply wanted them to fill out my little questionnaire first, as was my right under Section 337 of the Criminal Code. He was unaware of the PSQ, so I provided a copy of it for him. As he read it, his countenance changed. He glared at me over his glasses and asked, *"Who do you think this applies to? Are you trying to tell me I have to fill one out too?"* There was laughter in the courtroom. I explained how as a public servant, yes, he was required to fill one out, however, for the sake of not tying up the court, I wished to simply plead guilty and ask for a reduction in my fine.

It was very quiet as he read the questionnaire again. Then said, *"This is very interesting. Can I keep this copy?"* To which I replied, *"Of course, I have many more."* He then asked me if reducing the fine to $100.00 was okay with me. I agreed and that was that.

Another incident occurred at the Vernon BC scale a few years later. I was working for Rudy, delivering courier freight to Kelowna, then bringing new glass bottles back from a plant east of Vernon. We had been getting along quite well with the shipper there and she was starting to give me preferential treatment, which I didn't mind at all. What never crossed my mind was that there was already a trucking company that hauled for them regularly, and they weren't too happy with Jonny Upstart suddenly getting loaded before they were, even though they would drop and leave their trailers in the docks, effectively making them unusable until someone pulled their trailers out. No one wanted to touch them because of the liability issue, so out of six loading docks, it wasn't uncommon to find five trailers with no tractors, plugging up the works. The rest of us had to wait, and we don't get paid to wait.

One Friday afternoon, these trailers blocked every single dock. There was a long line of trucks waiting to get loaded and we were all stuck until Jerk Trucking moved their wagons. The shipper was livid, called them and yelled at them to get up there and pull the trailers out. Finally, I said, *"To heck with it. I'll pull one out. I just want to get loaded and get out of here."* It was Friday and they were going to shut down for the weekend at 5pm, leaving all of us stranded if we didn't get loaded. Another driver dropped his trailer and we moved their trailers to open two loading docks. I was out of there at 4:55pm, the last one out.

I didn't have to be in Vancouver until next Monday, so I had the entire weekend to visit friends. I decided to stop in and see Greg in Kamloops. As I came down the hill into Vernon, I was passed by a woman in a Jeep who stuck her arm out the window and gave me the finger. I had no idea why. I swung into the Walmart parking lot and parked, then went inside to buy some snacks for later. I came back out, jumped in the truck, and hit the trail. As I came up to a stop sign and applied the brakes, they seemed *"squishy."* But with nowhere to stop and check, I proceeded around the corner and onto the highway. The Vernon scale is just north of town and the first turn off after getting on the highway where I did. It was OPEN. I rolled in, using the engine brake to slow down, and rolled onto the scale pad. I had my drivers on the scale when the STOP light came on and stayed on. I knew something was wrong and had planned to pull in there and check it out anyway, but then the DOT guy came flying out of the scale shack and started taking pictures between my tractor and trailer. I stuck my head out the window and asked him what was wrong. He said, "You will find out soon enough. Park it and come inside."

I parked and got my papers together, climbed down and had a look at what the fuss was about. My service glad-hand was dangling. It was on when I left the bottle plant but, mysteriously, wasn't on at the scale. They don't usually come off by themselves either.

I went inside the chicken coop and the officers were both upset. I couldn't have agreed more. I tried to explain, but they didn't care. Four inoperable brakes, at $150.00 each, added up to a $600.00 fine. That was a week's wages right there. Obviously, someone had tampered with my truck while I was in Wally World, and it began to dawn on me, who and why. Jerk Trucking was trying to jerk my chain.

A $600.00 fine is worth fighting, so I did. The court date was almost a year from when I got the ticket. When I finally had my day in court, the same judge that presided over my other case a year or so before, heard this one as well. All the DOT officers were sitting there, plus a few extras, each of them with thick file folders on their laps, anticipating a fight. When the judge asked me how I pled, I said, *"Guilty your honor, but with a really good story."* I'm sure he remembered me as he said, *"This ought to be good. Go ahead."*

I turned to the officers in the gallery and said, *"Your honor, I would like to publicly thank these men. By them spotting my gladhand dangling there, and thereby knowing that I had no brakes on my trailer, they may have saved my life and the lives of others that day."* The look on their faces was priceless. *"Now, for my theory of what happened..."* I proceeded to tell the judge my version of the events. I concluded, *"Your honor, the competition in trucking is fierce. There are many not so honorable people in the industry. I can't prove that our competition undid my gladhand, but I do know that they don't come off by themselves. As I said, I accept my responsibility for the incident and I am simply asking you for a reduction in my fine, to say, $100.00."* There was chuckling in the gallery, then the Judge said, *"It is not often that I let an accused sentence himself, but in your case, I will make an exception. The fine is reduced to $100.00, have a nice day."* Okay, so it wasn't an earth-shattering victory, but I fulfilled the scripture that instructs us to *"Agree with the officer quickly, while you are in the way with him, lest he deliver you up to the judge and the judge throw you in prison."* What can I say, it was kind of fun.

I had a few more incidents with the police over the years. You drive a truck, they will want to meet you. Another scale incident was in Quesnel BC.

I was heading north to Ft. St. James to get a load of lumber. I was under the gun for time and didn't have time to lose. I pulled into the Quesnel scale, rolled beside it, since I was empty, and got the dreaded *PARK BRING PAPERS* light. I had my girlfriend with me and she waited in the truck while I went inside. The DOT officer took my logbook, thumbed through it, didn't see anything of note, and put it aside. He then took the registrations and my driver's license and went and entered the info in his computer. Not having anything to worry about, I was confident that we would be out of there and back on schedule in a few minutes. Then he announced, *"Your driver's license has been suspended. You're not moving that truck one inch, and if you do, I will have the police here arrest you."* I was in shock. *"Are you serious? How can that be? I don't owe ICBC anything, this can't be."* I called the boss on the payphone outside and he wasn't too happy. I said it had to be a mistake because I knew I didn't owe the government any money and I had completely paid off ICBC a month before. Hmmm, ICBC: Government mandated crown corporation insurance scam. I asked the DOT guy if it said anything on his computer about why and he said no. My boss asked me for all the information, told me to wait and hang up. I went back to the truck. It was winter, freezing cold, snowing, and dreary.

As we sat there, with permission to keep the engine running for heat, we began to pray, *"Heavenly Father, You know what is going on. You are not surprised by anything, so we won't be either, but my boss is another story. Thank You for making a way for us to get going again."* The DOT guy came out to the truck and knocked. I rolled down the window and he said he was starting his break and would drive me down to the DMV to see if we could fix things. I was taken aback but hey, they are not all jerks.

We arrived at the DMV and I found myself dealing with a nasty little woman. She was no fun at all. I tried to explain my situation, but she didn't care. She did offer me the information I needed to solve the whole mess. I had written ICBC four postdated checks for $500.00 each to pay for my outstanding debt. They had cashed all four and I had the cancelled checks at home, in the woods, 700kms away. As the teller explained that one of the checks bounced, I lost it because I knew it was a lie. She became more obnoxious, so I stepped back from the counter, dropped to my knees and raised my hands to Heaven, saying loudly, *"Dear Heavenly Father, You see what is going on here. You see the injustice that is happening right now. You know as well as I do that these lies are sent from the pit of hell to cause me to stumble. In Jesus name, I command that this situation be fixed right now."* I stood up and saw the look of pure shock on all the faces in the DMV, turned and told our new DOT friend that we could go back to the truck now. I had done all I could do. The poor guy was red faced but had a slight grin. As he was driving us back to the scale, he pulled into Tim Hortons and bought us coffee and donuts. He dropped us at the truck and went back into the scale shack. We waited in the truck and prayed.

About an hour later, he came outside and told me to call my boss. I called the boss and he told me he paid the $500.00 and I had better have a cancelled check so he could get his money back. I told the DOT guy that my license was being reinstated and was calling a cab to take me back to the DMV office. He said, *"No, I'm driving you."*

We were on our way there when I noticed he had a Masonic ring on his finger. Feeling bold, I asked him if he was a Mason, to which he said yes. I asked him why he joined, and he said he wanted to do good for his community. I said that was a noble thing to do, but had he ever heard the gospel of Jesus Christ? He had never heard the Good News. So, as we were on our way to get my new driver license, I shared the love of God and His plan of salvation with this man. It was amazing how he wanted to hear it. I told him plainly that Freemasonry is a cult. It looks good until you get in too deep, then you are trapped, but Jesus offers us nothing but love and forgiveness for our sins, then doing good things for your community just flows from us. He didn't stop the truck and kick us out, so that was a good thing.

We went back into the DMV. I got the same nasty woman as before, *"I told you before, your license is suspended, there is nothing I can do about it."* I asked, *"Can you check again please?"* She checked, and her eyes bulged as she saw that it had been reinstated. She was visibly upset but had to do her job, which included a new picture for my new license and everything. It was awesome.

Our new friend drove us back to the truck. I gave him a hug for being such a great guy and helping me out of the jam. He said, *"It didn't look like you needed my help."* He was right in the middle of the plan and God put him there for that purpose. I called the boss who had made arrangements for a forklift operator to wait for us at the lumber mill in Ft. St. James, and two and a half hours later, we arrived, got loaded and were back on schedule.

Driving Stories

I put on a lot of miles trucking. I started the way you used to start, at the bottom. After a while, I could get a driving job almost anywhere. I just needed to know someone who knew I could handle it.

I learned how to drive in Vancouver and the surrounding areas, through rain, and on steep hills with stop lights in the middle of steep hills, where stopping was a death sentence for the clutch. We were happy to get trailers that had brakes.

Front Street in New Westminster BC is a two-lane road all the way now, since they took the old railroad trestle *"dodge em poles"* out anyway, and it is the major truck route from South Burnaby and Richmond. Rush hour there can take an hour to get from the old Queensboro Bridge to the Trans Canada #1 Highway, about 2.5kms apart. To say it is an ancient bottleneck is an understatement. The City of New Westminster has refused to allow construction of at least a four lane with traffic lights.

One afternoon, I was sentenced to go across town to load in rush hour in a tractor/trailer, going to get a load of beer. Front St. intersects with Columbia Ave, like an on ramp, but with a traffic light. It is four lanes there for a very short stretch, going past the old BC Penitentiary gates on the hill to the left. You do get tired of the cars that see your slow start from a dead stop as the perfect opportunity to jump in front of you. After having this happen hundreds of times a day, I was done with being Mr. Nice Guy one last time before the right lane turned into Brunette Ave. then in the curb lane to the freeway, or in my case, to the LCB warehouse right at the interchange. The *"fast"* lane went straight up as Columbia continued and there is, to this day, a median with 18" high cement curbs.

Just before where the road splits is a side road that comes to a tee at the bottom of the hill with a pedestrian controlled traffic light. As I was sitting in traffic, inching along and just creeping into the intersection, an old Datsun car came flying down the hill and to a hard stop. The passenger jumped out of the car and ran to press the control button, then dove back into the car. I knew from the instant I saw them that they wanted to cut in front of me. I don't think so.

I was empty, and the truck had plenty of power, so starting in a higher gear was doable, like 6th gear. I was inches away from the car in front of me and sure enough, they roared up beside me and wanted to pull in front of me. With the truck in 6th gear, a little rev and release of the clutch and you can rabbit start like a car. That is what I did, and didn't feel bad about it one bit. They never did get in front of me before the median. The ramp curves to the right and becomes Brunette Ave which again opens to four lanes. Trucks just stay in the curb lane. I was creeping along, and the morons in the Datsun stopped beside me, yelling all kinds of profanity, and were a wee bit mad. I rolled down the window and asked them what their problem was, and the passenger replied with insults and profanity. It was starting to become annoying, so I grabbed my Bible from off the dash. I randomly flipped it open and hung out the window with it, and recited at the top of my lungs, from memory, *"For God so loved the world that He gave His only begotten Son that whosoever shall believe, the same shall be saved."* The passenger freaked out and yelled, *"He's got a Bible. Let's get outta here."* Yep, sharper than a two-edged sword, that Book.

Family of God

You know, few brothers and sisters in Christ have experienced the incredible closeness that comes from being a member of a true community, not just of believers, but of people from messed up back grounds, people of privilege who were dispossessed of their inheritances, the broken fisherman with no hope and no relationship with God, the guy who was hiding in the woods running from his past. These people were nevertheless a part of our community. God put them there for a very good reason, and that was to shine His divine light into these lost souls.

It seems like even the Christians have a warped view of what "church" is. Long before Christ, there were no shortage of places of worship. What they worshiped was questionable, and frankly, demonic. Idolatry is there because of the fall. No, the true Church is the gathering of the *'true born from above believers,'* voluntarily coming together as the Called-Out Ones. If they are listening to God through the Holy Spirit, they will all be gathered, at the right time and at the right place. Such was the little city on a hill known as Tranquility Station.

Living in a realm of miracles, among the brethren who are experiencing the same, in the bond of true brotherly love, it makes showing up at some building for a few hours a week seem lame. I am not knocking the churches out there at all. I know there are deep relationships and much good done through believers who are tied to the system in such a way as people with jobs in the city are. But when you have been utterly cast off, and don't want anything in any form from the government, living by faith is the only option. It turns out that it is the best option.

From Heidi's non-stop love of serving, to Richard's little generator and satellite dish where we sat and watched Pastor Arnold Murray broadcasting on his own private satellite channel, as the snow and cold were howling just outside. Pastor Murray would simply read from the Bible and spend a little time explaining what the Word was saying. I now know that some of his theology was off, but sitting in that cabin night after night, watching that man just read the Bible to us was amazing. It built our faith to keep trusting God no matter what happened, and Praise God, it was always rewarded.

There were quite the crew of unbelievers there though. There was Rick and Veronica his girlfriend. He was hiding in the woods from his past. He was kicked out of his family home when he was six years old and lived on the street, in Northern BC, back in the Seventies. He was miserable, mean, evil minded, and could be counted on in a pinch. In fact, he is somewhat of a hero to me. When I had visitation rights with my children every second weekend, I brought them up to Tranquility a couple of times. Brandon was about five and Christina was three. We camped out on Friday and Saturday, then I took them home to Princeton on Sunday afternoon. This was a year before ending up living there myself.

One afternoon, as we went for a walk on the trails, we had to cross the creek on a log bridge that led to the Summer Kitchen. It was planked and had a railing and Brandon was ahead and Chrissy was behind me holding my hand. She let go and as quickly as I turned around, she tripped and fell into the creek. Rick was right there and scooped her out like he was fishing. The horror of what could have happened if he hadn't been right there hit me like a wall. He had saved my precious Christina's life. He was certainly a challenging figure to me when God took me up there. I had to decide if what God was doing in me was worth putting up with some of these characters. I don't know if you noticed, but these special challenges are pretty much everywhere.

I remember Evan the junkie showing up one December. We hadn't had much snow to speak of by then, and Mountain Ed and Rick brought him up. Did I mention that the place was open and hospitable to strangers, and it was a drug treatment facility sometimes?

Evan was an outgoing and friendly guy. Everyone liked him, even though we all quickly discerned that he wasn't saved yet. A little more time revealed that he was from the streets of Vancouver, and he hated it there and couldn't believe that a place like ours existed. Mountain Ed said he was going to town for a few things, especially a pouch of tobacco, and would be back later, and here we were, with Evan. Then it started to snow. As the snow started to accumulate, mild panic started to appear in him. We were fine and had lots of supplies, at least a few weeks' worth, and tried to calm him down. But he was not a happy camper and finally just blurted out that he was a heroin addict and he only had enough for one more day. All right then, that makes it interesting. The snow was that wet heavy snow that was famous on the west coast, even far inland, and it was piling up at over an inch an hour. The hope of Mountain Ed coming back was getting slimmer and slimmer as the night came on. There was ten inches of snow by 8pm, and there was the usual sound of crashing trees and breaking branches that come with heavy wet snow.

We fired up the generator, tuned in Arnold, sat down in the little survival shack, and had dinner. When we were asking God to bless our meal, Evan suddenly realized he was surrounded by Jesus freaks. He started asking, *"What kind of place is this? When is that Ed guy getting back?"* We told him Ed probably wasn't coming back that night. We asked him if we could pray for him. It was obvious that he was going to be needing it soon anyway. He was a bit hesitant and wanted to know what to do. We told him we were going to ask God to deliver him from drug addiction and to bless him in his time with us. He looked terrified and relieved at the same time but agreed to let us pray. After we prayed, he was shaking, and it was a bit unnerving, so we continued to pray and cast out a few demons as well. He stopped shaking, sat, and we finished dinner, which was Kraft Dinner mac and cheese. We continued to watch Arnold read the Bible to us.

As the night went on, it continued to snow. We knew that breaking trail was going to be a challenge when we got up the next morning. There was one and a half feet of snow. Richard had a 4x4 but no gas and no money, especially not for breaking trail. I came down from my place and everyone was already awake at Richard's. I was most concerned about Evan. He was sitting there having breakfast, and seemingly happy. God really had delivered the guy from heroin. I was cautious though and didn't bring it up, and he did say he had enough for a day. As the day went on we would know whether he was truly set free or not. It was about noon when I asked him how he was doing. I reminded him of our prayer the night before and he reluctantly acknowledged it, but then told me he had thrown his last bit of heroin in the creek the night before. He said that *"Whatever you guys did, the addiction is gone."* I had to laugh as I explained that we didn't do anything, God did. He didn't want to accept that there was a Living God who delivered him from drug addiction. As the day went on, Evan wasn't showing any signs of withdrawals. He commented how he was amazed at how free he felt from the drugs. Since he was snowed in with us and couldn't go anywhere even if he wanted to, he settled in and helped out. Richard's generator started making a loud squealing noise, then it died. As night came on, we only had candles for light, as well as a few flash lights. It turned out that Evan was a mechanic, so he and I brought Richard's generator into the cabin to see if he could fix it. The rear support bearing housing was worn out. I had some two-part epoxy cement and we used it to build the worn-out metal back up. We left it overnight and in the morning put the generator back together. It started up and worked flawlessly. Four days after he had arrived, the snow had melted enough for Ed to make it back up to Tranquility, and Evan was ready to go, but not before he had given his life to Jesus Christ. As a new brother in the Lord, we blessed him and wished him well, telling him that he was welcome to come back any time. He left with Ed, and we never saw him again.

Chapter Seven

The Dream

In a dream, I was walking on a path in the woods, much like the ones I walked every day at Tranquility Station. I came to a fork in the trail. The trail to the left was dark and foreboding. There were snakes hanging from the tree branches, dried blood on the rocks, slime of some kind dripping off things, spider webs, and it stank. I could see a door about thirty feet away and it was black and thoroughly uninviting. To my right the trail was beautiful. There were flowers and it smelled nice. There were birds singing in the branches, rabbits hopping around, and it was very pleasing to the senses. There was a door, about thirty feet away on that trail as well, and it was beautiful.

I stood there, unable to decide what to do. The obvious thing was to take the trail to the right, but something just didn't seem right. It was too perfect. The trail to the left was scary and intimidating but somehow, I knew I was supposed to take it. The natural man and the spiritual man were battling it out while I stood there. There was a war going on in me and all I could do was wait until it played out.

If I took the dark trail I knew there would be pain involved. If I took the light one, it would just be too easy. If I took the dark trail, I would be forced to rely on God. If I took the light one, I could lean on my own resources. As much as the one was attractive and the other repulsive, I knew what I had to do. I started walking down the dark path.

As soon as I decided to go that way, I was attacked by unseen but very real beings. I was getting pushed. I was being spit on. I felt intense fear. It smelled worse than a public bathroom. I was dry retching. Stinging tears were in my eyes. I could see the other trail.

My mind was reeling as I wondered what I was doing on this nightmare trail. As I stumbled along, I was second guessing my choice. I turned to look behind me and there was nothing there. Going back was not an option. Then I remembered something I had read in the Bible, *"Fear Not!"*

With renewed determination, I began to move towards the dark door. The demons and creatures were mocking me, yelling at me and trying to trip me, but I simply ignored them and moved forward.

Finally, I was at the door. There was nothing inviting about it at all. Dried blood, pentagrams, skulls; every evil thing was portrayed on it. Knowing that I couldn't turn around, and seeing the other door off in the distance, I felt sick. I wanted to die right there.

I closed my eyes and asked the Lord to help me, to show me what to do. He said, *"Go through the door."*

I put my hand on it. It was hot to the touch. I thought, this is going to hurt. I gave it a good push and it swung open. I couldn't believe what I was seeing. It was paradise. All of the beauty of Heaven was right there, and I was overjoyed. The Lord was standing there, and I flew into His arms and melted into the most comforting hug ever.

I looked over an abyss, towards where the other door was, and what I saw was terrifying. Everyone who went through that beautiful door was grabbed by a demon and hauled straight down into a burning pit. The screams were agonizing. I had barely escaped the same fate and was so glad that I chose the ugly trail.

I woke up.

Epilogue

I realize that I have come to an abrupt ending. If I had continued to write, I could easily add another 100 plus pages. I plan to write a sequel so all the stories that weren't concluded in this book will be shared. I can tell you that God has brought many of these stories to a very happy ending.

When we are faced with various trials, and we lean wholly on God, we can be confident that He will bring them to a satisfying conclusion, and He will usually give us an amazing testimony to go with them. In my experience, God loves to surprise us, and everyone else, so that we can encourage others who are struggling. Salvation is an instant gift, but sanctification takes a little longer, usually the rest of our lives.

Abraham was given many promises. Some were fulfilled during his lifetime, and some are still awaiting fulfillment. It is the same in our lives. *Don't give up* seems to be the central theme of the Bible. Just when it looks the darkest and we don't think we can go on, God comes through. No matter what situations we face, we can always trust that God has our best in mind.

Some have died while believing God for healing. Some have gone bankrupt while believing God for prosperity. Some have lost marriages while believing for restoration. All these things can shake our faith in God. But they are never the end of the story. Those who died are now in Paradise where there is no sickness or death. Those who went bankrupt have been taken through those dark times to be a light to others who face the same trials. Those whose marriages have failed, God knows best. He tells us that He sees the beginning from the end, and all we need to do is lean on Him and trust.

The light at the end of the tunnel isn't a train. It is the hope that we have, knowing that God is in control of every situation. Since, if we are brutally honest with ourselves, nearly all the trials we face are because of our bad decisions, we should be grateful that God delivers us from our own self-made disasters.

It is my hope that these stories will encourage you to keep pressing on. When the world and the devil tell you that you should just curl up and die, look to the author of life and defy them. The hope that God gives is the true wealth we are seeking. By giving us His only Son, Jesus Christ, He has shown us the extent He is willing to go to save us from this sinful world and give us a future and a hope.

I pray that you will look to the author and finisher of your faith, Jesus, and, in the words of Winston Churchill, *never give up.*

www.ingramcontent.com/pod-product-compliance
Lightning Source LLC
Chambersburg PA
CBHW070534010526
44118CB00012B/1136